UNRECOVERABLE

An American
woman's rescue from
a Turkish prison

Shelly Lantz

FREILING
PUBLISHING

Published by Freiling Publishing, a division of Freiling Agency, LLC.

P.O. Box 1264,
Warrenton, VA 20188

www.FreilingPublishing.com

ISBN 978-1-950948-65-9

Printed in the United States of America

Chapter 1

UNCERTAINTY

An overpowering stench hung in the air, so thick I could taste it, and I wondered if the odor was coming from me.

Pressing my face against the jail cell bars, I searched for signs of life; a prisoner, a guard, anyone. I was nauseous, and my heart pounded in my ears. Looking around for a place to throw up, I found nothing for it – no toilet, no bucket. If I got sick on the floor, I realized it would just be another hardship, another disgusting odor in this already repulsive pit.

I needed to fight the nausea. I needed to regain control.

Calming down a bit, I peered down the corridor again. I still didn't see a soul, but there was a hopeful sign. A distant sound was reverberating through the stone walls. I strained to pick out familiar words from the muffled cacophony, but all of the voices were foreign to my ears. This left me feeling even more disoriented.

To take my mind off my fears, the stench, and my growing nausea, I studied the small part of the jailhouse I could see – my cell and the few areas within my view. The place looked ancient. Its crudely poured cement walls were coarse, unfinished, and cold. Its paint-chipped steel bars had been worn to the metal in several places. I shivered to think a captive's hands had wrung them bare, and I wondered if I would be begging through them in the years to come as well.

Again, the stink surrounded me like a foul fog, and I gagged in response. At first, I prayed my senses would dull so the stench might become tolerable, but then I realized the folly of that wish. God forbid I might ever become comfortable here. The idea I might spend days, weeks, or even years in that horrible place brought another surge of panic, and I pulled at the bars in frustration.

God, how can this be happening to me?

"I need to use the bathroom," I yelled – then flinched at the panicky tone of my voice. It was the voice of a terrified child, the voice of someone on the brink of madness.

Calm down. Get yourself under control!

"Guard! Please – I need to use a bathroom." This time, I forced myself to sound more rational. "Is anyone there? Is there a guard somewhere?"

Pushing my face against the bars, I searched up and down the corridor for some sign my shouting had been heard. Inside this cell, with no control over my circumstances, I felt completely powerless. If I could just get someone to answer my calls, I could regain some sense of autonomy. And, if I was able to leave the cell – even for just a few minutes – there would be a glimmer of hope for more freedom in the future.

"Please, get me out of here!"

Suddenly, a man with greasy black hair and a thick mustache appeared. I took a step back. He was oddly dressed, like some of the civilians I'd seen in town. He wore jeans and a pale blue shirt at least a size too small. Its cuffed sleeves rode high on his biceps.

Is this guy wearing a woman's shirt? Why?

The man brushed back the edges of his mustache and nodded as if urging me to speak.

"Please – I need to pee," I said sheepishly, motioning around my cell as if he hadn't noticed it contained no place for me to go.

He spoke, but the coarse words were incomprehensible to me. At first, I backed away a step in fear, but I quickly realized the message my actions might send and returned to my original position. I couldn't afford to offend him or inadvertently refuse whatever he'd come to offer.

"Restroom," I said again. "I need to use a toilet." I hoped at least one of these words would be understood.

He spoke harshly again, but this time, I held my ground. I was determined to get out of the cell. The burly man's gibberish ended with something sounding like "tum-um," and he stepped closer to unlock the door.

My heart began pounding again. Focus. Concentrate on everything you see from here on out. You need to find Susie.

The guard took my arm and led me away. Together, we moved down the corridor, deeper into the guts of the prison. It didn't take long for me to realize I wasn't going to escape the stench of my cell on this outing. I was, in fact, walking into the teeth of that terrible odor. Perhaps it was inescapable. Either the whole place smelled like a sewer – or it was me.

As we moved on, I felt a little hope. He took me past other cells and other rooms. Perhaps I would find Susie. Truth be told, I would have settled for seeing any American at that point. Even though I was walking directly beside the guard, I felt an overwhelming sense of isolation. The prison was completely foreign to me, and its people would never understand me. It felt like being lost in a deep desert or adrift in the ocean. There was no human connection for me anywhere.

All of the cells we passed were empty. At the intersection of two halls, I decided to take a chance.

"Susie?" I yelled out, feeling any answer in English would be a victory. Focusing all of my attention on the muffled sound of my voice reverberating through the place, I prayed for a reply.

Words drifted back a moment later. "I'm over here!"

My heart leapt, and I surged toward the voice, but the guard tightened his grip on my arm and held me in place. He clearly intended to keep Susie and me apart.

Risking his rebuke, I shouted back into the echoing corridor. "Are you OK, Susie? What's going on?"

Susie's answer was a kick in my gut.

"I'm bleeding, Shell." There was panic in her voice. "I'm hemorrhaging."

I gasped. Susie had experienced a miscarriage earlier in the week. It was possible something else had gone horribly wrong. I imagined her lying in a cell like mine with no access to anything – pads, toilet paper, even an old newspaper. She could be bleeding to death. She might even die before I saw her again. The thought of that was unbearable.

Oblivious to my panic, the guard moved steadily along. I fought back tears, racking my brain for a way to get Susie help. How can they let this happen? Are these people inhuman? The woman needs a doctor. Surely they can see that!

Desperate, I again moved in the direction of Susie's voice, but the guard was strong, and he pulled me forward. When I resisted again, he tightened his grip, sending a sharp pain through my arm and elbow. When my knees buckled, he jerked me up. There was no way I would ever reach Susie, I decided. There was nothing I could do – so I marched on.

Finally, the guard stopped at a doorway into darkness. He stood between me and the way back to Susie. I could see he expected me to go through. But this couldn't possibly be a bathroom, I thought. It looked more like the entrance to a dank cellar.

I looked at him with a pleading expression, unsure what he wanted me to do. He rolled his eyes, stepped into the little room, and pulled a string hanging down from somewhere above. A single bulb sputtered on, casting a harsh white light into the small space.

What I saw inside made me yearn for my cell. If this was a bathroom, it was repulsive. The unfinished cement walls were spattered with muck, and the floor was slick with an ungodly mixture of water and slime.

As I pulled back in disgust, the guard motioned toward something near the doorway. It was a pair of worn, soiled flip flops someone had tossed aside. When I didn't move, he grunted and pointed at them again. The jailers had taken my shoes from me earlier. These were being provided for my bare feet, I realized. Cringing, I stepped into the flip-flops and went through the doorway.

At first, I recoiled as a new wave of breath-taking odors enveloped me. The room was thick with the smell of feces, urine, and vomit. Although my mind screamed, "breathe," my body rejected the command. I coughed a few times to clear both my throat and my senses. The stench literally burned my eyes.

As I'd suspected, areas of the cement floor were extremely slippery. A culture of organic goop had grown in the standing water, and only by shuffling slowly and carefully through the room could I avoid sliding and falling.

Pushing forward, I passed under the light bulb and noticed the crudeness of the ceiling overhead. The light socket was attached to a tangled old extension cord strung haphazardly on beams above me. I prayed it would stay in place because if it fell into the soupy muck swishing around my feet, I'd surely be electrocuted.

"Hey, there's no toilet paper in here," I yelled out before realizing the comment was ridiculous. The guard wouldn't have cared even if he had understood me.

From his position in the hall, he pointed to one side of the room. I followed his gesture to a crude metal pipe and water faucet set low in one wall. When I turned the metal handle on the old nozzle, a stream of water gushed out, splashing into my open hand. In the midst of all the filth, its purity almost brought me to tears. It was probably only well water, but it was clear and cool, in sharp contrast to the murky, fetid room. Hands trembling, I poured it on my face and let it run down my neck and over my sweat-stained clothing.

With this little bit of relief, I felt human again.

Calmer and more focused, I rose from my stoop and checked out the rest of the room. Someone had hung an ancient shower curtain to serve as a door, so I slid it closed, blocking the guard's view. By now, my stomach was cramping, and I felt an overwhelming urge to relieve myself. I was still disgusted by my surroundings, but I knew this opportunity might not come again anytime soon, so I took care of my business quickly and returned to the faucet to wash off my body.

When the cool water touched my unclothed flesh, a sharp pain shot into my lower abdomen. I could tell something was terribly wrong. Along with the pain, there was also an odd odor – perhaps the smell of infection. My fear returned, and its impact was disorienting. I stood and tried to gather myself. This pain must be linked to some kind of cut or injury, I reasoned. How serious is this? Will the guard help me? The man hadn't shown any compassion for Susie. What reason would he have to treat me differently?

I had suffered from pelvic inflammatory disease before, and I'd been hospitalized with it several times in the past. This felt like it could be a reoccurring infection. If it was, my terrible situation could actually become worse. I felt myself tearing up. I was losing control again, and along with the panic, my anger was rising. I was furious with myself.

"This is your own damn fault! You did this to yourself!" I said nothing aloud, but I was screaming inside.

For a moment or two, I literally shook with fear and rage. Then, the storm passed. The emotions helped shock me into action, renewing my energy, and refocusing my mind. I pulled aside the tattered shower curtain and stepped back into the corridor.

The guard was waiting there, leaning against the wall. Glancing at me, he dug something out of his nose. In spite of everything I'd already experienced, this still shocked me, and my flesh crawled with disgust.

As I met the eyes of the guard, this loathing flared into panic again. Something new and frightening was sweeping over his previously blank expression – an unmistakable sign of sexual hunger. I'd seen it before in other men, in other places, and at other times. He was examining my body and evaluating my condition.

I immediately looked away, breaking eye contact and moving back down the corridor in the direction of my cell. I had been raped before when I'd worked the streets as a prostitute, and I knew how men could be. I was determined not to be taken now. Not by this filthy man. Not in this disgusting hellhole. It would be one indignity too many; one degradation I could not accept. As I passed by him, I vowed I would die before enduring it.

When I finally had the courage to look back, I expected to see him closing on me, an animalistic fervor in his eyes, but his face had changed again. His expression was vacant, his eyes cold and uninterested. Something had snuffed out his sexual desire, and he'd become his old self again, a bored guard unenthusiastically carrying out his duties. Thank God, I thought. Thank God!

Without a word, he moved to my side, took my arm, and led me back through the corridor. As we reached the intersecting hallways, I yelled for Susie again, but this time she didn't answer as quickly. When she did respond, her voice was faint and listless. "I'm here," was all she could manage, and I could tell she was in terrible pain.

I wanted to shout out to her – to tell her I was sorry for getting us into this mess – but I knew my words would be useless. Convincing the guard he should take Susie to the hospital for better care would be fruitless too. He wouldn't understand a word I said.

Dejected, I dropped my head, fearing I'd never see Susie again.

Back in my cell, the old smell seemed almost tolerable compared to the overwhelming reek of the toilet. With a grunt, the guard departed, and I was left alone with my thoughts. My mind drifted back to the interrogation I'd faced at the hands of the DEA agent. He'd flown in from The States shortly after Susie and I were picked up by the Turkish authorities. The locals had been pleasant compared to that guy.

As our conversation began, it was clear to me the DEA had no intention of helping us. Instead, the agent's plan was to break us. To him, we were just dumb mules. The real trophy catch was elsewhere, and the agent was simply using us to get to those higher up in the chain of command. He literally treated us like animals, berating us and threatening us as he pushed toward that goal.

Even without his insults and attacks, it was easy for me to feel like a stupid animal now.

Am I a complete idiot? Am I incapable of doing anything right? Am I unrecoverable? Those were the thoughts assailing my mind.

Bringing drugs into Turkey certainly wasn't "normal" or "reasonable." No normal person would do such a thing. Something must be very, very wrong with me, I decided.

As I sat in the cell, my mind also dredged up one of the last embarrassing moments I had spent with my family. It played back in my mind like a movie, rich with detail. I was sitting on the sofa in my parents' apartment, arguing with my dad. A man named Jimmy had told me I needed to get my passport to travel overseas, and I was determined to succeed.

"You've got my passport," I told my stepfather. "I need it – NOW!"

There was a look of concern on his face, but I could tell he wasn't up for a fight. He'd gone through this kind of battle with me dozens of times, and he knew I could be relentless. I would cheat, lie, or steal to get what I wanted. Weariness was already showing in his eyes.

As I stared him down, he looked away for a moment, as if considering his options. At that point, I knew I had him. I'd given him the passport because I hadn't trusted myself. Now, I was proving why those instincts had been correct.

"Shelly," he finally said, "this is on you now. Whatever you're planning to do down there, and whoever you drag into this thing, it's all going to be on your head. You're going to be the only one responsible. And you're going to have to pay whatever price it costs."

This was a new wrinkle for dad, but I didn't bat an eye. I was far, far beyond any guilt trip he might concoct to dissuade me.

"You worry too much. The trip is nothing. It's going to be fine," I said.

Still, something about our conversation made me uneasy. Maybe it was his expression. Perhaps it wasn't weariness but resignation I'd seen in his eyes. Is he finally and completely giving up on me? This thought was fleeting. Whatever. All that mattered to me was getting the passport, and I intended to leave with it.

He handed me the trim, blue booklet.

"Here, Shelly. Please, please don't do anything stupid."

Stupid.

Now, the word seemed to echo endlessly around me. To break the spell, I whispered it aloud in my cell. "Stupid."

The DEA agent had been right.

My dad had been right.

I was monumentally stupid, and this time, there would be no one to stop my fall.

Overcome by this terrible realization, I succumbed to my bone-aching weariness, curled up in the corner of my cell, and dropped into an uneasy sleep.

*   *   *

On my second day in the jail, the pain from my infection grew more intense. I could still move, but the area between my legs was beginning to burn and ache. I could tell my weakened body was failing to fight off the disease. The day before, I'd received a bottle of water and a simple meal – a loaf of uncut bread and some black olives served up on a piece of newspaper – but it wasn't enough to keep my energy up.

Sometime during the previous night, a group of men had been placed in the cell across from mine. As the morning hours passed, I exchanged stares with those new prisoners. They spoke in a language I couldn't understand. Eventually, I got bored and began daydreaming about home again.

I was lost in those thoughts when a guard cleared his throat. Startled, I looked up. Few guards had shown any interest in my fate before, and this one had come without being called. I stared at him blankly. He unlocked the door and motioned for me to come out.

By now, my sweaty body reeked again, so I asked him if I could take a shower. Like the other guard, he had no idea what I was saying. He just signaled for me to follow him.

Eventually, we entered a room I'd never seen before. Inside, on a table, was a plastic garbage bag containing clothes of mine they'd taken from my luggage. Maybe I'll get to take a shower after all, I thought optimistically. By that point, I was desperate to get out of my disgusting, sweaty things.

The guard motioned toward the bag, so I moved forward and rifled through it. It contained a full change of clothing, including a pair of shoes. Before I could examine these things any further, he took my arm and guided me out of the room, bag in hand. We moved down the same corridor I had taken the day before.

He's taking me back to that horrible bathroom. He couldn't possibly expect me to change in that pit.

My spirit sagged when he confirmed my fears, stopping at the dark doorway. I had to make the most of it. It would be better than spending another day in the rags I was wearing.

Seeing the muck on the floor, I was thankful to have my own shoes back. I took them out of the bag and slipped them on. As I went in, the stench of the place washed over me again, and I recoiled from its intensity. There was nothing for it, so I'd just need to change quickly. The things I was wearing were trash now. The sooner they were off my body, the better.

I cleaned up at the faucet, dressed in fresh clothes, and slid aside the shower curtain, ready to return to my cell.

My jaw dropped when I found Susie standing with the guard. It appeared she had changed her clothes too. She was wearing clean jeans and a fresh T-shirt.

Seeing her gave me a terrible stab of guilt. Her eyes were red and swollen from crying, and she was obviously struggling with intense pain. How could I have done this to Susie? I was worse than a stupid animal. I was evil – and dangerous. This girl had trusted me, and I had destroyed her life. Now she might never see her five-year-old daughter again. In fact, based on what the DEA agent had said, it was unlikely either of us would return to The States.

As I moved toward her, I wondered what was going through her mind. I tried to imagine myself in her place. If I were her, I would be screaming. I would attack the person who had put me in this place. Why was she so docile? She seemed to be a completely broken woman, and her vacant expression and weakened condition sickened me with guilt.

Susie seemed unfazed by any of these emotions playing across my face. She never focused on me or acknowledged what was happening around her. She just walked on zombie-like when the guard motioned for us to go.

We left the prison together in the back of a ratty, old sedan. After traveling through a few desolate streets, we arrived at a hole-in-the-wall doctor's office. There, the guard ordered us to get out. The place was nothing like the clinics I'd seen in the U.S. It seemed to be a black market operation of some kind – just a few simple rooms, crude equipment, and a few staff on hand. In spite of the conditions there, I was thrilled to be out of the prison, and when the doctor spoke English, I almost cried with relief.

He asked me a couple of questions, and I explained my medical history. Then, he did a brief physical examination. Within minutes, he found something he didn't like, and his expression became grim. He told me to lie down on an old medical table. It had a soiled leather top with cracked and peeling edges, but I did as I was told.

Without examining me further, he left the room, and a new surge of panic pushed into my throat. I had finally met someone in authority who spoke English, and now he was leaving. I wanted to call out to him and beg him to stay, but the idea was ludicrous. Of course, he had other patients. Of course, he would eventually return.

Although I probably waited on the table for less than twenty minutes, it felt like an eternity. Finally, a girl pushed a rusty old cart into the room. It was a small ultrasound machine. Just as she was finishing a pelvic ultrasound scan on me, the doctor returned to look over the pictures.

"You have a serious problem," he said matter-of-factly. "There's a cyst."

"A what?" I asked.

"A cyst. It's like a tumor. You also have a fever, and you're developing an infection."

The first thing to come to mind was ovarian cancer, and that thought terrified me. I'm going to die in this terrible Turkish prison. Oddly, the idea God might save me with a miracle also popped into my head, but that notion seemed crazy – even profane – considering my many faults and failures. There will be no rescues. Dad had said so when I left for Brazil. This trip and its consequences would be entirely my responsibility.

After the exam, the doctor prescribed two medications; an antibiotic and another drug for pain. Susie was finished with her examination, too, so we were both moved along. They drove us back to the prison, and we were returned to our cells. The experience had been so shocking neither of us spoke on the way back.

As I was getting settled back in my cell, a guard approached and started babbling and laughing. He was pointing to something in his hand. It was a tattered copy of the Istanbul newspaper. There we were, Susie and I, on the front page. The story and pictures filled the entire sheet. Two big photos showed us at the airport being led away by mustachioed police. My name was under Susie's picture, and her name was under my photo. Both names were misspelled.

When the guard moved along, his laughter still reverberating down the corridor, I turned my back to the cell wall and slid to the floor, disgusted and dejected. It was becoming dark, and I considered what the next day might bring. We had been told we would spend several more days in this place before being moved to a larger prison where we would eventually be sentenced. From what the DEA agent had said, I expected to get life.

The weight of such a terrible future suddenly overwhelmed me, crushing my soul. I was emotionally drained, and the soreness from sitting on the hard cement floor was becoming intolerable. My butt and back ached so intensely I could feel the stabbing pain all the way from my ankles to the base of my skull.

At least I was being cared for by a doctor. As backward as the clinic had been, it still offered some hope for the treatment of my infection. I prayed the tumors wouldn't grow unchecked until they killed me. That, I thought, would be a miserable way to go.

At this point, my guilty conscience kicked in again.

Shelly, you fool, you don't deserve even a little glimmer of hope. You've fought against authority all your life. You've spit in the face of everyone who has ever wanted to help you. Why should anyone care about you now? The world has every reason to leave you here to rot – to be destroyed by your own cancerous body. That's what you deserve!

Filled with this guilt and self-loathing, I eventually dropped off to sleep.

*   *   *

Sometime in the middle of the night, I woke up.

All seemed quiet, but I felt certain something was very wrong. Although it was dark, I sensed someone watching me, and my heart raced with fear. Has one of the guards entered my cell? What is he after? I remained completely still, waiting for some sound or movement – a clear sign another person was nearby.

When I didn't hear anything, I slowly rolled over to expand my field of view.

What I saw brought shock – then, relief. Standing in the corner of my cell was a young woman. She must have been put in with me during the night, I reasoned. She's probably awaiting sentencing like I am—just another drug mule. Thank God, I'm safe.

My initial impression of the woman might surprise you. I was impressed by the condition of her clothes and calm demeanor. Her dress was simple but unmarred by stains or sweat. Her face was clean, and her expression was serene.

I wasn't this cool when I was brought in. Why is she taking it so well?

As I slowly eased myself up into a sitting position, she smiled at me, and I wondered if she was American or European. Should I talk to her? Will she understand me? My questions were answered when she spoke in a soft whisper.

"My name is Anna," she said.

This made my mind race with even more questions. How had this new inmate gotten inside my cell? I had taken the pain medication from the doctor. Had it knocked me out completely? The cell door was old and rusty. It usually squealed when it was opened. To have missed her arrival, I must have been completely unconscious.

I looked down at her hands. They were clean and folded in front of her in a simple posture of contentment.

"So, you speak English?"

She nodded.

Before I could question her further, she turned toward the cell opposite mine. It was dark, but the male prisoners I'd seen earlier were still there. Most of them were now sleeping on the floor. As Anna approached the bars, a man stepped out of the gloom in the opposite cell, and the two of them talked briefly in whispers. Like Anna, he must have been a recent arrival. His face was shaven, and his clothes were much cleaner than those of his cellmates. Anna and the man shared a few words, then parted. He turned his attention to one of the men in his cell, and she moved back toward me.

"That's my brother," Anna said as she approached me.

Without saying another word, she sat down on the concrete floor of our cell, stretching out her long legs before crossing them Indian style. When she was settled, she patted the floor at her side, inviting me to join her. The extreme pain in my lower back had returned, so I chose to remain standing against the wall. I really didn't want to sit again.

I had no idea who the girl was, but I was thrilled to have her company. She seemed so calm, and her face and voice were soft and comforting. Everyone I'd met in the jail had been hard-edged and gruff. She was the opposite, and that helped ease my anxiety.

I was also excited to communicate with someone in English. I'd craved the sound of spoken English since my time at the makeshift clinic.

Before I could understand why, I began to cry. It was brought on by my sense of relief, I suppose. The pain in my body had been extremely intense, but these tears weren't born of that suffering. They were moans coming out of my brokenness. They were pouring from the depths of my soul. I had felt completely rejected and depressed for days. Through this encounter with Anna, I was finally being granted a shred of acceptance and hope.

As I cried on and on, Anna watched silently. She seemed to understand my need for emotional release because she wisely let my weeping run its course. When I finally opened my mouth to speak, I could only manage a few gasping sobs, like a child so upset she's unable to catch her breath. At that point, Anna leaned toward me, her eyes full of compassion.

"Shelly, look here," she said, trying to focus my attention. Had I told her my name? Probably – when she had told me hers. I couldn't remember. I looked into her eyes, still hiccupping for breath.

"Shelly, you are going to be fine. You don't need to worry," she said softly.

You don't know me, I thought. I've never been fine. My life has always been a complete mess, and this is the end of everything for me. I'm far from being fine.

When I still couldn't speak, Anna gestured again for me to join her on the floor of the cell. She motioned for me to lie down and put my head in her lap. I felt like a child being called to her mother, and deep emotions welled up again. Tears poured down my cheeks as I went to her.

"I promise – nothing here will harm you," she said as I let her guide me down. It was such a relief to hear English. It was so gratifying to be with someone who understood my situation and cared about me. No more isolation, I thought, with a swelling sense of joy. At least I won't suffer here alone.

With her gentle hand positioning me, I stretched out on the floor and eased my head down into her lap. Nothing about it seemed sensual or uncomfortable. She was like a sister to me. That's how I remember it.

"You need to get some sleep," Anna said, "but you will be alright, Shelly. I know you will. And all of this will work out in the end."

As she placed a hand on my hair, I recoiled slightly – not because I wanted to avoid her touch, but because I had suddenly become aware of my filthiness. I would never have touched anything as grimy as I was, and I wondered why she was willing to put her hands on me. I could smell the sweat on myself too. Why don't I disgust her?

By now, my sobs had subsided a little. Tears still came, but my crying had lost its uncontrolled intensity. The few remaining drops trickled down my cheeks and into the fabric of Anna's dress. I felt the cool of that moist cloth against my face, and my body finally began to relax.

As the minutes ticked on, she rocked rhythmically and gently stroked my hair. Slowly but surely, this took away more and more of my pain. It was a sweet escape, and the first time in days I had felt safe enough to let go of my fears completely.

That night, I slept more fully and deeply than I had since the arrest.

*   *   *

The next morning, I woke up in the cell alone.

A guard was banging on the bars, calling for me to get up, and I immediately sensed Anna was gone. In a panic, I scanned the other cell for some sign of her. Most of the prisoners I had seen earlier were there, but Anna's clean-shaven brother wasn't among them.

I called out Anna's name. I asked the guard where he had taken her. I questioned the men in the other cell. The guard and the prisoners in the opposite cell just stood there staring at me. They probably had no idea what I was saying.

Losing my connection with Anna brought back my sickening fears. She'd spoken English. She'd been kind. In that moment, her absence felt like a betrayal. I had been given a wonderful gift, only to have it stripped cruelly away. In frustration, I yelled out her name again, but the call just echoed in the corridor.

Finally, one of the men in the other cell responded to my panic in broken English. He said I was alone and had always been alone.

I was shocked and heartbroken. Wasn't she real? Had the encounter only been a dream brought on by the drugs the doctor had given me? It felt like she had been in the cell with me. It felt like she had held me while I cried. God, am I becoming delusional now? Am I losing it like Susie?

I fought to regain control and to calm myself. It was my third day in the cell. I had been told I would be leaving for the other prison soon. I had to accept that fact. Anna was a lost dream. I needed to focus on myself and on my future.

The guard, who had been watching me, shook his head and walked away. The men in the opposite cell eventually lost interest in me too. They began to chatter among themselves, and before long, I was alone again with my thoughts.

As I had on the first day, my mind fled into daydreams of home and of the people and places I had left behind. It was the only positive place I could go – but the thoughts of home also brought back my feelings of guilt.

How could I have turned my back on those decent people in my life? Would there ever be a way back for me, I wondered, or is this it? Am I finally and irrevocably lost? I searched my mind for the root cause of my disastrous life choices – for the seed of all my sorrows.

This was 2004.

As my mind wandered back through my life, a memory from 1981 surfaced. It was a particular day in Texas and a particular incident that had changed everything for me.

Chapter 2

UNPREPARED

I stand at a window, looking out on a sweltering Texas day – and feel cold inside.

Since high school, I had learned to read the cycles of my life, and on that day in 1981, I could tell things were moving toward a terrible downward spiral. I felt unfocused. My situation seemed chaotic, and I could tell a horrible bout of depression was just around the corner.

A few years earlier, when I was a high school student, I'd had episodes like this too, but they hadn't been as frequent or severe. Perhaps it was because those had been simpler times. In high school, I'd been a popular cheerleader, thriving in the sports clique where jocks, parties, and my popularity usually kept life stimulating and fun.

I had a special talent in gymnastics, which often made me the center of attention when we would lead a cheer for our team. The crowds would applaud wildly during my sideline stunts, and that attention really boosted my confidence. Being popular and praised, I found, could be like a drug, making you feel powerful and important. It could lift you out of the drudgeries of normal life and put you on top of the world.

My time in Texas had been a very different story. Things had started out fine, but they'd unraveled quickly. A boyfriend had lured me there at a time when I'd desperately wanted to get out of South

Florida. Then, our relationship had fizzled.

Being independent hadn't lived up to my expectations either. When I was in school, my life had structure. Now, without the stability of traditional family life or the routines of the academic world, I found everything nebulous and unsatisfying. Life had become a grind, and the few good days I occasionally experienced were always followed by long stints of depression, loneliness, frustration, and insecurity.

My "career" was floundering too. My first job had been as a waitress in a western bar. Then, I'd moved on to an even less satisfying position as a sales clerk at a mall.

After I'd left my boyfriend, I'd found a place to crash, but arrangements were beginning to sour there too. The friend who had invited me to share expenses on the apartment had eventually taken in a boyfriend. As a result, I always felt out of place – like an interloper in their lives.

Standing there at the window, looking out on the steamy Texas day, I wondered how to handle this mistake. Should I return home? Could I make radical changes to improve my life? As I considered the chaos I'd created for myself, I thought, this life is nothing, so I have nothing to lose by walking away from it.

At that very moment, the phone rang.

It's amazing something that trivial could serve as a catalyst for momentous change, but that was the case for me. Only minutes before, I had debated the simple choice of returning home or staying in Texas. In picking up the phone, I unknowingly opened the door to a completely unexpected option, a choice that would forever change my life by taking me down a much darker path.

"Shelly? Is that you? This is Jeff."

"Jeff, who?" I asked.

"Jeff – your father."

I was shocked. Then, almost miraculously, the malaise that had been on me like a fog was blown to smithereens. Seconds before, life had seemed like an unending death march with no end in sight. Now

– flash – something new and exciting was dropping into my lap. Jeff, my crazy biological father, was on the phone!

Although I hadn't seen Jeff since I was five, I experienced an instant connection with him. It's hard to explain the reaction to someone who has never experienced an unexpected reunion of that kind. Without warning, my emotions took over, and there was a rush of euphoria. It was as if I had walked out of a torrential rainstorm into clear blue skies.

When Jeff abandoned my mother years earlier, it had ended a long and painful relationship for her. Understandably, she had done everything in her power to eliminate the man from both her life and ours. My older sister understood how my mother felt, but I was too young to appreciate her pain. To me, Jeff remained mysterious and compelling – a man I knew by name but couldn't recall in any other way.

In spite of my mother's attempts to exorcise Jeff from our family, there had been many whispered stories about him and the wild lifestyle he'd embraced. I'd heard him described as a freewheeling drug addict who thrived on parties and prostitutes. Completely unreliable, he lived on the edge, they would say. While those stories frightened me as a little girl, they touched a completely different nerve now that I was a teenager who was also fond of challenging authority and experimenting in the drug culture.

In high school, when I partied too much or stubbornly fought to escape the conservative ways of my mother and adoptive father, I would be compared to Jeff. You're just like him, they would say. Now, for the first time in my adult life, I was suddenly in direct contact with the man himself. Long-lost Jeff was on the line, and despite all the negative things I should have felt about him, my mind still screamed, "Wow! This is my dad!"

As Jeff proclaimed his great interest in me, his encouraging words felt like cool spring water bubbling out on the sun-parched earth. Crushed by fears and insecurity, I longed for acceptance, so I literally drank in everything he said – and was thirsty for more. The fact that he had searched me out made me feel significant just when I needed emotional support most.

He asked me about my life. He commiserated with me and cursed my struggles. We talked about his house in Ohio, and he gave me an update about my two half-brothers, Jeffrey and Chad. Both were with him for the summer, he said. I was aware he had other children after leaving my mother, but I'd never learned much about them. I was thrilled when he told me they were eager to meet me.

Then, he dangled even more enticing bait. My great grandmother, Mama Dell, was also living with him, he said, and she wanted to see me too.

As the conversation went on, my mother's characterization of Jeff as a selfish, dangerous man began to seem ludicrous. In fact, I began to feel her warnings had been hurtful and judgmental. Jeff was like me – just a simple, easygoing guy who wanted to enjoy life. My mom and dad just didn't understand him, but I did, and I found his invitation to join him in Ohio compelling.

After all, what reason did I have to stay in Texas? What benefit would there be in returning to Florida? I was eighteen and unencumbered, a girl with no responsibilities, a young woman hungry for new opportunities. What Jeff offered was the perfect cure for everything that ailed me.

I told him I would come.

Looking back, I now realize this call was a huge turning point for me, but at the time, I had no way of knowing what would come of it. In the moment, it seemed like just another day and just another decision. If anything, I thought it would provide a welcome diversion in my otherwise humdrum journey through life.

* * *

When the plane landed in Ohio, I was almost levitating out of my seat with excitement. I was thrilled to be out of Texas, and the fact that my biological father was comfortable with my edgy lifestyle only heightened my desire to meet him. Although I wasn't sure what to expect, I felt real joy for the first time in months, and that alone was cause for celebration.

Earlier, on the plane, I had run through all of the reasons why this had been the right choice to make. Texas had been a dead end. This would be the beginning of something new. He was my biological father. What harm could come out of our reunion? If nothing else, the trip would be a vacation and a release from the drudgery my life had become – and who didn't need a break from time to time?

Although I was nervous, the feeling was a good kind of anxiety, like the anticipation you experience just before an important event. Even today, many years later, I remember our meeting like it happened yesterday.

After disembarking from the plane, I entered the arrival lounge and stepped on to the escalator bound for the main concourse. Halfway up, I saw Jeff. He was waiting on the floor above – a tall man with a big, puffy afro. Standing next to him was a small, Hispanic woman. The two of them were smiling warmly. He opened his arms as the escalator delivered me to him, and we embraced tightly. Rosita – who I later learned was his fourth or fifth wife – seemed genuinely pleased to welcome me too. Her eyes sparkled with admiration for Jeff, and that comforted me. It made my father seem more respectable somehow.

In our first meeting, I also remember being surprised by the ruggedness of Rosita's face. This was clearly a woman who'd lived a hard life, and I could tell there was still some burden on her soul. Before I could dwell on her strangely melancholy spirit, Jeff dominated the moment with his childlike exuberance.

"Jeffery and Chad can't wait to meet their big sister!" he said, pulling me close. "And Mama Del is waiting at the house too. It's going to be great having everybody together! It's going to be awesome!"

There was something so uncomplicated and warm about Jeff's welcome that I immediately felt at ease with him. The passage of time and our separate lives seemed irrelevant, and the fact he'd abandoned me as a child meant nothing in that special moment. Instead, my mind and heart focused on the fanciful hope this reunion would lead to a new and better future. In fact, my heart would not let my mind consider any other perspective.

This would be something great. I was sure of it.

On the way to the car, Jeff asked me if I wanted to get high, and without hesitation, I said, "Yes."

Rather than stir up fears from the past, Jeff's audacity and roguish personality stoked my rebellious, youthful spirit into full blaze. This guy is cool, I thought. He's nothing like Mom and Dad back in Florida. And this visit is just what I've needed. It'll be just like hanging out with my high school friends. No responsibilities. Just parties and fun. What could be better?

In all honesty, the drive from the airport to Jeff's house is hard for me to describe. It was a blur. We drove around for hours, drinking, laughing, and smoking pot. I remember the drugs and excitement of those hours being intoxicating, but any detailed memories of it have become as thin and ethereal as a wisp of smoke.

By the time we finally pulled into my father's neighborhood, night had become early morning, and the streets were empty of all traffic and life. I do remember having a good first impression of his house. He lived in a nice suburban area full of well-maintained homes, and there was a big, pink Cadillac in his driveway. Jeff was clearly doing well for himself.

Since it was well after midnight when we arrived, my great grandmother and half-brothers were already asleep. Mama Dell was slumped in a rocking chair with her knitting on her lap, and the two boys were sprawled on the floor at her feet. The moment was amazing, and its significance finally shook me out of my stupor. I hadn't seen my great grandmother for as long as I could remember.

When she woke, Mama Dell immediately held out her arms to welcome me. Hearing the fuss, the boys also stirred and jumped to their feet. Big smiles on their faces, they embraced me and jumped up and down, screaming, "Our sister, our sister, our sister!" as if a long-lost treasure they prized had unexpectedly been found.

Jeffery was eleven. Chad was ten. Both were adorable, and I fell in love with them the moment I saw them. They seemed just as enamored with me. The connection was mystical. Almost instantly, an overpowering bond formed between us. At the time, we had no idea our lives would soon take wild twists and turns, so at that moment we met, only one thought filled my mind – this acceptance is what I've been craving!

I really believed coming to see Jeff was going to be the beginning of something amazingly good for me, and I slept that night with greater contentment than I'd felt for years.

The next morning, I found an envelope waiting for me on the kitchen table. It was from Jeff. Inside were three, crisp hundred-dollar bills. I was surprised by the gesture but oddly reassured too. This was Jeff's way of making amends, a sign he wanted things to be right between us. I eagerly accepted the cash with that perspective in mind. What I didn't realize at the time was that the gift also symbolized something far more sinister to Jeff. For him, it signified my entry into his economy of life; a self-centered pursuit of drugs and good times. In many ways, the cash in the envelope was "a cost of doing business." With it, he was buying my pawned childhood out of hock so he could exploit it again.

With this purchase out of the way, Jeff lost no time in exposing me to the drug culture in Ohio. He never asked me if I was okay with trafficking in narcotics. My acceptance of the pot in the airport parking lot must have answered that question as far as he was concerned.

I met him in the living room as he was preparing to leave for the day. Glancing over as if he'd been expecting me, he motioned for me to come along. We sped away that morning as if an outing to score drugs was the most natural thing in the world for a father and daughter to do.

*   *   *

Our drive through town ended at a gorgeous house in an upscale, gated community. I was excited by the prospect of going inside. It was a huge, extravagant estate – nicer than any place I had ever seen – and pulling into the driveway felt like the beginning of an adventure story.

In my gut, I knew Jeff was probably involving me in something illegal, but I felt exhilaration, not fear. As we walked up, I remember thinking, I wonder if the cops will suddenly appear? Wouldn't it be amazing to be caught in the middle of a big drug bust? It all felt like an out-of-body experience, as if I was watching our actions play out in a movie. Everything was electric, and I felt an incredible charge of adrenalin.

Shortly after Jeff knocked on the door, I heard the click, click, click of high-heel shoes coming from somewhere inside. After a moment, a tiny woman opened the door. She was dressed entirely in white with fur-lined slippers on her feet. Her fingers, hands, and neck were covered with expensive jewelry.

She seemed surprised to find me standing at Jeff's side and appeared to be uncomfortable with the intrusion. Thanks to my unexpected appearance, her usual routine was being thrown out of whack. Stupid, Jeff. He was already screwing things up, and it was only our first day together.

The little woman's negative reaction was so obvious even he couldn't miss it. He mumbled his way through a list of excuses and explanations. He needed to bring me. I was cool. I wasn't going to be a problem. Those kinds of things. She seemed unconvinced but led us inside.

I was immediately captivated by her flamboyance and by the ostentatious interior of the house. Like the woman, everything in the place was white. White walls. White floors. White rugs. A white leather couch with white throw pillows. The only thing breaking with the white theme was a black, monolithic television set. It stood against one wall, creepy and completely out of place.

My father motioned for me to stand to one side while he and the woman whispered to each other. Like our arrival, this exchange also seemed like a cheesy scene from a low-budget gangster movie. Jeff was playing the drug dealer. The woman was the gangster's ditzy wife. If the moment hadn't been so tense, I probably would have laughed out loud.

Jeff must have soothed the woman's concerns about me because the two separated, and he returned to reassure me everything was cool. It's funny how the term "cool" has stayed alive in the drug culture for so long. It became unfashionable as slang long ago, but addicts still use "cool" to describe a situation that's under control or a person who's safe and can be trusted.

Once he was certain I was okay with the situation, Jeff left me and went upstairs. He was barely out of sight when the white woman approached me. I was wary, but those fears faded after she asked me a few superficial questions. It was clear I was nothing to her – just an inconvenient child who would soon be gone. Her business was with "daddy," not his snot-nosed kid, and I was glad when she finally abandoned me to do more important things.

Alone in the room, I took a seat on the big white couch. An old black-and-white movie had been running on the television since we arrived, probably to provide background noise, and I checked it out to fill my time. I had no idea what the film was, but it got my mind churning about movie plots again.

Maybe this is the point when the cops will bust in. I could almost see them in my mind's eye, assembling along the outside walls, preparing to smash through the front door or pour in through the back patio. My imagination ran wild. I got myself so worked up, I actually felt a tingle of anticipation.

You're not in Texas anymore, Dorothy. This is the castle of the white witch, where everybody has secrets and lives outside the law. Come to think of it – what exactly are they doing upstairs? Jeff looked pretty excited as he went up there. I wondered what he had gotten himself into.

After thirty minutes passed, hushed voices and footsteps brought me out of my daydreams. Looking up, I saw Jeff appear on the top landing. The sparkle was gone from his eyes. So was his bubbly personality. Jeff usually exuded the charm of a natural-born salesman, but his expression was now dull, and he seemed disoriented. He was clearly high on something. Whatever he had taken, sniffed, or inject-ed upstairs must have had a profound effect on him.

As I watched, a second man appeared next to him on the landing. This guy was tall and heavyset with a thick, black mustache. As Jeff descended, he followed a few steps behind. It was nearly noon, but the big guy still wore a bathrobe. An unlit cigar wobbled between two of his fat fingers.

Like the woman in white, the mustachioed man was a character perfectly cast for my imaginary gangster movie. He was the "mafia kingpin," but unlike the woman, there was nothing comical about him. He watched impassively as my father fumbled his way down the same stairs he had confidently climbed just thirty minutes before.

Like everything else about the house, the strange and dangerous overtones in this experience excited me further. That's the way it has always been for me. Others adopt either a "flight" or "fight" response when they face a threatening situation, but I've always been moved in an entirely different way. Instead of wanting to fight or flee, I feel energized by taboo experiences and drawn into emotionally-charged situations, as if pulled by a magnet.

In this case, I found myself attracted to Mr. Big. I was fascinated by his obvious power. His world seemed lavish, mysterious, and com-pelling. The edginess of it drew me in, and the undertone of danger charged my senses.

Realizing we would soon be leaving, I took one last look around the room. What a place it was! What an experience this had been! I had tasted something exotic here, and deep down, I knew I would crave the flavor forever. Although Jeff was little more than a jester in Mr. Big's court, I promised myself I would return someday as some-thing more.

As we left the house, Jeff stumbled on the lawn, nearly falling head-long into the driveway. Fishing around in his pocket, he had difficulty retrieving his keys, so I took his arm, and we shared a look. He smiled coyly. He was too stoned to take the wheel, and we both knew it.

"Maybe you should drive, Shelly," he said, chuckling with embarrassment.

As he handed me the keys, a rush of self-assurance filled me. This was good. Jeff wasn't treating me like a stupid kid or some brat he'd only dragged along because he couldn't find a sitter. It was exciting to be treated as an equal – as a true partner in crime. I was elated to have earned his confidence.

Swinging over to the driver's side of his car, I got in. It was a new Cougar with a sunroof and power everything. It would be a blast to drive.

Jeff plopped down on the passenger side and set a big bag between us. There must have been a thousand pills inside. He pulled one out and handed it to me. It was stamped with the number 714—a Quaalude. I'd never seen so many of them in my life.

"I think we should talk," he said, opening up to me about the drugs he'd scored and about his plans for selling them. Nothing he said surprised me. I'd expected as much.

"Do you want one?" he asked. I shook my head. It wasn't because I was afraid of doing Quaaludes. I'd popped them in the past. Quaaludes just didn't do anything for me.

"Then what about this?" he said.

Reaching back into the bag, Jeff removed a thick brick of hashish, bound in plastic. As he unwrapped it, the car filled with a sweet smell, and I began to feel old hunger pangs rise in me.

"I got this just for you," he said with a smile.

At that point, all resistance melted away, and I opened myself fully and completely to the possibilities his lifestyle presented. I was aware of where things were heading, but I was also convinced it was already too late for me to stop. The opportunity had passed the night I arrived. There was nothing left now but to fully embrace who I really was – crazy Jeff's daughter. A child cast in her father's image. The flesh of his flesh.

Together, we smoked fine, blonde Lebanese hashish all the way home.

Chapter 3

UNCONTROLLABLE

Coming downstairs, I found Rosita in the kitchen. I hadn't said anything to her about the mansion or the drugs, but I sensed she knew exactly what had happened. She handed me another packet of cash.

"Jeff left earlier this morning," she said offhandedly. "He's taken a trip. He'll probably be back in a few days." Rosita had obviously experienced this kind of thing many times before.

A few days came and went. When Jeff eventually returned, he didn't stay long. He picked up more drugs and took off again, leaving little or no specific information about his plans. Now I understood why Rosita had been unfazed by our visit to the mansion. Even Mama Dell could have figured it out. Rosita knew Jeff was a minor league dealer serving one of the local drug kingpins, and she'd come to accept that fact.

Eventually, Jeff's coming and going became routine, and I was forced to find a way to fit in. Although Rosita was always around, I got the impression Jeff wanted me to take care of Mama Dell and the kids, so I put my time and energy into that task. I found this new role surprisingly satisfying. I loved Mama Dell, Jeffrey and Chad, and taking care of them gave me a sense of self-worth and family pride. It was hard work at times, but I found it much more fulfilling than the waitressing and sales jobs I'd had in Texas.

During this time, I was also smoking hash regularly. I hadn't yet fallen into Jeff's hardcore drug habits, but I was completely comfortable with the carefree, no-rules lifestyle he embraced. Living in his world, hashish was no longer taboo or even a guilty pleasure. It was commonplace, like picking up a cigarette or pouring a glass of wine.

Eventually, the long summer came to an end, and things began to change. Mama Del packed her belongings and left us to visit the home of another one of my relatives. As we said our goodbyes, I was sad but not upset. I understood why she had to go. It would have been selfish not to share her with other members of my family.

I had a completely different reaction when I discovered Chad and Jeffery packing to leave. Upset, I confronted Jeff about it.

"I need to get these kids back to their mother," he said dismissively. "School is starting soon. What did you think would happen when the summer ended?"

It was a good question. What I hadn't expected was for the entire family to dissolve within a few weeks. Things had been good, and I wasn't prepared for it to end so abruptly. It was hard to imagine living at Jeff's house without Mama Dell and the kids around. To overcome feelings of resentment toward Jeff, I eventually rationalized his actions. The boys did have a mother. She was probably a good woman living in a nice place – like my own mom. With school starting, the boys would need a more stable life, and their mother would undoubtedly be better suited to organizing their school routines. By the time we loaded Chad and Jeffery's belongings into the car, I had convinced myself Jeff was making the right move.

I couldn't have been more mistaken.

When we pulled up to their mother's house, I was shocked by what I saw. The place was literally a four-walled shack on a weed-infested lot. It was like something you'd expect to find in the Appalachian backwoods.

"No."

The word came out of my mouth involuntarily, a whisper – or

perhaps a prayer.

I turned to face Jeff, and he pulled back a little. The look on my face must have stung him. Before I could speak, his eyes darted away, and he began to ramble. "They'll be fine. Their mother expects them. She's a good woman. She'll take care of them."

When my expression didn't change, he gave up this pleading tone and became more direct.

"Whatever you think, these kids have a mother, Shelly."

When I didn't back down, he became stern, and his words more biting. They left no room for argument.

"I wouldn't have let you come if I knew you were going to be like this. You'll just have to let this go!"

To this day, I remember what happened next as a kind of waking nightmare. The boys got out. I sobbed. They cried too. It felt as if I was about to throw someone I loved into a cesspool; to toss them headlong onto the city dump. No one treats their own flesh and blood this way, I remember thinking. These are innocent, vulnerable children. They only want to live a decent life. How can Jeff just drop them here and drive away?

Worse still, I felt I was part of this betrayal, and that had a devastating impact on my relationship with Jeff. As our car pulled away, the boys sobbing and waving from the yard, I swore I would never again feel any pride or respect for the man.

I cried over the loss for days. Even a week later, the pain felt unbearable. To escape it, I began taking more drugs. Each time a memory of the day surfaced, I pushed it down with Quaaludes or hashish. This tactic worked – unfortunately – and before long, I was wasted more often than I was sober. Within three or four weeks, I lost twenty pounds. Despair was literally swallowing me up. Deep down, I understood and feared what the drugs were doing to me, but on another level, I couldn't live without the release they provided.

I didn't recognize it at the time, but this was another pivotal moment in my life. It was the beginning of an insidious cycle – a defense mechanism – I would adopt later and use often. It is an "escape," I discovered, that only spirals down into greater pain and self-loathing.

Fortunately, an unexpected intervention pulled me out of that decline before too much harm was done. It came in the form of another phone call, this time from my older sister. There'd been a lot of friction between us in our teen years, so I wasn't sure what to say. Kim, on the other hand, seemed genuinely happy to have reached me, so I opened up and told her about my situation.

At one point, I explained what had happened to the boys and admitted to using drugs to deal with my pain. The weight loss came up too. I blamed myself, but she surprised me by coming to my defense. Perhaps my troubles brought out her protective "big sister" qualities. She was kind and sympathetic.

"I'm just three hours away, Shelly. I'll head over there now, and we'll get to the bottom of this," she told me.

Jeff was away when Kim arrived. I must have been starving for adult companionship because my heart swelled with love and gratitude the moment she confidently strode through the door. She'd always been a "take charge" kind of person – the type who doesn't easily back down – and that was a strength I desperately needed at the time. Her fiery spirit fortified me, pulling me out of my downward spiral.

"I'm going to stay here for a while, Shelly," she said matter-of-factly. "I want to see what Jeff is up to."

A few days later, the phone rang. It was Jeff. Before I could get a word in, he began pushing for something. He said he was in Toledo, in trouble, and needed a favor. I immediately shifted into enabler mode, babbling something encouraging. Fortunately, Kim was nearby and grabbed the phone before I could offer any specific help.

As they talked, her face registered irritation, then concern. Although I could only hear part of their conversation, I could tell something serious must have happened. Kim was strong and argued every point, but she eventually surrendered to Jeff, hanging up the phone, frustrated but focused.

"We do need to take care of something for him," she said to me, almost apologetically. I could see it aggravated her to lose this battle of wills with Jeff.

Together, we traveled to a nearby store and found a sinister man there, sitting behind the counter. He looked at us suspiciously, but after my sister introduced herself as Jeff's daughter, he took her into a back room. Within a few minutes, she returned with a paper bag.

Our next stop was a little diner in Toledo. As we pulled into the parking lot, we could see Rosita and Jeff inside having lunch. Kim stalked inside. I sheepishly followed.

"Your damn taxi service is here," Kim said, tossing the bag. It slid across the table. Jeff opened it and pulled out what looked like a thick stack of money held together with a rubber band. Before Jeff could nod his thanks, Kim had already turned and was walking away. I had to run to catch up.

Back in the car, she fumed. I could sense Kim had been pushed too far and could see she wanted to pay Jeff back for his insolence.

"Shelly, we're both getting out of here," she said. On the long drive back, we plotted the "when" and "how" of it. She was so confident in this decision, I couldn't help but feel optimistic.

*   *   *

On the morning we departed, Jeff was still completely unaware of our plans. A few weeks had passed since the Toledo incident, so he probably thought things had settled back to normal. Kim and I had actually spent the intervening time preparing for this day.

Each week, my desire to leave Jeff had grown stronger, and on one particular night, after my father had returned home, my feelings and fears were confirmed. Kim and I had gone out to a party that evening. When we came back, my sister noticed a paper bag tucked in the corner of the kitchen counter. It was full of u-100 syringes – a sure sign Jeff was back on heroin. Kim and I were both rattled. Things had gone from bad to worse. We needed to get out, and there could be no turning back.

Even so, I felt sick to my stomach when the day of our departure literally dawned. I tried to justify what we were doing by recalling the terrible things Jeff had done in the preceding weeks. Over and over again, I forced myself to relive the anger and pain I'd felt when he abandoned his sons to a life of misery. In spite of this, I couldn't help but feel sympathy for the man because I knew our actions would hurt him deeply.

I also pitied him. I had problems with drugs, but his situation was much worse. He had become a captive, enslaved to dope, to money, and to his crazy dreams. I could drive away and leave his hellish world behind, but he would remain trapped there, a lost soul, a true junkie. Strung out on heroin, he would be unable to escape.

I handed my bags to my sister, and she tossed them into the back of the van. At that point, I remember thinking, draw your strength from Kim. She knows how to handle this kind of thing. As I watched her begin final preparations, the inevitability of our departure suddenly became more real to me, and I began to tear up. When she glanced up from her tasks, she saw I was wavering and shook her head gently. Her unspoken message – be strong.

Suddenly, a jolt of panic shot through me. I'd heard a noise from inside the house. How would I hold it together if Jeff had heard us and was coming down to investigate? I had no idea what I would say to him.

Kim had noticed the sound too. She hurriedly arranged the last of the bags and motioned for me to get into the van. Just as she slid behind the wheel and turned the key to start the motor, the front door opened, and Jeff stumbled out, still groggy with sleep. He held up his hands to gesture, "What's going on."

I began to cry.

Kim took control.

Putting a hand on my leg to keep me from moving, she opened the van door and slid out, cutting Jeff off as he came toward me. I could see them talking, but I couldn't hear what was said over the rumble of the motor. Eventually, Jeff came to my side of the van, and I rolled down the window.

"Is it true? You're leaving?"

"I have to," I said, praying he would let it go at that. I didn't know what I would do if he challenged me.

Jeff seemed lost in thought for a moment. Perhaps he realized my departure would mean less baggage in his own life. Perhaps Kim had challenged him about the heroin, and he'd been humbled by the charge. He never expressed what passed through his mind, but he didn't argue with me either. He just stepped close, hugged me through the window, and whispered in my ear, "I'm sorry."

I nodded. As father and daughter, we shared a last intimate moment. Looking into his eyes, I could see he had picked up my unspoken message – I know you're sorry, dad, and I believe you. With that, Kim climbed back into the van, and we pulled out of the driveway.

As Kim drove on, the impact of what we were doing struck me. I was 18. Kim was 21. Although leaving made sense, it meant the two of us would be homeless. My parents had sold their townhouse and moved into a two-bedroom condo in Florida. Living with them clearly wouldn't be a long term solution for either of us.

As if Kim had read my mind, she offered reassurance. "Mom and dad will be glad to see us," she said. "I'm sure we can stay there until we get back on our feet."

When I didn't reply, she continued.

"You know you had no future with Jeff, Shelly. You were too young to remember what he was like when we were kids. He was terrible to mom. He was a hopeless addict. And he still is. This is the right thing to do."

I let Kim's confidence wash over me, and it did strengthen my resolve. I wanted to believe her. Those words became my mantra. This is the right thing to do. This is the right thing to do. This is the right thing to do.

And, for a short time, it was.

*   *   *

Those first weeks following my return to South Florida went well. I enjoyed the stability of living with my mother and stepfather again.

Life with Jeff had been chaotic and an emotional whirlwind, so it was a huge relief to be in a calm, stable environment. Like a hospital patient being treated for exhaustion, I desperately needed peace and quiet, so those weeks at home were the best medicine for what ailed me.

Unfortunately, even a helpful hospital stay can get old. Eventually, rest becomes boring, routines start to irritate, and caregivers annoy. Once I began to feel better, I became antsy and yearned for excitement again.

Mom had expected my life to change after my return home. She and Dad had never approved of my lifestyle, so they assumed I'd "learned my lesson" and would now adopt a more straight-laced way of life. Nothing could have been further from my mind.

My sister, on the other hand, did respond to their encouragement and set new life goals as a result. While I was floundering, she began researching opportunities with the U.S. military. Typical of Kim, she moved quickly and decisively. Within a few weeks, she had visited a recruiter, taken the tests required, and was accepted into the armed forces.

Not knowing what else to do with my life, I followed her like a lost puppy. I also went through the testing the recruiters required – but I failed. When the rejection notice came, I was horribly ashamed. I'm not even good enough for the army, I remember thinking. It was humiliating.

After Kim packed up and moved out, I settled into my parent's den. This was in the early 1980s – around 1982. It must have been strange for them. On one hand, they were happy to have me home and out of harm's way. On the other, they had no idea what to make of me. I had barely achieved a high school education, and I had no real job skills. It was a frustrating time for all of us.

Searching for answers, I eventually turned to my old high school contacts. Kathy, a cheerleader girlfriend from those days, suggested we sign up for cosmetology school. She had looked into it and told me financing was available for the classes. The idea thrilled me because I had always been good at doing my own hair and nails. This might be something I could do and succeed.

My hunch was right. Cosmetology school was wonderful. I had a real talent for the work, and as new fashions became popular in the 80s, it created a lot of demand for my services. I was so good I even built a clientele among the other girls at the school. Soon, those leads led to contacts out in the community, and I began getting calls from local salon owners who wanted to hire me immediately. With so many job offers on the table, I saw no reason to continue with school, so I dropped out and got into "the real world."

My very first job was at an upscale nail salon, and before long, big money was rolling in. The acrylic nail craze was exploding all over South Florida, and I was in the perfect position to cash in on the business it generated.

I continued to live at home and do everything I could to appease my parents, but the success and money actually allowed me to begin a double life – a very common skill among addicts. To pursue our goals, we quickly learn how to play the system. We placate parents and appease employers, but we live completely differently outside of work and home.

Double lives are much more common than you might expect. There have been plenty of famous cases. We've all heard of politicians who appear straight-laced but are suddenly discovered to have bizarre habits in their "personal lives." There are also pastors who have solid reputations in their churches but end up having multiple girlfriends on the side. For every one of those notorious cases, there are thousands if not millions of less newsworthy double-lifers; people like me who use the tactic to hide their addictions and deviant behaviors.

In my case, the reckless aspects of my lifestyle were always kept out of the house. Whenever I needed to cover for my drug use or partying, I would formulate some reasonable excuse so I could have my cake and eat it too. I could crash at home and still indulge my drug habit and my appetite for partying. My parents had their suspicions, but they would only push so far. When I felt cornered, I would pretend to be offended by their accusations, and they would back down. It was an ironic side effect of their high moral stance. They were afraid of blaming me unjustly, and as a result, their own good natures worked against them.

Among other things, money was always hidden. I made certain my parents didn't know my income or how much cash I was using to fuel my parties, promiscuity, and drug purchases. If they realized how much money I had, they would expect me to get my own place or pitch in on their expenses.

In time, another old high school friend, Sarah, became my "partner in crime," sharing in most of my double life's darker exploits. Sarah was my kind of girl. She thrived on frenetic activity and was drawn to the same reckless lifestyle I loved. Our weekends were filled with alcohol, drugs, and parties.

Eventually, our drinking became so obvious my parents couldn't ignore it. They began to ride me about the dangers of drinking and driving, and my usual excuses would no longer fly. To keep my lifestyle going, I switched to another tactic. I would manipulate my mother and play her against my dad to get my way. Using this strategy, I was able to wheedle out of their grasp awhile longer.

Then, things escalated to a new breaking point.

I had convinced my dad to lend me his car so I could join a friend at a midnight bowling league. I was misleading him, of course. The bowling league was real, but I actually wanted the car to drive to one of my favorite local hangouts called "The Chickee Bar." When I arrived, Sarah was already there. She was sitting with Mike, a mutual friend. On his lap were a small mirror, a razor blade, and two lines of cocaine.

I was thrilled. Tonight, I would try something new – cocaine!

My parents would have been horrified, but I felt no fear or guilt. Immature and completely self-absorbed, I'd always lived in the moment. Being reckless was exciting, and the consequences of my actions were rarely considered.

Sarah took the mirror first and snorted up a line. The two of us giggled like school girls, and after a moment, I asked her what it was like. She bubbled with excitement.

"Wow. It's an incredible high. A real rush! Try it!"

Without hesitation, I took the mirror and snorted up the cocaine, flinching at the slight burn in my nostril. The sharpness startled me, but the feeling wasn't unpleasant. Then, my mouth numbed, and a surge of euphoria followed.

In a matter of seconds, all the nagging little aches and pains I had been feeling were blown away like a coat of dust. My dullness and exhaustion vanished. I became completely alert and incredibly focused. This was like nothing I'd ever experienced before.

I remember thinking: This is amazing! I'll chase this high for the rest of my life. Whatever it takes, I want more. Like an infatuated lover, all I saw and craved was this drug and its warm embrace.

Within an hour, Sarah and I snorted our way through Mike's entire gram, and I learned that while a cocaine high was spectacular, it didn't last. After we talked awhile, Mike left our table, and I became depressed. Cocaine was $100 a gram. How and where could I buy more? The craving I had was already beginning to control me.

Just as my anxiety was becoming overwhelming, Mike returned with a stranger. He introduced the man as Smokey. The guy barely warmed his seat before he started bragging about a stash of cocaine he had back in his room, and I almost swooned with relief.

All three of us followed Smokey to his place. There, he produced a shoebox containing a huge baggie of white powder. Smokey chopped at the stuff carelessly, and I was shocked by his nonchalance. He seemed to have no regard for the value of the cocaine he was offering us. Then I noticed his wrist. He was wearing a gold Rolex watch with diamonds circling its face. His wealth and cocky attitude were intoxicating, and it all reminded me of the Ohio drug lord and the attraction I'd felt for his power and lifestyle.

Smokey finished, and the cocaine made its rounds. I was almost trembling with desire when my turn came. I snorted a line and was surprised by what happened – or rather, what didn't occur. Before, the cocaine had produced a harsh bite in the membrane of my nose. This time, I felt nothing. I waited for the jolt of energy, but it didn't come either.

As if he could sense our confusion, Smokey stepped forward to reassure us. "Hey, it may take a few minutes, but wait for it. You won't believe it. It'll be the best high of your life."

Another minute passed. Mike, Sarah, and I glanced at each other, then back at the white powder still clinging to the mirror. We were all thinking the same thing. Is this some kind of con?

I checked my watch. The hour was late, and I needed to go. Before Smokey could say more, I got up, excused myself, and headed for the door. Weird, I thought. The guy must be a conman. As I slid in behind the wheel of my car, I wondered how Mike and Sarah would handle the situation. Would they challenge Smokey? Had I just escaped a bad scene? Was the guy actually an undercover cop?

Forty minutes later, my head spinning, I was fighting to remain conscious. Hadn't I just left the bar? How had so much time passed? Where exactly was I? Struggling to make sense of the world around me was like fighting to wake from a nightmare. My surroundings seemed ethereal. Lights were spinning. Horns were honking. My mind was swimming.

Suddenly, something banged against my car's window. The hammering became rapid and insistent. Then, I noticed the lights. Red, blue, red, blue; flashes in rapid succession. A cop.

You're as high as a kite. You're under the influence of Smokey's dope. Panic helped pull my thoughts together. I had talked my way out of trouble with cops before. I needed a story. I would need to become a victim. I could hear myself speaking, but my words sounded distorted.

"Help. I think somebody slipped something into my drink. My dad. This is his car. He's going to kill me. I need help. I need to get home."

Blinded by the flashing lights, I rambled on and on. The fear in my voice was palpable. Good – my emotions may distract this cop, some distant but foggy part of my mind realized.

"You're OK, right? You need to slide over on the seat, honey. I need to get this car out of traffic."

Thank God! The cop hadn't pulled me out and handcuffed me. He was going to help me instead. I slid over, allowing him to get inside. Only then did I realize I'd stopped the car in the middle of moving traffic. The cop put the car in drive and moved it to the shoulder. Then, he turned to face me.

"You sure you're OK? Do you need to go to the hospital?"

I shook my head.

"Do you realize you were on the wrong side of the road? You were on the bridge over the Intracoastal Waterway. It's a miracle nobody hit you."

I shook my head again and wiped away a tear.

"I think somebody spiked my drink. My dad is going to kill me."

The cop nodded and squeezed my arm. He had bought the story, and he was going to help me get home. Thank God, I thought. What a disaster this might have been.

My parents didn't react well to having a cop deliver their daughter to the door, but their anger was balanced with relief when they heard about the tragedy I'd narrowly averted. I was punished, of course, but the storm passed surprisingly quickly.

In the following days, I traded notes with Sarah and Mike and discovered they'd experienced something similar.

"I found out Smokey's stuff was laced with PCP," Sarah said.

Angel dust. That made sense. It was my first encounter with PCP, but I had heard of it and was aware of its potency. I never asked any more questions. Mike took care of things with Smokey, and he eventually found another more reliable dealer.

Once the scare passed, I fell into a new routine, shifting from smoking marijuana to snorting cocaine. Weekend after weekend, we smoked, did coke, and partied. What had started as a single mind-blowing experience quickly became a habit. Doing cocaine had started as a special thrill. Now, it was my norm. I couldn't imagine a week without it. It seemed as natural as eating and drinking, and I often felt anxious and depressed when I wasn't under its influence.

The drug also robbed me of any sense of purpose. I saw men and women around me living traditional lives and pursuing normal career goals, but I never considered those options for myself. I now thought of myself as an outsider. I could observe the "real world" but was only able to live in my drug-addled fantasyland.

I didn't see it at the time, but this was another pivotal stage in my decline. I had reached a turning point and had chosen a life path that would shape my entire future. I was no longer playing games. I was entering the drug culture purposefully and completely. I was giving up "normal" and moving into the shadows – into the artificial, skewed world of a dedicated drug user.

Jack became my next guide down this rabbit hole.

I ran into him at a local club I frequented, and it wasn't long before we were living together. This solved two problems. It got me away from my suspicious parents, and it provided another distraction in my otherwise shiftless, unsatisfying life. Jack was a drinker, a drug user, and a lot of fun. He worked two jobs. He served as a valet at a local hot spot and moonlighted as the drug dealer for nearby strip clubs.

My parents had been furious about most of the choices I'd made in life, but my decision to move in with Jack angered them most. It also cut off their access to me, so their opinions rarely reached me. Once I was living with Jack, they were "out of sight, out of mind," and there was nothing they could do to influence me.

For a while, Jack and I thrived as functioning addicts, and our abuse of drugs and alcohol reached staggering levels. Then, thanks to our high-strung emotional state, our carefully constructed fantasyland began to fray at the edges. We would fight, break up, make up, and fight again. At first, this added to the thrill of the relationship, but eventually, any positive feelings ebbed away, and only an empty, aching misery remained.

"We need to get out of here," Jack said one day. He explained his mother lived in Michigan, and we could move there for a fresh start.

"She loves the idea of us coming up," he told me.

As Jack explained it, his mother would happily open her home to us, and she and her husband would help us find work, get our relationship stabilized, and make a new start. This scenario sounded appealing. It reminded me of how I felt the first weeks I had spent with my father in Ohio. Though brief, those were good times, and I had positive memories about it.

My mother hated the idea. She feared the worst and felt she might never see me again. She knew all about the fights Jack and I were having and had seen the signs of his violent temper. There had been bruises, black eyes – even hospital visits. She believed Jack would eventually fall into a drunken rage and kill me.

What she didn't know was that most of my fights with Jack were sparked by my theft of his cocaine stash. Jack was a social cocaine user and could stop at any point. Alcohol was actually his drug of choice. I, on the other hand, had become an insatiable cokehead. Once I started, I couldn't stop. I would go on and on, even if it meant secretly stealing the supply of cocaine he sold to support us.

My mother only relented after I promised those days were behind me. I didn't need her approval, of course, but gaining her favor was comforting. I was nervous, leaving my family and home again, so having her on my side helped calm my mind.

On the day I packed my things for Bloomfield Hills, I felt certain my life would improve. It didn't seem possible it could get any worse.

*   *   *

My face was a mess. A stream of blood ran freely from my broken lip, and a purple-blue bruise was forming around my right eye. Within hours, the eye would swell shut, and by morning, I knew I'd look like a train wreck. How could I go to work?

My boss knew Jack and I fought occasionally, but she tolerated my behavior because the salon's nail business was thriving, thanks to my clients. Even still, this incident would be impossible to ignore. I had to go in – Saturday was our busiest day – but I would need to concoct a cover story to deflect her questions.

Once the bleeding stopped, I sought solace with alcohol. I was already smashed, but I needed more booze to soothe the pain.

After medicating myself, I plopped into bed and stared up at the ceiling. Michigan was supposed to have been the beginning of something better, and it had been for the first few months. Jack and I were occupied with getting jobs and setting up a home. Those had been helpful distractions, normalizing our lives a little. At that point, it really had felt like a second chance.

Then, the alcohol and drugs began to pollute everything again. As before, it started as a way to get thrills but quickly became an enslaving routine. In a matter of months, we were again spending embarrassing amounts of money on cocaine. Moving to Michigan had accomplished nothing.

Lying in bed, I pondered how wrong things had gone. Eventually, my thoughts returned to the face in the mirror – my face; broken, bruised, and fearful. My emotions overwhelmed me, and I sobbed, buried my head in a pillow, and relived the attack.

In my mind's eye, I saw it all again. Jack stalking out of the house. Me screaming as I followed behind. The terrible moment when he turned to face me. The full force of his punch. The hard fall I took. Jack waving off a friend who had moved to help me. His leering expression and harsh words. "Leave that bitch. She deserved it!"

I was so disoriented by the blow his words barely registered at the time, but I remembered them now. I could also recall his laugh and the way he stalked away, never looking back.

Overwhelmed by these memories, I began sobbing again. My face burned intensely from the pain and from shame. Under the weight of it all, I curled into a fetal position and tried to escape into sleep. I was grateful when the alcohol finally sent me off into oblivion.

When I woke, it was morning. A pang of fear swept over me. I was certain I had just heard the sound of a door closing. Was it, Jack? Had he returned? It must be him. I could hear someone stumbling around in the other room. Then I realized I would need to get moving too. It was Saturday, my work schedule was packed, and I couldn't afford to lose the business – or worse – my job.

Just as I pulled myself up from the bed, Jack stalked into the room. He stared at me with unfocused eyes.

"What happened to you?"

Infuriated by his outlandish remark, I snapped. I screamed. I cursed him. I said I would press charges and moved toward the phone to make good on the threat. It was foolish, but in the moment, I'd lost my temper and my mind.

As I fumbled with the receiver, Jack swept in. He yanked the phone out of my hand and savagely smashed it against the side of my head. The casing disintegrated, fragments flying in every direction. In shock, I gasped and held up my hands to ward off a second barrage of blows. He shoved through my feeble defenses, grabbed a fistful of my hair, and pulled me off my feet, marching me toward the bathroom.

My heart raced. My head pounded. I could feel blood running over my cheek and down my neck. Frantic, I searched his eyes but saw no light there – not even a sign of simple recognition. Jack was so drunk he probably didn't even know who I was.

At the open bathroom door, he stopped abruptly and heaved me inside like a tattered ragdoll. I tumbled to the floor, slipped on my own blood and tears, and smashed into the cabinets and toilet. Before I could rise, I was knocked back again by a savage kick. He pulled his heavy boot back and kicked again and again and again. My pathetic attempts to stop these blows were completely ineffective. In that terrible moment, I wondered if I was about to die, everything ending there on the bathroom floor.

Just as I found myself slipping into darkness, Jack stopped. As suddenly as he had attacked, he turned and walked out of the bathroom. Heart pounding, fighting for breath, I waited for some indication of Jack's intentions. It was possible he was looking for a weapon. Within a few minutes, I heard a familiar sound and realized what had happened. Jack was sprawled out on the bed and snoring. He was out cold.

Using the toilet and sink to steady myself, I rose to my feet, got into a pair of jeans, pulled on a blouse, and slunk out of the apartment. I was a bloody mess. I couldn't go to work, but I was determined to get away. Anywhere would be better.

A few weeks later, I slid even further down the rabbit hole. If Jack had been the frying pan I'd leapt from, Debbie was the awaiting fire. Rebounding from my broken relationship with Jack, I quickly fell into her equally twisted world.

Very much like Sarah before her, Debbie was a spirited girl with an easy-going nature and an adventurous streak. I was desperate for love and acceptance, and she welcomed me with open arms.

Over the next four or five months, Debbie and I lived for drugs and parties. As the cocaine use skyrocketed, my health and weight plummeted, and after five months, I looked emaciated and hollow-eyed, like I'd stumbled out of the Auschwitz camp. I was, in fact, a prisoner of a different kind. I was unable to escape my addictions in spite of what the cocaine was doing to me.

The fire grew even hotter as I took my next steps toward hell. Debbie was my introduction to freebasing. I had been aware of freebasing even before my time with Jack, but I'd always considered it a crazy extreme, something only the most strung-out addicts dared to dabble in. Most of us still remember the accident involving comedian Richard Pryor. While freebasing, which often involves cooking up dope with a blowtorch, Pryor set himself on fire and was horribly burned.

During my thrill-seeking days with Debbie, I'd been through booze, marijuana, pills, and cocaine. Freebasing, I concluded, would just be the next new thrill.

Like the euphoria I had felt with my first use of cocaine, freebasing brought a new rush and a new high. I still remember the guys who introduced us to the technique. They seemed amused by our excitement, and one responded with an ominous warning.

"Enjoy every second of it, baby," he said, "but know you'll be chasing this high for the rest of your life."

I spent the rest of the night freebasing cocaine and called in sick on the following day. Through the next several weeks, every paycheck I got went to cocaine, and virtually every night was devoted to freebasing. Although I'd considered Debbie a great friend, I no longer found her company necessary. Cocaine was all I cared about, and I would spend night after night alone, freebasing in my apartment.

Less than two months into the habit, my already unstable life was on a countdown to self-destruction. Bills were unpaid. My health faltered further, and I began to call in sick and make ridiculous excuses for my behavior. I also became desperate for money to buy drugs, so piece by piece, I sold all my things – electronics, furniture, clothes – anything I could unload for cash.

Hiding this drug use eventually became impossible, and my boss finally stepped in. She insisted I call my parents and explain what was happening. I cried and pleaded, but she would not relent. As a concession, she agreed I could confess my cocaine use without mentioning the freebasing in order to save face.

The day I called home felt like the end of the world. My mother cried and could not be consoled. My father pushed relentlessly for more facts and explanations. Both reactions filled me with guilt and self-loathing. I've finally reached bottom, I remember thinking. As painful as it is, I have no choice. I have to seek help. This madness has to end.

Chapter 4

UNREPENTANT

Rehab rarely works for the unrepentant.

After leaving Michigan in 1986, I was broken and ashamed, but I remained hard-headed and self-absorbed. I was an addict at my core. Rehabs were tried, but they were never successful at ending my destructive, addictive behaviors because I was prideful, stubborn, and fixated on self-gratification.

By the time I entered a Christian program in Florida, I had also become a skilled con woman, able to manipulate my family and friends to achieve my own ends. Those who wanted me to change tended to be empathetic and good-hearted – two qualities I could easily turn to my advantage.

That said, I wasn't a fool, and I could see why a rehab might be worth trying. Addiction includes a lot of downs and emotional turmoil, and I could see the value of overcoming those problems. As my parents drove me to the rehab's compound, I lowered my defenses slightly and considered giving the process a try. Maybe this will help me manage my situation – to minimize the bad times. Perhaps, I'll be able to take away a few good things without relinquishing my control.

Like many drug rehabs, this program was located in a fairly remote location to increase security and reduce the number of runaways. This particular place was tucked among the orange groves in

Winter Haven, Florida. As we drove by long rows of well-manicured trees toward the entrance, I finally made up my mind, pledging to give the program a sincere try. After all, what could it hurt to memorize a few Bible verses and follow a few rules for a month or two? I could always bail if things got really creepy.

Thanks in part to this positive attitude, my first week at the rehab was much more pleasant than I'd expected. Most of the girls I met were close to my age, and we all got along well. As I'd expected, there were religious parts of the program and plenty of rules, but I found I could live within the staff's expectations without feeling too caged in.

I even found the spiritual parts of the program thought-provoking. If nothing else, they made me reexamine my own views of God. Of course, once things moved from broad ideas to specific teachings and their practical application, I became less interested in what they had to say. I preferred a vague God – not one with defined expectations.

Nothing in this Christian rehab program contradicted what I remembered about "the faith" my parents professed. As I expected, they portrayed God as a father figure who was angered by sinful living, and their plans for my improvement revolved around me making changes in my life, I presume, so God would be happier with me. After a few weeks of this, I lost any positive expectations I had about their approach and simply concentrated on making it through the program so I could return to my old life and go back to doing things my way.

Then, something unexpected happened.

A young woman on the staff approached me as I was working on my laundry. Her name was Tina, and most of the girls liked her because she was approachable, kind, and thoughtful, much more vulnerable and compassionate than other members of the rehab team. To us, Tina was "one of the girls," and she fostered a very positive, peaceful feeling everywhere she went.

When Tina saw I was frustrated and asked me why I was so upset, I told her about the dogs.

Because the rehab compound was located in a remote grove, there were always stray animals around the place. This included wild pigs and a pack of feral dogs. When we hung clothes on the line and left them there at night, the dogs would often maul them. It was common to go to the lines in the morning to collect your things and find them trampled on the ground or dangling in shreds.

On this particular day, an outing was planned, and we would not return until after dark. I had been told to do my laundry, but I was worried it would all be for naught. There was a good chance the things I was hanging out to dry would be destroyed by the dogs while we were away. I had little regard for the rehab or its programs, but I did value my own clothes. It was frustrating to be put in this position.

Tina heard me out, then smiled.

"Who do these clothes belong to, Shelly?"

I liked Tina but laughed inwardly at this smarmy comment. I knew where this would be going. Defiantly, I claimed the clothes were mine.

"No, like everything else, these are God's things," she said. Her response was soft and innocent; nothing about it was critical or challenging. "When you hang these things, just tell God they are important to you, and ask him to protect them for you."

I felt silly but said I would do what she suggested. After she walked away, I stared into the basket of clothes feeling ridiculous – but also challenged. I thought about her words and her faith. What she had said seemed ludicrous, but something about her confidence made me waver. Wasn't this just another example of naïve Christian thinking? Why would the God of the universe care about small things that were only important to me?

As I hung the clothes, I decided to play Tina's strange game. While pinning each item to the string, I told God my clothes were important to me, and I asked Him to keep the dogs away. Eventually, I reached something in the basket that didn't belong to me. It was a sheet from one of the dorms, something owned by the rehab itself. When I saw it, I chuckled and changed my prayer.

"This one the dogs can have," I told God. After finishing up, I rushed off to prepare for the field trip, never giving the clothes a second thought.

Many hours later, my group returned to the compound. We'd had a great time. The van slid to a stop, and we all piled out. It was dark, so we were told to gather our things and return to the dorm. My roommate helped me gather our stuff, including the clothes on the line. We were energized by the outing and excitedly chatted about the things we had seen and done. Both of us were distracted by this conversation as we folded our clothes. Suddenly, my friend gasped and cursed. She held up a piece of ripped fabric, something the dogs had destroyed. It was dirty and savagely torn.

I immediately assumed it was mine and began to frantically reexamine each item to see how many of my outfits had been mauled. As I finished the search, my jaw dropped. Piece after piece was perfect and clean. The only things on my line that had been lost were the items I had not prayed to protect. The dogs had shredded those things, focusing all of their fury on them.

The words I'd prayed reverberated through my mind. This is important to me, God. Tears welled up in my eyes as I imagined saying those words to my loving stepfather. Yes, he and my mother might have cared enough to concern themselves with such things, but why would God? The notion was mind-boggling, and it impacted me profoundly. Although some of the power of that experience has faded over time, it did alter my concept of God in the years that followed. In fact, it became a puzzle piece I would later use to construct a new image of the Divine.

Unfortunately, that was probably the only thing of value I took away from that rehab experience – though much of that failing certainly rests on me. After a few run-ins with the program's directors, I began to resist their help and defy their rules more openly. By the time the program ran its course, I was ready to leave and get back to my old life.

Less than three months later, I was back in the full throes of my addictions and starving for a high. Incredibly frustrated, I felt like a balloon stretched to its limit and ready to explode. When my old friend Sarah called, it was like a pinprick to my self-control. Bang went that balloon – along with any healthy habits I'd developed while in rehab.

"You need to come over tonight, so we can party," she said, adding she had an ounce of cocaine I could share with her and another friend. She said she knew I was adept at freebasing and asked if I would be willing to give them a lesson. I said yes, of course.

After I hung up, I considered how casually the conversation had gone and how easily I'd disregarded everything my parents wanted for me. It seemed to confirm my worst fears about myself. Nothing in any of my rehab experiences had given me the strength to overcome my addictions. I was clearly a lost cause, so why fight it any longer?

Without a second thought, I hatched a plan to deceive my parents. I would need a strategy to attend that party without mom and dad becoming suspicious. Luckily, my parents' own plans played perfectly into a scheme. My mother would be flying to the Bahamas with a girlfriend that night, and she needed me to drive her to the airport. This would provide me with transportation and a reason for being out. I hadn't been allowed to use the family car since returning from rehab. Now I would have that opportunity – and my parents would actually want me to take it.

After saying goodbye and watching mom's plane take off, I called Sarah to make sure the plan was still on. She begged me to hurry. They'd botched their first attempt to cook up some coke, and she needed me to play Chef Boyardee.

I couldn't get to Sarah's apartment fast enough. In fact, I was so taken by an urge to get high; I was practically hyperventilating on the drive to her place. When I walked in, Sarah and her friend were in the kitchen. There was a box of baking soda on the counter, and they were trying to cook the cocaine in a spoon. I laughed and pushed them aside, intent on showing them how it was done.

A few minutes later, I was as frustrated as they had been. Something was clearly wrong. The cocaine wasn't coming together. It must have been cut with inferior stuff. It would be useless for freebasing. Using a makeshift pipe, I tried to smoke what little I could collect from the process. It tasted strange, and I set it aside, disgusted and disappointed by the whole experience.

The three of us argued about what to do next. As the evening wore on, things got more and more tense. Finally, after one shouting match, I realized I had an uncashed check for about $400 in my purse. I didn't need the hassle of working something out with Sarah and her friend. With that check, I could buy my own dope and get high myself. I broke off from the argument and told Sarah she could do whatever she wanted – without me.

After a quick visit to a check-cashing store, I used my old drug contacts to locate a crack house nearby. The place was a dump, dirty and empty except for some makeshift furniture and a filthy, old couch. I bought some crack there and took a hit. The high was incredibly satisfying. Slow down. Get the most out of this. It may be weeks before you get out of mom and dad's house again.

That thought brought up a surge of panic. It was late now, and I was sure I'd be facing repercussions. My father would have a thousand questions. At the very least, he'd want to know why my trip to the airport had taken so long.

When the cocaine was gone, I headed for the car. I needed to get back. I'd be in trouble for sure. I was shocked when the car came into view. Someone had taken off the expensive tires and rims and replaced them with an old, worn set. The lug nuts were still lying in the dirt. The thief hadn't even finished the job!

My stomach roiled. This was serious. I would never be able to talk my way out of it. My parents were going to kill me. Frantic for a way out, I got a guy from the crack house to help me tighten the lug nuts. One thing led to another, and he suggested we go to his buddy's place to score more dope. I still had fifty bucks in my pocket, so I agreed.

Less than an hour later, I was accepting another crack pipe with trembling hands. Somewhere in the back of my mind, I realized things were rapidly spiraling out of control, but my desire to get high overwhelmed that still small voice. With only $50, I hadn't been able to afford much, so I'd had to settle for the dealer's offer. She would let me smoke the resin she had scraped from a glass bowl that had been used for freebasing.

As she handed me the pipe, she added a note of caution.

"Are you sure you want to try this? I've seen people collapse after smoking this crap."

I nodded and drew deeply from the pipe. The flavor seemed sweet and smooth, so I eagerly drew in more.

"Don't hold the smoke for so long, you fool. You'll have a freakin' seizure!" She reached for my arm, but I pulled away from her.

The little voice in my head resurfaced. It was screaming now, but the warnings sounded distant. Any fears I may have felt were being swallowed up in my stupor.

You're losing control.

The voice in my head was just a whisper. Too late, I understood that something really was going wrong.

Frantic to avoid disaster, I quickly exhaled. Sirens went off in my ears. Hallucinations followed. I saw huge spots coming and going, and my legs became rubber. I swayed back and forth. My mind and body were no longer attached. It was as if I had become an observer of my own life, watching my slow, steady collapse from afar.

The woman saw my reaction and ran to the refrigerator. She grabbed a handful of ice and rushed back to apply it to my neck and wrists. Somewhere in my hazy mind, I could hear my companion from the crack house laughing loudly. I was scared to death because it seemed possible I would die.

Slowly, the ice did its work. A little control returned to my body, and my mind started to clear. When I felt capable of functioning, my first thought was to flee. I mumbled something about needing to go. The woman turned to my friend, but he just shrugged.

"Are you sure you want to do that?" she asked. "Are you sure you can drive?"

I felt the urge to flee increasing. Hiding my dizziness and discomfort, I said I was fine. They were unconvinced, but they stepped aside. "I think you're crazy, but whatever."

The guy who had brought me to the house opened the front door, and I stumbled out. It was now mid-morning, and the sun was blazing. The house had been cold, but the driveway was hot. It felt as if I had stepped out of an icebox and into a furnace. Still dizzy, I made my way to the car. My ears roared with white noise, and the colors of the world dimmed as huge spots danced through my view.

Get to the car before you pass out. The voice in my mind was no longer soft or distant. It was shouting and filled with panic. I responded by pushing on.

Fortunately, the car started. I'm not certain how, but I made it to a nearby phone booth.

When my stepfather picked up the phone, the best I could do was spew out a lot of gibberish. Amazingly, his own voice was remarkably calm. There was no anger, no string of accusations, no venom. He must have understood something was very, very wrong.

"Are you OK, honey?"

I was too frightened for pretense. I begged for his help, telling him I didn't want to die. With directions I was able to give, he said he could find me. He told me to be calm and said he'd soon be on his way.

I made it back to the car and plopped into the seat. Looking down, I saw my white pants were soaked with blood. Oh, my God! I'm hemorrhaging! Another overwhelming surge of panic washed over me, and I passed out.

*   *   *

If you are fortunate, you've never heard of the Baker Act. It's also known as the Florida Mental Health Act of 1971. It's a Florida statute used to take control of individuals who have become a risk to themselves or others, and it's most often used by family members or the state to remove people from endangering environments and place them into institutional care.

You need to be pretty desperate to Baker Act someone, and to be Baker Acted, you need to be frighteningly self-destructive.

I was Baker Acted, so you can guess the scale and scope of my situation.

I have a difficult time remembering what happened to me after the call to my father. There are only a few sensations and images. I remember having people all around me. I recall something pressing in on me and my throat being blocked, but after that, I was swallowed up by darkness.

My memories from my time in the hospital are much clearer. I remember the bed, the tubes in me, and the heart monitor beeping. I knew I had been close to death and was in extreme pain, but I wasn't clear on why I'd had blood on me at the phone booth. Had I gotten into a car accident?

I was struggling to make sense of these things when my father and a doctor entered the room. Their eyes were full of pity. The doctor spoke first.

"You had an incredible amount of cocaine in your bloodstream. You're very lucky to be alive."

My father told me that some of the cops considered my overdose a suicide attempt. His other remarks stung too. "How long will it take for you to realize you're a serious drug addict? The next time, you may not make it."

I wasn't surprised this intervention had become necessary, so I didn't protest. Still, it was painful to learn I had been Baker Acted. Was I completely out of control? What would they do to me now?

These thoughts were interrupted when a woman entered the room. She'd come to explain the first steps in my treatment. She handed me a makeshift pajama set – and diapers. I couldn't believe my life had come to this. She explained that the diaper was necessary because my stomach had been pumped with some kind of charcoal, and it was common for patients to lose control of their bowels after-ward. The woman said the diaper would protect me from soiling my clothes, the furniture, and a car I'd be taking to the treatment center.

When we arrived at that center, I was taken to a waiting room where a nurse asked me some questions. That's when my stomach began to rumble. I rushed to a nearby bathroom, barely making it there in time. The charcoal stuff literally poured out of me. It was awful, and I felt miserable and ashamed. I also felt dehydrated. Rushing to the sink, I began guzzling water, glass after glass. I remembered the nurse saying I should avoid drinking anything for eight hours, but I didn't care. I was so thirsty I took in water until my stomach hurt.

Three minutes later, I was Linda Blair from The Exorcist. A stream of black slimy stuff shot out of my mouth like water from a firehose, coating the furniture and walls. Then, my bowels opened, and a clot of greasy black stuff filled my diaper. I couldn't control that or the vomiting, so before long, the mirror, sink, and floor were covered with black smears. It was everywhere – and it had all come out of me. Sobbing, I dropped to my knees.

The nurse must have heard me getting sick and guessed I had gone after water in spite of her warnings. When she opened the door, her eyes flashed with anger. I'm sure the scene was pitiful. I was mortified, but there was nothing I could do.

When the ordeal was finally over, I was taken to the showers and given clean pajamas. As I walked back to that part of the center, I passed the bathroom where I'd gotten sick – and shuddered. Two women were on their hands and knees, cleaning up my mess. Burning with shame, I slipped by, praying they wouldn't notice me.

Eventually, I was taken to a nice, hotel-like room where another patient had already been admitted. She was sleeping, and I was eager to do the same. Exhausted, I crawled into bed and quickly fell into a deep sleep.

Two days later, the new rehab program began. The coordinator for my floor arrived with a manual and workbooks. More papers were filled out, and I was given a schedule of activities for the week. The classes were called "12 Steps for Recovering Alcoholics and Addicts." I assumed this was either an Alcoholics Anonymous program or some variation of their concept. I had no experience with AA, but I had seen their group therapy approach depicted on TV shows and in movies.

My class was filled with twenty girls of various ages. Early on, I found the experience very enjoyable. I liked it much better than the Christian program I'd been in earlier. The people in this rehab seemed more like me, and their openness was refreshing. This group valued self-expression, while the Christian program's approach had focused on performance. When you were good, you were rewarded. When you were bad, you were labeled rebellious and told you needed to change.

This rehab staff asked questions rather than issuing commands. They seemed more concerned about how I felt and cared less about how I performed. I had never experienced this approach before, and I was happy I could open up and say what I was really feeling.

My parents also came to some counseling sessions the program provided. Under the guidance of a psychiatrist, my Mom and I were challenged to address what the doctor called our co-dependent relationship. I was surprised when he told her she needed to get help too. According to the psychiatrist, my mom was one of my biggest enablers. She was so eager to avoid conflict with me that I could manipulate her to achieve virtually anything I wanted. The psychiatrist said I needed to take responsibility for myself.

My parents were also asked to express how I had hurt them. That was tough for them, but they eventually shared their resentments, explaining the frustration they felt when they had to pay my debts and clean up my messes. As painful as this was, I think the meetings were helpful. Through them, I began to understand the pain I was causing, and I started to develop a greater trust in people who challenged me because they had my best interests at heart.

In another session, called "Healing the Child Within," I also faced an incident I had never shared before. After six other women described terrible things that had happened to them as young children, I told my story.

When I was just seven-years-old, I had been molested by one of the men in our neighborhood. It was tough to talk about, particularly because my parents had been angry about my fear of the man immediately after the incident. They saw my refusal to be friendly and visit his house as acts of disobedience and defiance toward them. As a child, I explained, I had felt violated, betrayed, and trapped.

The fear and shame I'd felt during that nightmarish experience resurfaced in that session, and I sobbed cathartically. The other girls cried too. More than twenty minutes passed before we could regain our composure. At that point, the group leader walked us through an exercise to help bring closure to our traumas. It wasn't a cure, but it was liberating, and it did help me make sense of my struggles with intimacy, guilt, and anger.

When the four weeks of rehab therapy were completed, I moved back home. My parents again assumed this would be a new start for me. I had been detoxed, purged of old traumas, reprogrammed, and supplied with a new set of psychological tools for fending off future threats. Surely this would be enough. Surely this would put me on the straight and narrow.

After going to just a few of the follow-up meetings, I bonded with one of the girls from the rehab, and, after a session, she offered me an opportunity to get high. I accepted, and we partied all night.

Thanks to the rehab, I had just become a well-adjusted addict, it seemed. None of the training had ended my obsession with drugs. Their allure remained as strong as ever. Next time, I thought, I should suggest my parents pick a rehab out of state. That way, I could at least enjoy a change of scenery during the ordeal.

Chapter 5

UNEXPLAINABLE

The hotel I'd picked was unremarkable – just one of the many dingy, sunbaked places that line the highways in central Texas. It was basic, cheap, and had a pool, making it the perfect place for my simple needs.

After all, I wasn't vacationing. I was hiding out.

Weeks earlier, I'd fled from another rehab program in Texas with no specific plan for the future, other than to get high and stay high. I hadn't worried about what might come next – until now. Suddenly, I was facing an obstacle I couldn't ignore. I was being thrown out of my cracker box room because I'd run out of both cash and sob stories.

Uncertain what the next day might bring, I went to the pool to ponder the possibilities. Honestly, since I was trashed and broke, there really wasn't much to consider. The pool would simply be a diversion – a last chance to enjoy myself on this final day of my drug binge.

At times like these, I always felt a little ashamed, but the guilt was never enough to produce any significant changes in my behavior. It just made the day a little more depressing. Glum and groggy, I plunked myself down at the edge of the pool and tried to figure out a way to squeak out a few more days of freedom. If nothing came to me, I would have to return home.

Perhaps, I thought, I can skulk back to the hotel after dark and crash on one of the pool chairs? Anything would be better than walking the streets all night or being roused from a park bench by the cops.

Like the motel, this pool was nothing special. It was just your typical, rectangular cement pond with a few worn, plastic-banded chaise loungers lining one side. The hum of the pump equipment created an annoying buzz, and the air was pungent with the smells of chlorine and musty towels. All of these things conspired to deepen my funk.

The place was devoid of energy and life too. No one was moving around, and even the traffic along the fronting street seemed unusually sparse. Suddenly, I realized why. It was that peculiar time of day between the morning rush hour and lunchtime when most people are either at work or in school.

For normal people, experiencing this mid-morning malaise can be disconcerting, but for those of us who do dope, "dead times" like this are both familiar and comfortable. In fact, we are most active during the strangest hours of the night and day. While others are occupied with work or are asleep in their homes, we can do our own thing surreptitiously. There's no one around to get on our backs, no deadlines to meet, and no responsibilities to distract us. For all of those reasons, addicts thrive in the dead times of the day and night.

As you might expect, we also cringe when it comes to following routines and adapting to life's typical nine-to-five schedules. That's part of what makes most rehabs so daunting. A daily structure is typically the first thing they want to impose, and I'm always glad to be free of it – to do what I want when I want.

At the hotel, that moment, what I wanted to do was dangle my feet in cool pool water – so that's exactly what I did.

As the minutes passed, my mind wandered, and the late morning became midday. The hot sun washed over me, and the funk that had plagued me earlier began to fade. I had nothing in my pockets, no place to sleep, and no friends to turn to, but I still felt there was no reason to worry. My situation, my parents, and the future would take care of themselves. For now, all that mattered was the sun's warmth, the water … and finding one last way to get high.

Suddenly and unexpectedly, a young man strolled up. He had a lanky, boyish frame and a distinctive mop of frizzy, red hair. Without saying a word, he went to the far end of the pool, rolled up his jeans, and plopped down, dangling his feet in a position that mirrored my own.

I lowered my head and fought back a chuckle. A picture had flashed into my mind. We were two desperados laying low at a desert watering hole. It was funny, but I didn't betray my thoughts by laughing. That might have spoiled my prospects. I'd already sized up the guy, and I saw the opportunity he represented. My instincts told me this stranger was a drug addict, and with luck, I could find a way to use him to my own ends.

Remaining quiet, I let my head lull down coyly, hoping he was sizing me up. Most of the hardcore addicts I knew were capable of reading people as easily as I could. We all knew how to manipulate and how to avoid being played. I hoped this new guy wasn't in my league. I needed him to believe I was vulnerable.

Over the years, I'd learned the best tactics for reeling in a guy. I would either play the damsel in distress or bait my hook with the promise of easy sex. Both work best if your mark believes he is in control. Since "Firetop" didn't seem like the sex-crazed type, I opted to play the girl in trouble.

I glanced up and flashed a sad half-smile. He caught the gesture, just as I'd intended. He'd been casually stirring the water with one leg, but the movement stopped when our eyes met. More importantly, he smiled. My ploy seemed to be working, but I still wondered if it would take sex to close the deal.

As if he was reading my mind, he hoisted himself up on his feet and came toward me. My mind raced. What's up with this guy? What will he want?

What he actually did shocked me.

In plain sight, he produced a small plastic bag full of crack rocks, shaking them as if to say, "Hey girl, look at what I've got." I was thrilled, of course. The guy had realized I was a crackhead too, and he wanted to party. Considering how precarious my position had been just hours before, this score from nowhere seemed like a miracle.

Firetop introduced himself as Larry.

After a few minutes of small talk, he led me to his room at the hotel. As I'd suspected, he was an addict who'd made a recent score, and he was looking for a way to share the experience. I'd seen his type many times before. In fact, I often had the same desire for company when I did drugs. It was always more enjoyable getting high when the experience was like a party – or like some twisted science experiment shared with a lab partner.

I never had as much fun getting stoned when I was alone.

As I scanned Larry's room, he suggested I crash there. I was grateful, and I told him my story, explaining how I had escaped a nearby Christian rehab, spent a few weeks doing drugs, and had now reached the end of my stash – and cash. He said he had no problem with me sharing the room, but he expressed surprise when I mentioned the rehab. Then he explained what he was doing in Texas – and my jaw dropped.

"Believe it or not, I just bugged out of a Christian rehab program myself – in Colorado," he said.

My God, I thought, we both came to this hotel for the same reason! We really are desperados on the lam, like Butch Cassidy and The Sundance Kid, or better yet, Bonnie and Clyde. This was a strangely compelling idea to me, and it filled me with an odd sense of anticipation.

Larry went on to explain the how and why of his current situation.

"I owned a nice truck, but I decided to sell it and get something cheaper with smaller payments. One of my relatives heard about my plans and agreed to buy the truck to get it off my hands. He gave me $4,000."

According to Larry, this relative expected the vehicle to be delivered when his cashier's check arrived, but once Larry got the cash, he had "detoured" to crack town and made a score. The truck was now parked outside the hotel.

"I came here to party," he said, smiling and shaking the bag of crack rocks. "What do you think? Want to join me?"

As bizarre as it sounds, I considered this chance meeting with Larry, a mystical event. It fascinated me that we'd both come from Christian treatment centers and that he'd waltzed into my life just in the nick of time, with both drugs and a solution to my problems with the hotel.

Believe it or not, I actually wondered if God orchestrated the connection. Clearly, neither of us had any interest in living like Christians, so I have no idea why our religious backgrounds would have been relevant to me at the time. Perhaps it was just another sign of my deeply buried desire to come to terms with God.

Larry mentioned this spiritual connection a few times too. He seemed to think there was something to it, but in the end, the only mystical mission we shared was our selfish desire to get wasted at someone else's expense.

Once the introductions were over, Larry pulled out a crack pipe, filled it, struck a match, and began puffing. Almost immediately, his mood changed. He'd been bubbly, almost childish when we met, but the dope brought him to a much darker place. Larry literally seemed to deflate in his chair as I watched. His face fell, and a wave of intense emotions seized him.

Another observer might have been disturbed by this transformation, but I didn't worry too much about Larry or his funk. I had freebased crack before, and I'd seen lots of different reactions from users. I had experienced far, far stranger things.

For example, some guys on cocaine become extremely paranoid. They spend hours looking out of windows and reporting everything they see. They become incredibly edgy and excitable – usually because they're convinced the police are lurking nearby, ready to swoop down on them.

Other crack heads turn into furniture movers.

It sounds nuts, but this happens fairly often. Once, I entered my kitchen and discovered a guy pulling my refrigerator away from the wall. When I asked him what he was doing, he said he had to shove it to the front door. I challenged him about it, and he became extremely agitated, insisting the fridge had to be moved. I couldn't stop the madness, so I threw him out of the house.

Another time, while some of us were getting high, a guy suddenly jumped up, threw open the front door, and ran off down the street. I had no idea where he was heading, but I knew he'd be back. He'd been barefoot and had left everything behind, including his stash of drugs. I just got up and closed the door.

The only people I feared while doing drugs were those who became angry or violent on crack. A few addicts were known to carry concealed weapons, and they would pull out a knife or gun after taking a few hits. I once smoked with a guy who seemed very normal until he did crack. Two puffs and he switched like Dr. Jekyll into Mr. Hyde. One moment we were talking calmly. The next, he pulled out a gun, threw me face down on the bed, and began screaming that I was a narc who'd planned to bust him. It was a miracle I got out of that situation alive.

In light of experiences like those, Larry's funk seemed like a shade of normal.

Then, he began to talk.

He started with a story about his girlfriend. Larry explained how they'd both been raised in Christian homes and had great families. Little by little, she and Larry had gotten into drugs, and eventually, they had cut all ties with their church friends. Then their lives spiraled completely out of control. They became enslaved to the routines of their addictions and to all the crap that goes with it – the conning, the manipulation, and the obsessions.

One day, Larry and his girlfriend teamed up with another guy to rob a store. Afterward, they ditched their accomplice and used the money to buy cocaine, driving off to Vegas to get away. While on the road, Larry pulled out a big glass bong and started smoking. Every time he took a hit, the smoke inside would swirl into images – something he described as "mysterious omens." At one point, Larry became convinced the smoke was trying to warn him about trouble awaiting them in Vegas. Supposedly, it revealed he and his girlfriend would be busted when they got to the city, betrayed by the partner they'd duped and left behind.

As I listened to Larry babble on about this, I became more and more freaked out. Messages in bongs? Smokey portents of the future? Eventually, Larry said, it all came true, exactly as the bong had foretold. Their partner did turn them in. When they arrived in Vegas, the police were ready and waiting for them – and they barely escaped capture.

"Laura and I were always having creepy spiritual experiences like that when we got high," he said. "God warns us about bad things coming our way."

I had an odd reaction to this story. It made me depressed. God never sent spiritual warnings to protect me. In fact, the opposite seemed to happen. When I was on a drug binge, God would ambush me with trouble or an arrest. Things never went as I hoped or planned. I was constantly being thwarted in my attempts to live comfortably in my addiction.

As afternoon turned to evening, we smoked on and on, sharing other stories about our miserable lives. We even talked about our families and how we had failed them. But at the same time, we also planned our next score. That's the way it was for me through most of my drug-using years. One moment I would be angry about the terrible influence dope was having on my life, and the very next, I would pursue those destructive cravings in earnest. I was like a dog, continually returning to my own vomit.

That first night, Larry and I smoked and talked until the wee hours of the morning. I hadn't had a wink of sleep in days, and I'm guessing he hadn't either. When I finally fell asleep, it was a deep and dreamless release.

Hours later, I woke up in the exact same position, still with the crack pipe in my hand. Groggy, I opened my eyes to find Larry already awake and intent on getting high again. This time, he was fidgety and energized. Before I could get a word out, he told me about a great dope connection he had in Houston.

"We need to get moving as soon as possible," he said. "We're going shopping!"

*   *   *

During the next couple of weeks, Larry and I went on a full-scale drug binge. Using hotels as a home base, we would travel to Houston for an ounce of cocaine, then scurry back to a room to smoke ourselves into a stupor. The next morning, we would wake up antsy and feeling down from the previous night's high, so we would repeat the cycle again. Our goal was to remain as high as possible, for as long as possible.

As the days passed, our paranoia increased. Under the influence of crack, addicts often become anxious about every person they meet and every decision they make. There were times when Larry and I changed our hotel room three or four times in one day, convinced that we were barely evading the cops by getting out when we did. Of course, it was unlikely any police were ever on our trail. We were just conjuring up this threat in our drug-addled minds. If we really had been under surveillance, the police would probably have considered our antics laughable.

One morning, about three weeks into our binge, Larry became even more paranoid than usual. No longer satisfied with changing rooms, he wanted to move to a hotel in an entirely different part of the city. The place he picked was a stark, ten-story tower in a very rough area of Houston – the kind of place addicts and prostitutes frequent because the rooms are cheap, and the staff is either complicit or intentionally oblivious to what's going on.

I cringed when we pulled into this place's parking lot. Everything about it was dingy, and parts of the building's exterior were dilapidated. Most hotels have welcoming decorations or signage to lure in tourists. This place looked like a bleak tenement building you might find in the nastiest part of town.

Even the weather had turned ominous and uncomfortable. I got out of the truck and was immediately struck by the stifling heat and oppressive humidity. To make matters worse, a smoggy, acidic smell hung in the air. It took a moment for the odor to register. It was the tangy stink of asphalt, urine, and smoke. Disgusted, I wrinkled my nose but couldn't ward off its intrusion.

Before I could comment on the bad vibe I was feeling, Larry strode off. If he hadn't been so intent on getting inside, I would have begged him to consider another place, but that moment had passed, so I plodded on after him, sullen and depressed.

Things didn't improve when we got inside. The lobby was dank and musty, with discolored walls and a stained carpet. I felt dirty, just standing there. Thankfully, Larry rushed through the check-in, so we could move along.

By the time we dropped our things inside our third-floor room, I was incredibly edgy. My whole body felt sticky and grimy, and nothing about the place offered me any hope of relief. Driven on by my growing aggravation, I focused on the one thing I knew would blow away the dark clouds encircling me – a reality-shattering high.

Times like these are particularly dangerous for an addict. Desperation makes you impatient. Impatience leads to sloppiness. And when a high doesn't come quickly enough, things can get even worse. In those cases, accidents can happen.

Larry saw I was getting jittery, so he moved fast to cook up some crack. As soon as it was ready, we climbed into bed and took a hit. It didn't go well for either of us.

Almost immediately, Larry started behaving strangely. It was as if the dark, oppressive atmosphere in the hotel had gushed up from the lobby and poured directly into his soul. There's no better way to explain it. Under the influence of the dope, Larry seemed to have opened up to all the negative qualities in that creepy hotel, falling completely under its influence.

Being stoned, I became very susceptible to his delusions, and they dragged me down too. Within a few minutes, things were spiraling out of control for both of us. As Larry became more and more agitated, waves of fear washed over me, and my imagination took flight to very frightening places.

Larry's earlier babblings about spiritual messages and mysterious forces flooded back into my mind. My heart began to race, and I became convinced malevolent creatures were stirring in our midst, just outside the range of my perception. Was it real, or was it a manifestation caused by the drugs? I couldn't be sure.

Suddenly, Larry seemed to actually see the evil things I was sensing. Without warning, he sprang up and crawled under the bed, moaning and grunting as if he was fleeing from something threatening in the room. That was more than I could take, and I snapped. My heart felt like it would explode. A cold shiver shot through me, and I pulled the blanket up and burrowed down to escape whatever unseen thing had been set loose in the room. As Larry continued to thrash around under the bed, yelping, and growling like an animal, my body trembled uncontrollably.

Seconds passed – then minutes. When nothing worse occurred, I began to calm down. My mind turned away from irrational fears of unseen threats, and I began to consider my real problems. This was becoming a disaster. Larry had lost control, and if he snapped completely, what would I do? He had been striking out at invisible creatures he believed were stalking the room. What if he went crazy and attacked me?

There were other fears too. It would be hard to cope if Larry's sanity didn't return. I didn't know this part of Houston. I wasn't even sure how to get out of the area. Panic began to roil in my stomach. Fighting to regain control, I peeked out from beneath the covers.

At that moment, Larry unexpectedly skittered out from under the bed. As I watched, he got to his feet. His expression was wild and frightening, but he also seemed more focused – oddly intent on some specific goal. He moved to the table and picked up the crack pipe. As he took a hit, I held my breath, uncertain what to expect. Was it possible Larry might veer even deeper into madness? I had no way to defend myself and no means of escape. If he snapped, there was little I could do.

I expected Larry to become violent. Instead, he ripped off his shirt and bolted out of the room. His reaction was so abrupt it left me in a state of shock. For several minutes, I was frozen in place. Then, not knowing what else to do, I got up and closed the open door.

After the turmoil of Larry's fits, the room had become eerily quiet. I crawled back into bed. Deep in my gut, I was convinced the lull was just the calm before another storm, so I waited anxiously for the next disaster – for cops to show up, for Larry to return enraged, or for some other terrible sound to break the silence.

Nothing happened.

Minutes ticked by. Then an hour passed. When Larry still didn't return, I felt lost. I had no idea what to do or where to go, so I stayed in the room and continued to wait.

Several hours later, the door opened, and Larry staggered in. At first, I thought he had been beaten. His face was red, his remaining clothes were soiled, and his feet were smeared with blood. Only after I moved toward him did I realize he was suffering from trauma and exposure. He was literally sun-baked. His shoes were gone, and the undersides of his feet were completely seared off from running barefoot on hot asphalt. Blood oozed through his toes. I'd never seen anything like it, and I was stunned.

Larry seemed to be in shock too. No longer under the influence or tormented by unseen bogeymen, he seemed much less threatening – almost vulnerable. For a moment, our eyes met, and something human within us connected. His eyes welled up with tears, and I could see he was struggling with a new set of demons: humiliation, self-loathing, and regret. I'd been there many times myself, and I knew exactly how he felt. Empathy flooded through me. My lip began to tremble with emotion, and when Larry saw this, he let go too, sobbing openly and gasping out apologies between rasping breaths.

At that moment, we both felt disgusted with ourselves. Such is the life of an addict. When we feel pain, we use drugs. Then, ashamed of our weakness, we seek another escape with more dope. It's a cycle that repeats itself over and over; again and again.

As I cried with Larry, I wished with all my heart that I could make his pain go away, but I knew his rescue was beyond my control. He and I were too screwed up. It was impossible for me to save either of us, so I did the only thing I could think of at the time. I lay down next to him in the bed, sharing his pain until we both fell asleep.

When I woke the next morning, Larry was moving busily around the room. He had already showered and gotten some medicine for his feet. When he saw I was awake, he urged me to get up immediately and pack my stuff. We were leaving, he said. This evil place was the source of our troubles and the reason he had freaked out, he explained. We needed to go somewhere else.

As much as I hated the hotel, the thought of striking out in search of yet another one overwhelmed me. I was exhausted. In the two-and-a-half weeks I had spent with Larry, I had lost nearly fifteen pounds. My body literally looked as if I had been beaten. Fever blisters from the pipe filled my mouth, and dehydration was making my lips crack and swell. I was a mess and getting worse with each passing day.

Things were probably as bad for Larry, but he rarely spoke of it. Instead, he always wanted to press on, probably because he feared what awaited him at the end of our binge. At that point, he would need to return home to face the disappointment of his family. He would do anything to avoid that.

On the way to our next hotel, I told Larry it was becoming harder and harder for me to get high by smoking. I had experienced this phenomenon before. After a few weeks of doing crack, the sores in my mouth, and the exhaustion of my body would begin to dull the impact of the drugs. Hearing this, he suggested I shoot up cocaine with a syringe. Larry claimed it would give me a much better high. I'd never banged coke before, but I was desperate, so I told him I would try it. I didn't even consider the dangers this might pose.

After driving for almost three hours, Larry finally found a little hotel that was suitable for our needs. Even before he turned into the place's parking lot, we both realized this would probably be our last stop. We were nearly out of cash, and our bodies were too fried to continue the binge for more than another week. When Larry handed me money and told me to check in for only three nights, I felt a surge of relief. There was an end in sight, and on some level, I craved that change, whatever it might bring.

We agreed that while I checked in, Larry would go to a local drug store to buy a box of syringes. As he drove away, I entered the little lobby – and immediately noticed the walls inside were decorated with signs about Jesus.

"Jesus loves you. Life without Jesus is a dead-end road. Jesus is the answer!"

I cringed, but it was too late to change the plan. Larry's truck was already out of sight. Damn him. Larry had picked a motel owned by a Bible-thumping Christian. That was all I needed. Even more pain. Even more guilt.

As I neared the counter, a pleasant, round-faced woman appeared from the back to welcome me. Her smile was disarming. I'll never forget her for as long as I live. She seemed imbued with a peace that was completely missing from my own life, and she carried herself with confidence and conviction – things I also lacked.

I'm sure I blushed as she looked me over. I certainly felt ashamed. I couldn't remember the last time I'd washed my hair. I must be a frightening sight. I'm a greasy, sweaty mess. Surely I smell. A flood of these negative thoughts poured into my mind.

Following her eyes, I saw that she was examining my swollen lips. She's wondering what's wrong with me. She must see crackheads all the time. I bet she realizes I'm one of them.

While I struggled with these terrible thoughts and feelings, the woman waited patiently. The smile never left her face. It was a sincere, welcoming expression, and it spoke to my heart. I desperately wanted to say something positive in response, but I held back. I just gave her my driver's license and signed the paperwork. She gave me the room key.

The little hotel was shaped like the letter "U," with our room at the bottom of the curve. Shortly after I got inside, Larry returned from the store, and without saying a word, he piled everything from the truck on the bed and cleared off the dresser. Within a few minutes, he had set up beakers and a Sterno tin and was busy cooking up the cocaine. I cleared off the bed, sat down, and waited. Eventually, he turned to me.

"Are you ready for the best high of your life?"

I asked if he was going to shoot up the coke too.

"No, no, no," he said. "If you think I get crazy when I smoke crack, you should see what happens to me when I bang this stuff. We'd probably both end up in jail – or dead. I think it's better if I pass."

Oddly, I remember being relieved. Since the experience at the creepy hotel, I'd been worried about being around him when he got high.

As I sat there and watched, Larry added water to the cocaine on his spoon and drew the goopy liquid up into the syringe. Excitement grew in the pit of my stomach. My craving to get high had grown so intense it felt like the sensation of extreme hunger. I was literally starving for a high.

Smoking has failed me. This is what I need now. Something more powerful.

After the syringe was ready, Larry put a belt around my arm to slow the blood flow, just as they do at a doctor's office when drawing blood. I felt a bit of apprehension at that point, but I allowed him to continue. We were too far along now to stop. By the time he found a good vein and wiped the spot with an alcohol swab, I was all in. I didn't even wince when the needle went into my arm.

Once the contents of the syringe were delivered, Larry released the tension of the belt and tossed the strap aside. He walked over to his pipe and turned back to face me. There was a strange "wait for it, girl" grin of satisfaction on his face. Clearly, he was convinced I'd be blown away by what I was about to experience.

I waited – but nothing happened. For two or three minutes, we just stared at each other. It was obvious something wasn't right, and Larry's smug smile faded.

Having never banged coke, I wasn't sure what to expect.

"I don't feel anything, Larry. What should I do?"

Larry couldn't believe it. He clearly expected me to be sky-high. He checked the coke, looked at my arm, and ran his fingers through his hair in exasperation. Without saying a word, he went back to the table, filled the spoon again, and repeated the entire process.

For a second time, he banged the coke into my arm.

A minute passed. Then a few more. From the clarity in my eyes, Larry could see I still wasn't high.

"What is going on with this damn stuff? It's no good – or did you switch the bag on me?" There was growing anger rising in his voice. He continued to rant at me as he shuffled through the stuff on the table and reexamined the cocaine. I was hurt that he was blaming me. I fought back, arguing that I hadn't touched anything and had no motive to lie. For whatever reason, I valued the bond I'd formed with Larry during the past weeks, and I was deeply wounded by his attacks.

Overcome with frustration; he told me to take one more hit. This time, he said, I would definitely feel it.

As Larry stepped away to prepare that third shot of cocaine, an intense dread came over me. Warning lights flashed in my soul. I could see what was happening. Larry was angry, and I was about to become a victim of his frustration. These fears were balanced by an equally powerful force – a deep desire for peace between us. I wanted things to return to normal; I wanted us to be friends. I couldn't decide whether to confront Larry or to placate him.

Ultimately, I did nothing.

Then, something frightening happened. As Larry was preparing the third syringe, I began to feel a bizarre change coming on. I lost my ability to move or speak. My body remained seated on the bed, but my mind was no longer able to control its movements. I had become a spectator rather than a participant in what was unfolding around me.

I watched dumbly as Larry drew the third hit of liquefied cocaine into the syringe. A sick sense of desperation came over me, but I remained unable to act. I remember thinking – this is the end.

A surge of physical warmth ran down my throat and into my guts as Larry mainlined the third syringe of coke into my body. My ears filled with the roar of surging white sound. Every bit of pain I had been feeling melted away, and my sense of detachment increased tenfold.

Now seeing the scene from the perspective of an outside observer, I watched Larry step away. He moved to the dresser. He picked up his pipe. He took a hit. He looked into the mirror. Each of these actions felt like a dreamy step in some unstoppable mechanical process, and I perceived them that way – mechanically – without emotion. Then, Larry saw my face reflected in the mirror, and he turned back toward me with a terrified look in his eyes.

At that moment, a terrible spasm pulsed through my body. Violently, I flopped back on the bed. I could feel no physical sensations, but I knew I was jerking back and forth with convulsions. As before, I didn't feel anything. I simply understood the convulsions as a fact. That's how everything happened in those next few minutes. Each thing occurred to me as a detached observation. There was no physical feedback of any kind.

Simple thoughts began to flow into my mind, one after the other.

I am overdosing.

This is bad.

Larry is screaming.

I hear his voice.

He says, "Noooooooooooo."

Although I'd lost control of my body, my mind still accepted and processed these little details as they came to me.

Larry is on top of me. Larry is pushing my body down. He can't stop my convulsions. He is losing control too. I will die. I will face God. I will go to hell.

In spite of the trauma my body was experiencing, each of these thoughts was remarkably clear. I was also very aware of a distant but growing fear. As this fear grew into a terror, I became more and more certain I would die.

For what felt like a lifetime – though it was probably less than a couple of minutes – I hung in a state of cold, raw anguish. Detached from any connection to my physical body, I became intensely focused on my soul and on the steady flow of thoughts that continued to pour unbidden into my mind.

Time is ending. My body is meaningless. The world is meaningless. Something else awaits me. Something more real. Something unseen.

At that point, I also remember crying out for Jesus. I remember begging Jesus to forgive me – pleading he would not abandon me. I'm uncertain if these words were spoken aloud or were only thoughts in my mind.

Eventually, even the flow of facts and fears began to lose sharpness and intensity. It was as if reality itself was beginning to fade. Colors, once vibrant, became muted. Objects, once detailed, became soggy. Sounds, once distinguishable, melded into a steady white noise that pounded in my ears.

Larry probably sensed I was slipping away because he held me close. My head sagged down into the crook of his neck. I vaguely recall saying, "It's over," into his ear.

At that point, Shelly ended. And there was no tunnel of light.

I heard no comforting voices. No one came to escort me. I felt no sense of peace. I understood no purpose at all. Instead, there was only emptiness—an endless void. I was utterly alone and completely untethered from reality.

Then, something like a vacuum's suction gently pulled at me.

At that point, I realized I'd been floating weightless in space. Now, something was drawing me up and away. It was a tiny, indistinct force, barely perceptible. It drew me from the bed and toward a corner of the ceiling. From there, I suddenly saw and heard everything clearly again.

Below me, I could see both Larry and the body sprawled on the bed. I saw the pale face. The eyes were open. The lips were blue. The body's clothes were wet with sweat, and its sopping hair was tangled and disgusting.

As I looked into the glassy eyes – my eyes – I remember thinking, who is that? I can see, and I can think, but I'm not present in that body. I know my body is on the bed, but I'm also aware the hunk of flesh is not me.

Fascinated, I watched Larry intently. He seemed shell-shocked by what was happening. His eyes were bloodshot, and his face was soaked with tears. For a moment, I wondered if he would collapse with exhaustion, but he rallied and began CPR. He breathed into my body's parted lips. He pushed on my chest. He begged me to come back. The pattern was repeated over and over. Clearly, he believed this was his only hope to revive me.

This went on for a long time. I watched mesmerized, but I remained detached, still floating in the upper corner of the room. I knew I was no longer human. Although I could see my lifeless body and Larry working to revive it, I felt no connection between its dead flesh and my living mind.

What am I now – a spirit? Is everyone like this? Are we all souls stuffed into containers of flesh? I was surprised it had been so easy to "slip out" of that body and become a spirit.

Looking back at the bed, I also realized I was no longer interested in returning to my physical form. Whatever I had become was infinitely better than what I had been. My body and everything it represented now seemed unbearably ugly to me. It was broken and repulsive.

Spurred on by this realization, I began to yell at Larry. I screamed at him to stop the CPR. I didn't want him to resuscitate me. In my mind, the words I shouted were clearly expressed, but Larry didn't hear or notice. He never acknowledged my hovering self. Instead, he continued to breathe into the body, push on its chest, and scream out my name.

Then, unexpectedly, Larry stopped. I watched with curiosity. He seemed to gather himself. Had an idea occurred to him? Had he given up, or was he preparing to use some other strategy to revive me?

With clear purpose, Larry rolled off the bed, crossed the room, and opened the door. As he disappeared into the night, a strange new emotion pushed into my consciousness. It was anger. How could Larry leave me here! He was abandoning me!

As quickly as those feelings came, they melted away, and another emotion flooded through me. It was grief. It grew more and more intense with each passing second, eventually morphing into a darkness of spirit that literally stole the light in my mind's eye. The room became dim, then darker, then black. I knew I had no physical eyes, but it felt like I had lost my sight.

Then, there was a sensation of falling.

It's hard to explain, but on some level, I also felt a release. It was not the sense of leaving my troubled past behind. Rather, it was a profound liberation from self, something like a shedding of selfishness. Perhaps I was experiencing what it felt like to be released from sin.

Although I didn't speak aloud, a clear thought began to fill my mind. I was falling into the great unknown, and I found myself repeating: I give up everything. I give up, I give up, I give up…

With those words still echoing in my mind, I felt a presence in the darkness beside me. Even though it was indistinct, it provided something for me to grab hold of – to stop my long fall into nothingness – so I eagerly reached out for it.

As I did, it spoke to me. And it used my name.

"Yes, Shelly, you are right to let go."

I could sense this was more than a statement. It was some kind of promise. This was not a final judgment. It was an opportunity to help me find something better in life. Giving up didn't mean letting myself slip into death. It meant abandoning my self-destructive pattern of living and allowing something better to govern my choices in life.

This may not be the end, I realized. There might be a second chance.

There was no reply from the darkness, but I began to whisper those words to myself as if they were a mantra: second chance, second chance, second chance…

Then, in one shocking instant, the void was suddenly gone, and I was back in my broken, pain-filled body. I was sprawled on the soaking wet bed, packed up to my chin in cubes from the motel's ice machine.

I tried to sit up, but as I did, another bucket of ice rained down on me. My body ached. I could feel every pain again. I also realized I was extremely hot. The ice seemed to melt as soon as it touched my skin. Before I could make sense of what was happening, my body was again racked by a wave of violent convulsions. Frantically, as if my life depended on it, I pulled the ice around me.

"More ice. More. More." The hoarse words were mine, but they seemed strange to my ears. Larry reacted immediately to my croaking and redoubled his efforts. He rushed out of the room, returned with another bucket of ice, tossed it on me, and flew out for more. Every time he returned, he would reassure me, saying, "You're going to make it, Shelly. You're going to make it."

Slowly, I began to feel more "normal" – more grounded in the physical world. The sights and smells of the room came back to me. They and Larry became my new reality. I concentrated on the compassion in Larry's voice, and it comforted me.

I am getting a second chance, I thought. I am going to survive.

I took in the scene around me. It looked as if a tornado had smashed through the room. The door was wide open, furniture was toppled, and our belongings were tossed everywhere. Most bizarre of all, tiny squares of ice were scattered across the floor like wayward hailstones. Larry hadn't been very discreet about what he'd been doing, so I was amazed we weren't also facing a visit by the cops.

When I finally gained full control of my body and mind, I told

Larry to get up and shut the door. There was an uncomfortable moment immediately after it clicked shut. When he faced me, Larry's expression should have reflected relief, but what I saw in his eyes was fear. He expects me to yell at him, I realized. He expects me to blame him for what happened. Instead, I only felt sympathy for him. He couldn't have known it, but I'd witnessed his actions, and I understood what he'd just experienced.

"I just need rest," I said softly, trying to keep any hint of anger or frustration out of my voice, "but I'm afraid I might die in my sleep." Our eyes met, and we seemed to really see each other for the first time. Even before he spoke, his eyes were pleading with me.

"Let me take you to the hospital, Shelly," he said. "I need to…"

In that instant, my old self rushed back in and seized control. My voice became firm.

"No! We'll both go to jail. I'm not going to jail. Forget that!"

I told him to call someone he knew in town. I insisted he find another place for me to sleep off the trauma. Although his face still registered concern, he dutifully picked up the motel phone and dialed. Someone answered almost immediately, and from the conversation that followed, I could tell the person on the other end knew about Larry's addictions.

Many questions were asked, and Larry answered each in turn, explaining what had happened. Then, he shared the details of my overdose. Larry said he was convinced I was going to die. He said he was amazed I was back.

Larry must have trusted the person on the other end of the phone because he openly talked about using the needle to bang the cocaine. There were some tense moments during the call, but in the end, Larry appeared visibly relaxed. He smiled at me and nodded his head as if to say things would be fine.

The days that followed are vague and difficult for me to recollect now.

I remember stumbling out of the icy bed and into a running shower with my clothes on. I remember slumping down under the stream of water, my back to the tiled wall. I remember falling asleep in Larry's arms. We both sobbed out the last of our physical energy that night, and I remember sleeping for long stints during the time that followed, waking only when Larry urged me to eat. When he could rouse me, I would gobble up a few M&Ms and wash them down with orange juice. Then, I would slip back into sleep.

I later learned that I slept through most of three days. When I finally woke up, it was to one of the most shameful experiences of my life.

The morning of that third day began bright and promising. I opened my eyes to a room awash in soft, warm light. A cool breeze fluttered through the drapes of a nearby window. It was the first time since the night of the overdose that I felt clear-headed.

I probed my memory for details, but the last thing I remembered was the hotel room in chaos. This place was clean and orderly, sparkling with sunlight. It couldn't possibly be the same room.

The last time I had seen Larry, he'd been a broken man. Now, he was sleeping quietly in a nearby chair, his hands folded across his chest. It was such a peaceful scene – so warm and innocent – it made my heart hurt. Everything was a complete contrast to what we'd endured just a few days earlier.

I wanted to call out to Larry, but I held back. He was already experiencing deep serenity. What could I add?

Larry must have sensed my eyes were on him because he slowly woke. Realizing I was conscious and alert, he smiled warmly. Then he got up, moved to my bedside, and gently stroked my hair, asking how I felt. I was still trying to make sense of where I was, so I struggled with a reply. My memory was in fragments, a muddled mess of disjointed sounds and actions, and I found it impossible to place anything in sequence. Only one fact seemed concrete. Only one thing seemed certain.

"I died," I said.

As the words were spoken aloud, it clearly triggered a pang of guilt in Larry. His head dropped, and his shoulders slumped. I hadn't meant to wound him. I was simply in awe of the incredible nature of the experience.

"You scared the crap out of me, Shelly," he said. "I didn't expect what happened. Who could have?"

It was then I realized he had a very narrow perspective on that night. Larry thought my last moments of understanding had ended with his final injection of cocaine. He had no knowledge of the other things I had seen, heard, and experienced.

I shared the entire story, telling him I had been aware of things even after my death. I told him how I had escaped to the corner of the ceiling and explained the appealing sense of release I'd felt once I'd left my physical body. I also told him about my fears of abandonment when he bolted from the room.

"I saw everything that happened. I saw you screaming and pounding my chest and begging me to come back," I told him. "And I saw you leave the room."

As I explained this, Larry's expression changed from shame to confusion to shocked disbelief.

"Shelly, you couldn't possibly know any of that. You were dead. You weren't breathing, and you had no pulse," he said.

As he spoke, I nodded confirmation. I knew I had died, but I was also certain of what I had seen. I was aware of his actions. It was proof that something in me had transcended my death.

He listened intently while I told my story, but he appeared most moved when I shared the part about falling into the darkness – of letting go and sensing the presence of God. Hearing that, Larry's eyes filled with tears. Within moments, he broke down completely, crying like a baby. I sat there dumbfounded, not knowing what to say. Why was he so affected by something that had happened to me?

As his sobbing continued, I began to feel less and less sympathy for Larry. In fact, a deep sense of frustration settled in. This was just a bizarre twist of fate. Larry is taking it far too seriously. What does he think this was – some kind of mystical experience from God, like those ridiculous visions he saw while smoking his bong?

One after another, these angry thoughts came. Rather than sharing Larry's experience of brokenness and repentance, I saw his reaction to my story as a growing threat to our relationship and to my access to his cocaine. Within minutes, everything about the bright and peaceful room became annoying. The once noble things Larry had done to rescue me began to seem dirty and trite. I was angry – because he was complicating everything!

I also had an overwhelming urge to get high.

"Larry, why did you leave me alone in that room?" These stinging words were meant to break his trance, but they failed to have the desired effect. I had wanted to refocus his thoughts on me, to force him to move beyond his self-examination, but my question did the opposite.

Larry looked at me and said, "Shelly, you weren't the only one who experienced the presence of God that night. I did too."

Between sobs, he explained how he had run from our motel room to save his own life. Realizing his actions had caused my death, Larry said he feared arrest. Murder was punishable by death in the state of Texas.

"I was scared, and I had every intention of leaving you there, but something stopped me. It literally froze me in my tracks. I couldn't move. At that point, I looked up in the night sky, and it was clear and full of stars, so peaceful and orderly. So I asked God what to do. I begged him for help. I told him that if he brought you back, I would turn my life over to him completely. I said I would stop with the drugs, go home, and never look back."

I could see Larry was serious – and I began to panic. What has he done with the cocaine? Oblivious to what was going on in my head, Larry continued.

"I think God answered me. A voice in the back of my mind told me to pack your body in ice. So, I ran to the motel's ice machine, grabbed a small garbage can, and started to scoop up ice cubes."

Larry's words sparked memories. I suddenly recalled that crazy flurry of activity, the wet bed, the ice being poured out across my body.

"I kept going back and forth until you were completely covered with ice," he continued. "All the time, I was praying for God to intervene and bring you back. When I saw your eyes flutter open and you said, 'more ice' – that's when I knew it would be OK. God was going to save your life."

Now, Larry's earlier reaction to my story made perfect sense. We were both troubled, empty people. I could understand why he was seizing this moment to make his life right – even though I still felt as detached as ever about the whole experience.

In spite of my frustration, cravings, and fears, I couldn't help but tell Larry I forgave him, and after hearing those words, his body seemed to unclench with relief.

"During the convulsions, you started saying, 'Jesus, forgive me,' and I felt a terrible surge of shame myself," Larry said, beginning to tear up again. "I was the one who should have died, not you. I felt completely helpless, and I wanted forgiveness too. I knew I'd be damned to hell for what I had done to you, and I had nowhere else to turn."

Something in my soul winced at this. It was an indisputable confirmation Larry had gone through a profound transformation, but I saw nothing beautiful in it. Now, I would be alone. That prospect scared me, but I never once considered making a similar change myself. Instead, I just wanted to escape from him, to be away from him and his demanding new perspective on life.

What I wanted was the wonderful, dulling stupor of drugs.

Larry could see I was beginning to tune him out, but he stubbornly finished his story. "I made a deal with God, Shelly, and I am going to keep it. Believe what you like, but it's a miracle you're alive."

I honestly didn't know what to say next. I felt conflicted – happy for Larry, but intensely angry with him at the same time. I could see he intended to do everything he said, but I had no intention of following in his path. Even though I felt grateful to have survived, I was still fuming because Larry's decision to return home would hinder my selfish goals.

Larry expected his emotional story to arouse a change in me, but his words actually had the opposite effect. Rather than eliciting a new sense of hope in me, his epiphany brought a return of the guilt and pain that fueled my desire for drugs. I had stayed high as often as possible to avoid this kind of emotional turmoil. Drugs allowed me to feel nothing, and that's what I needed now – to be free of his guilt; to find an escape.

Before I could stop myself, I said, "I'm happy for you, Larry – but where did you put the dope? I need a hit."

He stared at me in disbelief; his expression betraying what he must have been thinking. We've just had this incredible experience with God, and you want to go back to living in hell? Instead, he said, "Shelly, you need help." Then, he offered a dozen reasons why I should change my ways.

In the face of all this pleading, I remained resolute. Over and over, I rebuffed him, and as I did, he seemed to deflate before my very eyes. Eventually, hope disappeared from his face, and his shoulders slumped. Larry knew all about the drug lifestyle, and he could see I was completely lost to its power.

Seeing his weakness, I pressed an attack. I said he had no right to control my life. I insisted I needed to get high. Finally, he relented.

"Shelly, if you want the stuff that bad, get out of bed and dig through the dumpster. It's all there somewhere in a garbage bag."

I'm sure he meant the remark to shock and challenge me, thinking I would be repulsed by the idea of leaving the comfort of my warm bed to dig through reeking piles of trash, but instead, I simply took him at his word, thankful that he was offering me his valuable stash.

I got out of bed, threw on some clothes, and marched out to the dumpster.

After a few minutes of digging through the fetid garbage with my hands, I finally saw a bag I recognized. Pulling it close, I looked inside. Pay dirt! It contained the pipes, syringes, and baggie of dope from our room. Seeing it stoked my urgent cravings, and as weak and exhausted as I was, I experienced a rush of excitement, anticipation for the coming hit, and the relief it would bring.

Pulling myself out of the dumpster, I headed back to the hotel room, bag in hand. When I returned, I assumed Larry would change his mind and get high with me, but he seemed completely uninterested in what I was doing. He was on the phone with someone in his family, explaining how he planned to return home with the truck. He told the person on the other end of the line, he was ready to get serious about changing his life.

After Larry hung up, he asked me to reconsider – to come back with him. He said he would find someplace safe for me to recover. I refused. Even as he was talking, all I had been able to think about was ending the conversation, so I could use the drugs and escape into a high.

Convinced I wasn't going to turn away from my self-destructive course, Larry finally gave up. He told me he would drop me off at the house of a drug addict he knew in town. He said I could probably crash there for free.

We drove to the place in silence.

As we said our goodbyes, Larry pushed a torn piece of paper into my hand. His home phone number was scrawled on it. "Call me if you ever change your mind and decide to get help," he said. Nothing in his tone of voice suggested he believed I would ever call. Still, I took the slip of paper, and we hugged. Without another word, Larry returned to his truck. He never looked back.

A few weeks later, I tried the phone number. I wanted to speak to Larry, but I never got the chance. His parents knew my story, recognized who I was, and asked me not to rekindle a relationship with their son. He was doing fine, they said. He was on the right track. He needed a clean break from his old lifestyle – and with me.

I honored their request.

My memories of that call are bittersweet. At the time, part of me was relieved to be completely free of Larry and the nagging guilt his final words had evoked. But another part of me wondered why – as miserable and lost as I was – the strange experience of my death and encounter with God hadn't led to something better for me.

Clearly, I was still too deeply mired in the quicksand of my addiction to change. I wasn't yet prepared to "give up" as I had promised.

To bring about real change, it would take something even more traumatic than death.

Chapter 6

UNSAFE

When the taxi pulled up to the address I'd been given, I hesitated for a moment. The apartments were dark and dingy, and the parking lot was littered with trash. Like most things touched by addiction and addicts, it was a sullen, disheveled, and hopeless place. I had seen my share of crack houses, but this place still raised red flags.

I was desperate, but not stupid.

The taxi driver, no happier to be in this neighborhood, glanced back at me expectantly. He probably thought I would ask him to drive on, but instead, I shook off my discomfort and smiled.

"I don't see my friend," I said. "Can we wait for a minute? I'm sure he'll show up."

The driver's face registered surprise. He must have been thinking I'd balk when I saw this place. What sane person would want to stay? But he underestimated my hunger. Addiction is an amazingly powerful motivator, and red flags or not, it pushes you forward with little regard for your safety. All it seeks is satisfaction; the next high.

Unhappy but compliant, he turned off the cab but kept the meter running, and I wondered how long he would wait before challenging me to pay. The delay was a problem because I wanted to save every dollar I could to purchase cocaine.

The "friend" I was waiting for was a man I'd never met. His name was Sammy. Carla, a dancer at the strip club, had recommended him. She claimed he was a good source. More importantly, she said he sometimes traded dope for sex. Although I'd come with a hundred dollars – enough to score a little crack – it would be nice to have another bargaining chip if I needed more.

In spite of how that sounds, I didn't consider myself a prostitute. As I saw it, sex was simply a tool resourceful women could use to achieve their goals, the way men use their muscles or a weapon to get what they want. Sex is a way of life for hookers. For me, it was just a tactic, a means to an end.

In other words, I rationalized my behaviors away.

Fortunately, it didn't take long for Sammy to appear, and he fit Carla's description perfectly. He was a young Spanish guy with a long, thick mane of black hair running down to his waist. As I watched, he exited an apartment and cautiously crossed the lot toward a parked car. I paid the driver and got out of the cab.

I'm ashamed to admit it, but I was reacting like a hungry animal drawn to the smell of food. Addiction is a raw, base thing. As it grows stronger, it overrides everything else – your willpower, your common sense, and your pride. Eventually, there's nothing but the hunger and the need to satisfy it.

Pausing for a moment, I tried to regain my composure. I didn't want to tip Sammy off, and he hadn't yet noticed me approaching. A drug dealer can easily turn desperation to his advantage. Addicts must never show weakness.

Sammy finally saw me approaching, and he sized me up, just as Carla said he would. I could see the questions passing through his mind. Was I attractive enough? Was it worth trading sex for drugs? Would this be a one-time thing, or was I likely to stick around? Sammy was like many of the dealers I'd met. He was an addict himself and, therefore, willing to use junkies, as well as drugs, to meet his own selfish needs.

He smiled coyly before asking, "What's up?"

Trying to remain nonchalant, I told Sammy I'd heard he sold

crack. I asked him to show me what he had to offer. He nodded, gestured for me to follow, and we headed back up to his apartment.

Considering the huge sums of money that pass between junkies and dealers, you might think crack is bought and sold in nice, well-appointed places, but that's rarely the case. In fact, the opposite is more often true. Drugs are usually peddled in slums, seedy hotels, fetid alleys, and dank tenements. Dope does make its way into the lavish homes of the rich, but it usually originates in hell holes like this one.

True to form, Sammy's apartment was a stark, shabby pit. Its living room was empty except for a drum set and a tattered bar stool positioned at the pass-through to the kitchen. That was it. It looked like an abandoned home that some squatters had claimed.

As we entered, a young couple looked up at us with blank expressions. They were sprawled on the floor, blithely smoking crack from a crude pipe they'd fashioned from an old soda can. Both were trashed, completely useless.

If I'd been wise, I'd have seen their lives as a cautionary tale – another warning of where my own path was heading – but the thought never occurred to me. Few junkies see the folly of their ways when they're caught up in the full throws of addiction. Logic is lost on us by then. Instead, we just dig in. Move on. Survive.

Of course, this obsession also makes us extremely good targets for the unscrupulous in society – particularly men who use the weaknesses of addicts for their own gain. These predators typically manipulate addicts for easy sex or quick cash to fuel their own drug habits. They're particularly attracted to the disoriented, disillusioned and desperate, and will feed on them until they are completely used up.

While dangerous, guys like Sammy are trivial compared to the real monsters in the drug culture – the guys who manipulate addicts on a larger scale and in more systematic ways. Those people strategically control large groups of dope-enslaved junkies for profit, sometimes even trafficking them as salable property. Many strippers and porn actresses are victims of such men and women. The girls turn to stripping and porn for money to feed their habits and ultimately become a captive to that lifestyle. Unscrupulous club owners and porn producers count on these addicts to keep their stables filled with girls who will literally do anything to stay high.

Even knowing this, most crack addicts knowingly and eagerly seek out such predators for the cash and dope they need. I was an example of this sad reality. No one forced me to go to Sammy. I went to him willingly.

I crossed the living room in Sammy's apartment and hopped up on the barstool near the kitchen. I hadn't expected to find the other junkies in the place, and I needed a minute to size up the situation. Who were these kids? Was he already hooking up with them?

I tossed my jacket aside to provide Sammy with a better view of my body. It was important to keep sex on his mind and to distract him from what was going on with the other junkies. Sammy glanced at me and smiled. He seemed to approve. Strolling over to the couple on the floor, he grabbed the makeshift coke-can crack pipe out of their hands and offered it to me.

I was expecting this. It's typical for a drug dealer to literally smoke out cops by insisting every buyer do crack before getting down to business. While I was happy to take a hit, I was disgusted by the grimy can. Instead of taking it, I reached into my purse and pulled out my own glass stem. Once the crack was in place, I took a long drag, held it for a good twenty seconds, and then blew out a perfect smoke ring. Sammy grinned and moved to the drum set. He pulled a small plastic bag from a hiding place between the cymbals.

As the high washed over me, all the tensions from the cab ride melted away. I'd experienced this euphoria many times, but the initial impact of smoking crack always thrilled me.

"Stark reality. That's no way to go through life, baby," Sammy said as if reading my mind. "Much better to escape, isn't it?"

I nodded dreamily. I was being swallowed up, and Sammy knew it. Smiling with satisfaction, he opened the plastic bag and showed me the two large crack cookies it contained. Without a word of negotiation, I offered up my hundred dollars. He broke off a generous chunk of the cookie and offered it to me. I knew the game. This was the initiation of our new relationship. It would start with me spending every cent I had. It would end with me doing anything he wanted, for as long as he wanted.

Eventually, Sammy shooed the couple out of his place and focused entirely on me. Before dawn, I'd smoked almost everything he had, only holding back a small rock for a morning hit so I could get stoned before heading off to work.

* * *

Guys driving the northwest freeway in or out of Houston have probably seen the strip club's flashing purple lights many times. The sign is considered a local landmark. That stretch of 290 is cluttered with buildings and signage, but the club's lavender neon glow still stands out, enticing truckers and businessmen to stop in for a good time.

Like many temptations, the place's flashy appeal fades on close examination. The two-story gray, concrete building is blocky and bland. It's a good thing most of the business there is done at night because darkness definitely improves the character of the place.

When I worked there, the club was actually pretty nice inside – better than a lot of places I'd plied my trade. Its interior color scheme was red and black, and its walls were covered with carpeting, muffling loud sounds, and giving the rooms a warmer, more hospitable appearance.

The layout of the club was simple. An elevated stage ran through the middle of the ground floor's main room, with a couple dozen round tables and cubicles on either side of the runway. Upstairs, the owners had put in a "champagne room" where the more affluent clientele could arrange private dances and other services away from prying eyes.

On the floor level, such sexual dalliances were handled in the little cubicles, which offered much less privacy. To protect themselves, the owners had informed all of the girls that illegal sex was not allowed, but they rarely enforced those rules, and the clients and the club's strippers were both glad for the freedom. Many of the girls who work at clubs are addicts and alcoholics. They need a steady flow of cash for drugs or booze and having this lax enforcement of club rules suits their needs.

By the time I met Sammy, I'd been working at the strip club for nearly a year, and I'd developed a decent clientele there. Regulars are important to a girl's survival in that business. Some girls were only "favorites" to a few, but my gregarious personality made me popular with a wide range of clients.

Although I didn't realize it then, I suppose most of the men who frequented the place were addicts of a sort too. They only felt good when they got their fix. Ironically, that made me something of a dealer. I was turning their sexual hunger into a steady flow of cash.

By this time, I was also a veteran of strip club life. I'd even been through a raid or two. One night, while I was taking part in a private dance upstairs, a group of twenty SWAT team agents stormed through the first-floor entry. They had masks on their faces and guns in their hands. The place was normally very dark inside, so it was a shock when the cops turned on all the lights and stopped the music. One of them commandeered the microphone and began calling down specific girls, using both their stage and real names.

After they separated out the men and collected the specific girls they wanted, the rest of us were told to wait in the main room while a few guys from the SWAT team went through the dressing rooms, searching for drugs and other contraband.

One of the girls later explained the process to me. The cops prepare for a raid like this, she said. They come into the club and solicit illegal services for several weeks prior to the bust. Most of the veteran strippers spot them because they are very forward, aggressively asking for sex. Real customers are typically much more skittish about making those arrangements, probably because they fear accidentally soliciting an undercover cop in the process. Such are the games strippers and cops play.

One night, a few weeks after my first encounter with Sammy, I'd had a particularly good shift at the club. In five or six hours, I'd taken in more than three hundred dollars. I desperately needed to get high that night, so I headed off to Sammy's apartment. This time, I decided I would not stay. I'd only go in to pick up the drugs. Then, I would take the stash back to my own place. Staying with Sammy would make things too complicated. I couldn't afford to give him too much control over my life.

My own apartment was small, but it was secure. Once there, I wouldn't need to worry about anyone pilfering my money or drugs while I was high. I also knew I'd need to hold back some of the cash I'd earned. I had back rent to pay and there were a few overdue bills to clear out too. I couldn't afford to have Sammy wheedle this money out of me.

At Sammy's place, these carefully conceived plans had fallen apart. He'd welcomed me with a smile and a ready supply of crack. I went through all of my money, buying everything he had, so my precious cash literally went up in smoke.

By the end of the binge, Sammy had also convinced me to leave my apartment and move in with him "for free" – a deal certain to include sex on demand and the end of my personal independence. High as a kite, I'd eagerly accepted.

My submission to Sammy had probably been inevitable. I had no self-worth, I was about to be evicted from my apartment, and my addiction was compelling me to secure more and more dope. In other words, Sammy could meet my every need. His sexual desire for me also played on my need for acceptance and self-worth. So, in spite of what this surrender would cost me, I'd convinced myself that hooking up with Sammy was the right thing to do. At the very least, its benefits would outweigh any loss or indignity the relationship might bring.

At that moment, a realization had struck me. I was no longer a woman with a foot in two places – the "normal" world and the world of addiction. The drug culture had finally and fully claimed me. Its language had become my language; its people, my people; its routines, my reality. A few years earlier, surrendering to a man like Sammy would have been unthinkable to me, but on that day, I was completely comfortable with the idea. I was no longer a woman with a drug problem. I was a true junkie – unworthy of respect, undone by my addictions.

I was unrecoverable.

This realization had sickened me a bit after that day – but the pain was soon gone. Recent events had taught me nothing would change. Nothing could. So, I simply had to be honest with myself and accept what I had become.

In the weeks that followed, I fell into the typical, terrible patterns most addicts accept as a way of life. Every night, I worked the strip club, and after every shift, I would bring my earnings to Sammy for the drugs he would supply. Hour after hour, day after day, week after week, this routine continued. It was a life many of the strippers had succumbed to – and most never escaped.

I might be there still, if not for an unexpected event that took me down a different path.

*   *   *

One night, before my shift, I sat in a bathroom stall at the strip club, smoking crack and thinking about my troubles. Suddenly, a thought popped into my head. I wondered what had happened to Larry since my overdose at the motel. Was he staying clean? Did he ever think about me? This made God come to mind too. He had rescued Larry during the downward spiral of his life. Why hadn't I experienced something similar?

There, in the bathroom stall, a small voice within me prayed for an escape from the mire my life had become, but as soon as this thought came to mind, another part of my ego fought to snatch the prayer back. Every other time I had prayed to God for help, the answer came in some painful, nearly catastrophic form. "Be careful what you wish for; you might get it," was the old adage that came to mind.

Stoned, I headed back to the club's main floor, and something odd there caught my attention. I noticed three new men had taken seats at a table in the corner. None of the girls had seen them before. All three were clean-cut and well dressed, much more polished looking than our typical patrons. One of the men, much older than his companions, wore a cowboy hat. All three shared a family resemblance.

As I drew close, the older man in the hat introduced himself as Ray Sr. He explained his tablemates were his two sons, Ray Jr. and Ronnie. They had come in to celebrate Ronnie's birthday, the older man explained. All three wore lots of gold, and packets of cash were scattered across the tabletop. Clearly, the older guy in the cowboy hat wanted us to think he was a high roller.

"Join us, young lady," Ray Sr. said. "And bring over another girl. Show my sons a good time. They're in from Chicago. Make 'em feel welcome."

Thrilled by the prospect of working a big spender, I quickly grabbed Keri, one of the younger dancers. She was too green and too passive to move in on my call. Together, we slipped into their booth. I took the spot between Ray Sr. and Jr., leaving Keri on the outside position next to the youngest son.

In the hours that followed, I hit it off with all three guys. We joked, we drank, and Keri and I danced every time a good song was played. Everyone was very nice, and the buzz from the alcohol kept our mood light and freewheeling. Ray Sr. clearly loved the spotlight and took control of the situation, reveling in his role as the family patriarch. He lavished us with fifty and hundred dollar bills every time we danced, and as the money flowed, I began to think about how this unexpected payday might change my situation.

I knew it would be folly to go back to Sammy's place with the cash. I'd collected almost a grand that night, and he would likely get all of it out of me. Perhaps, I thought, this is a God-sent opportunity for me to escape. I could use the bankroll to get a place for myself again. I had prayed for a change. Maybe this was the answer. A door was opening for me.

As if Ray Sr. could read my mind, he pulled me close. "I like you. So do my sons. Why don't you come over to our place when your shift is over? I'm staying in a hotel nearby. We can party there."

The warm, lulling embrace of alcohol smothered my usual caution, and my growing desire to protect my money from Sammy urged me on. Even if it was just for one night, it would be worth it to go with these men. I'd have a chance to regroup and evaluate my options afterward. When I paused for a moment to consider the idea, Ray Sr. misread my hesitation. Thinking I was apprehensive about joining him at his hotel, he sweetened the pot.

"We have lots of cocaine back in our room," he said.

Clearly, this was a promised payment of sorts. Rather than give me money for sex, he was offering me a supply of crack for my services. I nodded my approval of the deal, and he smiled.

When we left the club, all three guys were smashed and glassy-eyed. Even so, Ray Sr. insisted on stopping at a liquor store before going to the hotel. By the time we reached his room, Ray Jr. was fast asleep, and young Ronnie was in the last, lethargic stage of drunkenness. Seeing their condition, Ray Sr. urged me to leave Ray Jr. in the truck. I helped him get Ronnie into the room.

Within minutes, the birthday boy was out cold, flopped across one of the room's two beds. He was a cute kid, and I felt sorry for him. I wondered about his childhood. I sensed his father's lifestyle was strange and disorienting for him. Perhaps Ray Sr. was using this visit to introduce his sons to the dark side of the family as my own father had. At least, that was my impression at the time.

The old man seemed unfazed by the strangeness of the scene. After busying himself with a few details, he turned to face me. His mood and demeanor changed. He was less playful, more businesslike. He pulled a plastic bag from his coat pocket and dangled it in front of me. Inside were two huge crack cookies.

Before I could react, he opened the bag, pulled out one of the cookies, and set it on the room's small table. Then, with a few careful blows of his fist, he broke it into pipe-size fragments. I must have looked comical as I watched him, wide-eyed. Even under the influence of alcohol, I understood the value of that dope. There was enough cocaine on the table to keep me stoned for days, but Ray Sr. acted as if it was nothing – just a little treat he happened to have on hand.

Greed overcame me, and my mind raced with ways to exploit the opportunity. How much crack did these guys have? Was there a way to tap their resources? What would they expect from me in return? Was it as simple as sex, or did the old man have something else in mind? Perhaps he wanted me to sell dope to the other girls at the strip club. That could get me kicked out of the place.

One thing seemed clear. This opportunity – this score of free crack – was too big to leave on the table. The dope these guys carried was worth thousands. I needed to decide. What was I willing to sacrifice to remain close to Ray Sr. and his "business," whatever that might be?

As this debate raged in my mind, I went into my purse for a lighter. Like most addicts, I had more than a dozen of them. Cops often use a girl's purse to confirm their suspicions about drug use because Crack-smoking junkies are never far from a good supply of lighters.

"Go ahead," Ray Sr. said, motioning to the broken cookie on the table. "It's all for you."

I lit up and smoked a rock. While I got high, Ray Sr. talked. He told me about his ex-wife in Chicago. He filled me in on the lives of his sons. He spoke quietly and gently, like a man speaking to his daughter or girlfriend. Though older, he was a big, handsome man – more than six feet tall and well-muscled.

As he talked on, a crack-induced euphoria swept through my body, and I relaxed. I began to share a few things about my own life, and Ray Sr. seemed sincerely interested in what I had to say. I told him about growing up in Florida. I explained my move to Texas and shared a few details about my years as a stripper and my time with Sammy. I also told him I was looking for a way out of my current "relationship."

At that point, Ray Sr. opened up with more information about his business. He was supplying dope to more than two hundred women he housed in hotels all over the city. He said that his girls ranged from fourteen to about twenty-five.

"I put my girls to work as lot lizards," he explained.

The numbers stunned me, but I tried to remain composed, asking him what he meant by "lot lizards." I wasn't familiar with that term.

"Never heard of lot lizards?" he said, laughing with surprise. "They're the whores who work the truck stops. There's good money in it. Really good. And my girls are the best."

This shocked me too. Once again, he had called them "his" girls. Kids as young as fourteen were being sold for sex, and he was clearly using drugs as the means to control and bilk them. Stoned as I was, I found his remarks unbelievably callous and his attitude frightening. Although part of me craved his drug stash, another part of me screamed, "escape from this man!"

Before my fears could show on my face, Ray Sr. defused my anxiety with more kind words.

"Shelly, you're different from the other girls," he said. "You're mature with a good head on your shoulders. I saw that in you when we first met."

His tactic worked. I still considered his business disgusting and dangerous, but I no longer felt personally threatened by him. As long as I stay out of his business, I thought, things will be OK. I just wouldn't let him turn me into one of his whores.

"You know, it's important to surround yourself with the right kind of people," he went on. "That's why I'd be willing to take you on as my girl."

"What do you mean by your girl?" I said, the fear returning. "Are you talking about a girlfriend?"

"That – and more," he said. "I need a woman like you to help my other girls out. A lot of them are very young and don't know how to take care of themselves. They need guidance – someone to keep them straight. You could also deliver my dope to the hotels, drop off packages, and collect money. I'd involve you in that part of the business too. The girls will like you. They'll trust you. And you can let me know if any of them are trying to rip me off. Once you befriend them and supply their dope, they'll confide in you, and you can help me take care of any problems that pop up."

My fear grew, but I was careful to remain outwardly calm. This man wants me to be a pimp. He wants me to handle the dangerous part of his operation. If I carry dope and cash, I'll be the one at risk if the cops move in.

To avoid appearing too compliant or too confrontational, I asked, "So what's in it for me?"

"Plenty of drugs. All of your needs met," he said matter-of-factly. "You'll also have a place of your own. There'll be no need to strip for a living anymore. You'll have complete control of all the girls and nobody to answer to but me."

Angry thoughts ran through my mind, but I said nothing, hoping he would take my silence as thoughtful consideration. I was alone with Ray Sr., and that made me vulnerable. I couldn't afford to do anything that would aggravate him. Who knew how he might react.

Just as the silence was becoming uncomfortable, there was a loud knock at the door, and we both flinched. With the drugs in the room, there was reason to be cautious. In a deep gruff voice, Ray Sr. asked who was there.

"It's me."

Relieved, I opened the door for Ray Jr., and he pushed inside, berating his father for leaving him asleep in the truck. What Ray Sr. probably saw as an unwanted interruption, I considered a Godsend. The younger Ray's arrival had gotten me off the hook.

While the two men grumbled at each other, I moved back to my place on the bed. Eventually, Ray Jr. calmed down, took a beer from a nearby cooler, and sat beside me.

"You don't prefer the cocaine?" I asked. He shook his head.

"I haven't smoked in two years," he said. "I've cleaned up my act."

"We'll see how long that lasts," his father challenged, and the two argued a bit more.

As I listened, I felt sorry for Ray Jr. He seemed sincere about wanting a better life, but his father belittled him mercilessly. It was odd. I could feel pity for these sons, but I never equated their situation to my own struggles. Though I was always quick to feel empathy for others, I rarely had any sympathy for myself.

Ray Sr. seemed to sense my affection for his son and moved to cut it off. He turned the conversation away from the boy and toward his goals for the family business.

"My son Ray is ready for more. I set the business up. Now, he can take the reins. He's a young man. He's got brains and energy. It's time for him to take over – to look after the girls," he said.

This idea must have reminded him about our earlier conversation because he shifted his focus to me again.

"All Ray Jr. needs is a woman like you, Shelly," he said. "I can train you. The two of you would make a great team."

This remark seemed to irk Ray Jr., and the two men went back to their bickering. I stayed out of their way, taking another crack rock for my pipe while these verbal jabs shot back and forth. I had no intention of becoming Ray's pimp, but I couldn't be seen as bucking his plans either.

Thankfully, the late hour began to take its toll on the older man, and his energy waned. When Ray Jr. ducked out to use the bathroom, his father tossed his hat on the bed and flopped back on the pillows to rest. By the time his son returned, Ray Sr. was asleep. He snored so loudly that Ray Jr. began to laugh, and the absurdity of it made me join in too. As the sound got louder and louder, the two of us laughed all the more.

"Let's take another room," young Ray said after we'd regained control of ourselves. "Grab the crack and come with me."

In the breezeway, we ran into one of the girls I knew from the strip club. She was stumbling down the corridor, clearly stoned. I stopped to speak to her, and Ray went on to the hotel office, telling me he'd return soon with a room key.

Moving toward me, the girl lost her footing again and almost knocked me over. At one point, she literally hung on me for support.

"Hey, can I join you guys? Do you have any dope you can spare?" she asked, slurring her words.

Realizing that Ray Jr. would be expecting sex, I pushed her away. I felt sorry for her, but I didn't want to complicate this night any further.

When she lingered nearby, I shoved a fragment of the coke cookie into her hand. "Here, take this and go. You can't share our room. This is a date. You need to find someplace else to crash."

The girl's glassy eyes looked from my face to the crack, then back again. Slowly, her scrambled mind processed what I'd said. She took the cocaine and staggered away.

*   *   *

"So, did my father talk to you? Did he ask you to work for him?"

Only a sliver of morning sunlight gleamed through the thick hotel curtains. Its harsh slash fell across my face, making Ray's question feel like the beginning of an interrogation. Fresh from the shower and wrapped only in a towel, I felt vulnerable again, so I tried to buy time, pulling a brush through my wet hair before answering.

"Nothing against your dad – or you, Ray," I said, "but I don't want to get involved. And I'm sure you can find somebody better."

Ray didn't reply immediately, so I filled the uncomfortable silence myself.

"I won't say anything about what you guys are doing, of course. There won't be any trouble from me. I just can't do the job he wants done. I definitely couldn't snitch on the other girls. You know, I'm just not cut out for that kind of thing."

"It's OK. I get it," he said, no malice in his voice. "I'll take care of things with him." The words left me breathless with relief.

"But maybe you can stick around," he added. "I like you. We could have a great thing together – whether you work in the business or not."

I was surprised and pleased Ray hadn't made a big issue of my refusal. I also liked what his response implied. It sounded like he wanted me to leave Sammy and stay with him. It would be a similar deal, but a much better situation for me. Unlike Sammy, Ray was a gentleman – and he didn't seem to need my money for the drugs he was supplying.

He did have one demand.

"I just want you to point out girls at the club who are junkies," he said. "You don't have to sell them anything. I'll take care of that."

Once I agreed to this, we jumped into a cab and headed for Sammy's place. I was edgy about leaving Sammy, but I was confident he wouldn't give me any trouble with Ray there. Ray Jr. was a big, well-muscled man like his father. Sammy was a skinny, paint-huffing junkie. If things got heated, I felt certain Sammy would back down.

It never came to that. Everything went very smoothly. When we walked in, there were several stoned kids crashing in the place. Sammy was surprised to see me with someone new and asked what was up, but he never got in our face or challenged me when I said I was moving out.

When we returned to the hotel, Ray gave me some cash and told me to get another room under my own name. I immediately slipped into the routines I had followed while living with Sammy. After unpacking my clothes and putting away my few belongings, I got ready for work while Ray watched something on the television. As I was leaving, he told me he would be coming to the club later that night.

"When I get there, we'll sit together for a few minutes," he said. "That way, you can point out the girls who do crack."

The early part of that night was typical for a weekday. It dragged on and on. Then, just before midnight, young Ray showed up. I was surprised to see Ray Sr. had joined him, but even more shocked that another woman had come along too. She was about my age, and I quickly got the impression she had taken the pimping role they'd offered me. Part of me was relieved, but I was also a little angry and jealous about the attention she was getting.

Ray Sr. stopped to introduce the girl as Jackie. When he and Jackie stepped away for a moment, I cornered young Ray, asking him if his father knew about my refusal of their business offer.

"Yes, and it's not a problem," he said, confirming my assumption about the new girl. "Dad's going to use Jackie instead."

In the weeks that followed, Ray Jr. and I fell into a pattern, working nights and sleeping most of the day. Jackie remained a fixture at the hotel, but I had very little direct contact with her. Because I was Ray Jr.'s girl, I would occasionally accompany him, or his father to the truck stops where their prostitutes worked. A lot of traffic moved up and down the interstate, so business was brisk. Most of the girl's clients were big-rig truckers just passing through, but there were locals who frequented the truck stops too.

The more I learned about the business, the more I hated it. The system Ray Sr. had set up was frightening, degrading, and inhuman. His "girls" were little more than animals to him. They were housed in small, dingy hotel rooms within a few miles of the truck stops and were kept high on drugs to ensure their compliance and loyalty. Most were shockingly young, clearly lost, and motivated mostly by fear. You could see the dread in their eyes when Ray or his father approached. They reacted like trapped animals, no longer able to imagine a world outside the truck stops. They were trapped in these horrible, nightly rounds.

Because the "business" Ray Sr. had developed offered a range of services at different costs, he and his son were ruthless about ensuring girls remained honest about the tricks they turned and the money they collected. I was present on several occasions when a girl got caught holding back cash. In those cases, Ray Sr. would become a terrifying sight. The huge man would shake the kid violently or send her sprawling with a savage slap. I winced and trembled during these assaults, only able to overcome my anxiety by rationalizing away his actions. The girl had lied or tried to cheat him, I would tell myself. It was her own fault.

Deep down, I was fearful something similar would happen to me someday.

Through this experience, I also learned that violence is a powerful tool for evil men to control the weak. I'd seen it used before, but never in such an intentional or systematic way. My exposure to Ray's strategies helped me understand how all of the dark businesses work – the strip clubs, the porn producers, and the drug world itself. In those "industries," the ultimate goal is to exploit girls and boys as both "products" and "consumers" – selling their bodies while grooming them as buyers in the drug trade. Make a hooker or stripper into a drug user, and you achieve the highest level of success. This is why a stripper or porn star dependent on supplied crack was considered the ultimate mark.

Even though I understood this terrible truth, it really had very little impact on my personal life during those years as a stripper. I knew I was being used and played for the benefit of others, but I felt incapable of changing my circumstances. I lived in a cage I had constructed myself, so I considered this abuse a fate I deserved.

In the days that followed, I often saw this same sense of resignation in the frightened eyes of Ray's girls. I understood why they accepted his savage blows and returned meekly to their lives of desperation. They were like me. Hopeless. They were women on a death march through life, pushing forward step by step, just doing enough to make it through another day – just enough to reach the next drug-induced high.

* * *

One day, a couple of weeks into my time with Ray, we moved out of the hotel. Ray Sr. had finished working that part of town and wanted to set up shop in another area of the city. This would be good for me, Ray Jr., said, even though it would mean leaving my job at the strip club.

At first, I was concerned about losing my job and the financial independence it offered. I pushed back a little, but my arguments proved fruitless. Ray Sr. always got what he wanted. Ray Jr. might argue the point with his father, but he would rarely win over the man.

The move to another part of Houston started a rapid downward spiral for me. Within a week, I found myself in a rundown hotel, cut off from my old friends and places I knew. To my credit, I did not surrender to despair. Pride and stubbornness were – for once – my allies. Rather than fall into mind-numbed complacency, as so many of Ray's girls did, I became frustrated, and a smoldering anger fueled a will to fight. If not for my obstinacy, I doubt I would have survived.

In the days following our move, Jackie became much more active in running Ray's business, and things in my daily life changed radically. The room I lived in was shabby, and I lost most of the privacy I had enjoyed before.

I remember one of those nights distinctly. There were four other girls in my room – two getting ready for their shifts at a new strip club and two preparing to do their rounds at the truck stops. As I sat fuming, even more girls came and went, using the room to stash their stuff or to take a shower.

Finally, Ray Jr. appeared, and all of the girls filed out. He must have seen the frustration on my face because he quickly brought out some dope and suggested I get high. As I took the crack out of his hand, there was a knock at the door. I asked who it could be, and he responded with a shrug.

When Ray opened the door, Jackie marched inside. I wasn't surprised. The two of them often talked shop, sharing war stories about the lot lizards and the stupid things they had done. But on this night, their conversation was very different. Jackie's mood was much darker, and her remarks more pointed. She confided in Ray about her frustrations with his father.

After the two talked for nearly twenty minutes, she reached for a big cookie of crack and broke off a piece.

"Is that yours?" I asked.

"It is now," she said with a laugh.

Uncertain what she meant, I looked to Ray for some sign of approval, but his expression was blank. Was she taking this dope without the men's permission? Red flags went up, and I stepped back into the shadows.

Ray Jr. seemed oddly quiet as Jackie lit up the rock and started to smoke. She continued with her tirade against Ray Sr., criticizing how he ran the operation and whining about the things she had to do to keep his business moving smoothly. At the end of this rant, Ray Jr. nodded and made a negative comment about his father too. I was surprised. I'd never heard him criticize his dad in front of Jackie or the girls.

Again, I searched his eyes, looking for a tell – some sign all was not as it seemed – but I couldn't get a good read on the man. My anxiety doubled. Ray must be playing along. He must want to know how far Jackie will go. I could feel the dangerous charge of electricity in the room, but Jackie seemed oblivious to it. Would she continue to throw fuel on the fire?

"You're right. My dad is a complete ass," Ray said, urging her on. "At some point, I'll be comfortable running this business. Then I'll take it all right from under his nose."

As I listened to them conspire, I never said a word, and Ray never looked my way. I was mesmerized. It was like watching a frightening movie scene. Deceit and betrayal were playing out before my eyes. Finally, Jackie broke my trance.

"I've got to go make a few pickups," she said. Getting up from the bed, she tossed the cookie and a wad of cash on a nearby table.

"I'll see you later, right?" she asked. Ray nodded as she left the room.

I didn't move a muscle or say anything. Ray got up, walked to the table, and picked up the money and dope. Without turning to me, he said, "You did good, girl."

Did good? His comment confused me. What had I done? I remained frozen in place as he left the room.

Several minutes ticked by. I was still struggling to make sense of what had happened. Had Ray played Jackie as I'd suspected? Or was I misreading the whole thing. Perhaps Ray was part of a plot against his father. Maybe he and Jackie were secret lovers, and I was the one being set up for a fall. My stomach roiled at these thoughts, and nausea pushed up into my throat.

I looked at the clock. My shift at the new strip club started in less than an hour, but I found it difficult to get ready. I was an emotional wreck, struggling to concentrate on even the simplest tasks.

Finally, just as I was finishing up and getting ready to leave, the phone rang. My heart jumped, and adrenaline surged through me. When I picked up the receiver, the voice on the other end was calm and deliberate. It was Ray Jr.

"Come to my father's room," he said. "Drop whatever you're doing and come here now." A little moan escaped before I could stop myself. I quickly recovered and stuttered an "OK." There was a brief hesitation on the other end of the line as if Ray considered making another comment, but he never did. The line just clicked dead.

The fear smoldering in my gut now stoked into full blaze. My imagination ran wild. In a panic, I looked around the room at my scattered belongings. Should I gather them up? Should I try to flee? I looked back at the phone, half expecting it to ring again. I could almost hear young Ray's voice and sense his impatience. Come on! Come now!

Desperate for some relief from this stress, my eyes settled on a crack pipe in an ashtray nearby. I retrieved it, lit a rock, and took a long hit. I had to go to see his father, I decided. There was no other choice. I grabbed the room key and headed off, praying my fears were unwarranted – that this was something simple; nothing to worry about.

When I reached the room, I put an ear to the door, hoping for a clue of what was going on inside. At first, I heard nothing. Then there was the sound of a breaking bottle. I knocked once and opened the door.

Time seemed to slow. The room was thick with crack smoke, and it took a moment for me to make sense of the scene. Two lot lizards from the truck stop were kneeling atop a bed that had been pushed out of position to a spot against one wall. Both looked up at me with terrified eyes.

Ray Sr. stood near the bed, a broken Jack Daniels bottle in one hand. The muscles in his shoulders, neck, and arms were tense, and his forehead was beaded with sweat. The expression on his face will haunt me forever. Eyes blazing, mouth contorted with rage, he looked more animal than man.

My mind raced to understand what was happening. It didn't make sense. Why was he so angry with these prostitutes? Who were they? What could they have done? Why had I been called in?

Searching for answers, I scanned the rest of the room. Ray Jr. caught my eye. He was sitting atop a dresser. There was an odd twinkle in his eye and a tiny smirk at the corner of his lips. I felt drawn to join him, probably hoping for his protection.

As I moved toward the dresser, a low moan redirected my attention to something I had missed. It was a woman previously hidden from my view by the bed closest to the door. She was sprawled at Ray Sr.'s feet. It was Jackie.

I may have gasped. I don't remember. It was such a shock to see her there, curled in a fetal position, her body bruised and bloody.

"Do you think Jackie is a liar?"

It took me a moment to realize the snarl had come from Ray Sr. and that the question had been posed to me. Still dazed and confused, I asked what he meant.

"You know she is, Shelly," Ray Sr. continued. "She's a liar."

I looked to Ray Jr. for support, but his eyes remained focused on his father.

In the seconds that followed, I remember babbling. "You're freaking me out. I don't know what's going on." I think I said something like that, but I can't be certain. By this time, a feeling of lightheadedness was swallowing me up, and my knees began to buckle. My ears were filled with the roar of static, and I found it hard to focus. I was about to pass out, so I stopped speaking and concentrated on keeping my feet under me.

Suddenly, I found myself looking up into young Ray's calm eyes. He had moved to me while I was swooning. I wanted to fall into his calmness. I wanted to escape, but the situation didn't allow it.

"Tell my dad what Jackie was doing. Tell him what she said," Ray offered in a slow, deliberate tone.

Red flags shot up again. I need to be very careful. What I say next might threaten Jackie's safety – or my own. I looked imploringly at Ray Sr. but found only cold anger in his eyes.

"I don't know what she was doing. I wasn't paying any attention to her ranting. I have no idea what she was up to."

Eyes still on me, Ray Sr. pulled his leg back and drove the pointed toe of his cowboy boot into Jackie's crumpled form. Air rushed out of her in a gasp and blubber. Wincing, I held my hands up as if to say; I have no more to offer – there's no more I can say. There was another low moan, but Jackie didn't move.

"Shelly, why didn't you touch the cocaine Jackie brought to our room? Wasn't it because you knew where she'd gotten it – who she had taken it from?" Ray Jr. asked.

Ray Sr. kept his stare on me. I tried hard not to look away.

"I would never take someone else's dope unless they offered it to me."

"And you knew that was dad's dope – right?"

Again, I remained silent, but I knew Ray Sr. could see the truth in my eyes. I hadn't wanted to incriminate Jackie. All I wanted to do was escape. All I wanted was an end to it all.

At that moment, the old man moved with surprising speed. His arm came down in a ferocious sweeping arc. The bottle he'd been holding struck Jackie's head with a terrible, bone-cracking sound, and a thick spray of blood spattered across the bedroom wall.

The two girls who had been sitting on the bed leapt to their feet, clearly horrified. I stumbled backward toward young Ray. As I took a rasping breath, I could feel my knees giving out again, but Ray Jr. moved in lithely and caught me in his arms.

Although my view of Jackie was partially obscured, I was certain

I'd just seen her life taken. Deep in my gut, I knew she was dead.

The room seemed to spin. In the minutes that followed, I have no idea where the two prostitutes went. Everything from that moment became a blur. Ray propped me up, intent on refocusing my attention, but I was a ragdoll in his arms.

"Dad had to do that, Shelly," he said. "Jackie was a liar and a thief. You know that. You saw what she did. Dad gave her everything she ever wanted, and she still betrayed him."

These words flooded into, through, and out of my mind. I couldn't focus. The scene was too surreal. As I began to pull away from young Ray, his father continued with his attack. As I moved toward the door, he savagely kicked Jackie's broken body again and again. With each blow, her limp arms and legs flailed erratically. She made no attempt to defend herself. She seemed a limp, lifeless thing.

I finally reached the room's door and pulled, thanking God when it opened. It was an incredible relief just to see the world outside. At that moment, it felt as if I was escaping hell. One of my flip flops caught in the door jam and was yanked off, but I never stopped to retrieve it. I just started to run. But where could I go? I needed to escape, but I had no option other than to return to my room.

When I got inside, I locked the door. Then I rushed to the bathroom and emptied my stomach in the toilet. The retching brought some relief, but fear still overwhelmed me. This was a living nightmare. Nothing seemed rational. My hands shook, and the objects in the room pulsed with each of my pounding heartbeats.

All of my previous decisions flooded into my mind. I'd made one stupid choice after another. Going to Sammy. Leaving him for Ray. Now, I would get exactly what I deserved. These evil men trafficked truck stop whores, yet I'd stayed with them for the dope they could provide. I was a fool.

Self-loathing and the haunting experience of seeing Jackie savagely beaten bore down on me with a crushing force. For a moment, I considered suicide, but I was too much of a coward to go through with that. Please God, just help me escape this somehow, I prayed.

I forced myself to focus. You need to wait for the cops. You need to stay safe until help comes. That's your best option. Just try to keep your head.

Minutes ticked by, but nothing happened. Eventually, my fears began to subside. They were replaced with more self-hatred. I needed to push down the pain. Then, I remembered the stash of crack we still had in the room. It would help me escape this stress. I ferreted out the dope and lost myself in its numbing stupor. Another thirty minutes passed. Then, the door opened.

Ray Jr. walked in, and I was surprised by how calm he seemed. Without saying a word, he quietly crossed the floor and entered the bathroom. He shut the door behind him, and I heard the shower start. My anger with myself shifted to disgust for him. He's washing off the filth, but he'll never be clean. He's a monster, just like his father. I need to escape somehow. Even if I'm arrested – so be it. That would be better than a life in their world.

With those thoughts spinning through my mind, I pulled back the sheets and crawled into bed. I would formulate a plan to get out. As I huddled in a fetal position, I closed my eyes tight and tried to wish all the craziness away.

When morning came, I woke with a start. Ray was by my side, but I couldn't remember when he'd gotten into bed. The trauma and cocaine had clearly drained me, and I'd slept soundly through the night.

Then, I remembered the attack on Jackie. I couldn't understand why everything seemed so normal. Where were the cops? Things couldn't possibly have blown over. I began to question the whole incident – and my own sanity.

I pulled out my pipe, lit up, and began to puff. Perhaps Jackie had only been injured. Maybe she was actually in the hospital now. How else would any of this make sense?

I turned in the bed and saw that Ray was awake and watching me. He seemed to be waiting for me to say something. Afraid I might set something terrible in motion, I remained silent. His eyes said everything I needed to know. Keep your mouth shut, Shelly, or you'll be next.

Finally, Ray got out of bed and ordered me to pack my things. We were leaving the hotel, he said. He told me to shower and dress.

Standing under the shower's stream, I sobbed. The flow of my tears joined the rivulets of water running over me. God, I prayed, how will I escape now? I saw no way to free myself, and I had no confidence there was any path out of the situation I could take.

God must see I am powerless. He must know the grief of my heart. As I prayed, I also felt unworthy of any help He might bring. In the end, I decided I should only beg for forgiveness.

As we prepared to leave the hotel, I imagined how things would go. Ray and I would carry our bags to the big Pathfinder his dad drove. I would crawl into the back. Ray Sr. would get behind the wheel. We would leave this mess behind and find a new hotel. Ultimately, it would all end badly, and I would experience Jackie's fate.

The next few minutes played out almost exactly as I had imagined. As we pulled away in his truck, Ray Sr. made some trite comment to his son, and the younger man laughed before saying something equally crass. They acted as if nothing had happened.

Show no fear, I thought. Pretend you don't care either, and eventually, you will find a way to escape.

Weeks later, my chance came – ironically through my arrest over a bad check I'd written months earlier. Thankfully, going to jail over that separated me from Ray and his sons, but it didn't end my destructive pattern of life. Once I overcame my legal challenges, I was back to my old ways and looking for trouble again.

Chapter 7

UNSPEAKABLE

Flipping through the yellow pages, I found the listings for escort services. After scanning the page, I looked away, uncertain about the choice I was making. It was 1994, and during my ten-plus years as an addict, I'd had sex with men to achieve my goals, but I'd never considered myself a prostitute.

If you call one of these places, all of that will change, I remember thinking.

These misgivings didn't last long. I had an intense desire to get high, and while my mind might struggle with the moral implications of my choice, my addiction was stronger. It produced its own twisted logic. Do the math! Sex equals money. Money equals drugs. Drugs will solve your problems. Had there been a devil on my shoulder, whispering in my ear, he couldn't have stated the case more effectively. By now, my addiction was its own dark spirit, and it knew exactly how to exploit my weaknesses.

I picked up the phone and scanned the top of the listings. "Abracadabra" was the first to catch my eye. I almost laughed out loud. Such savvy marketing! The "A" entries come at the top of each category, and this Madame had picked a name guaranteed to put her business in the best possible position.

I dialed. A woman answered.

"How can I help you?"

Help me? Before I could consider a sincere answer to that profound question, my addiction reasserted itself with its powerful mantra: sex equals money, money equals drugs, drugs will solve my problems. I felt like replying to her question with, "Yes, you can help me with money for drugs," but what I actually said sounded more like the pathetic ramblings of a loser.

"Um, OK. I was – you know – interested in… How do you become an escort?"

Miss Abracadabra didn't seem fazed by my floundering. She fell into a pleasant, professional pattern. How old was I? How would I describe my appearance? Those kinds of things. On some level, I wanted to escape the conversation, but I was swept along by her forward motion. As I answered each question, I rationalized why none of it really mattered. This escort thing might never happen, and even if Miss Abracadabra offered me the opportunity, I could always refuse her and end the whole process.

Then, she asked for my address.

"I need to come over to take a few pictures and go over some paperwork with you."

Suddenly, everything became very real.

Suddenly, it was time to decide.

The dark spirit's voice pushed its way back into my mind. *You've already gone this far, Shelly. Give her your address. What can it hurt? You can still refuse later if you change your mind.*

I told the woman what she wanted to know.

I felt dazed when I hung up the phone. Miss Abracadabra had said she was coming over immediately. There was nothing to do now but wait and see how it would all play out.

A couple of hours later, a tall blond showed up at my door. She was about my size and age. She wore shorts and flip-flops, but her attitude was all business. With an air of authority, she stepped inside and sized me up. Then, her eyes scanned my apartment. From the look on her face, she seemed satisfied. Apparently, I was escort material.

"My name is Susie. I'll need your driver's license," she said, pulling a few papers from her purse. "Then, you'll have to sign these."

While she took down info from my license, I scanned the documents she'd handed me. They looked as complicated as my lease agreement, a solid page of legalese. After reading a few lines of it, my eyes began to glaze over. I skipped to the end and put my signature on the dotted line. Satisfied, she took a few pictures of me.

"Sit down, and I'll go over a few things."

In the twenty minutes that followed, Susie explained the rules of escorting – how it was done, how the money was collected, even how to run a credit card slip if a john wanted to pay with plastic. Frankly, I was surprised by how easy it was. The payoff, she said, would be about $200 an hour. I would keep $100, and she would get the other hundred.

As I listened to Susie speak, I noticed her delivery was a bit off, and the pupils of her eyes were dilated. She must be stoned, I thought, and I wondered what she was on. Pills? Crack? No matter. What she described sounded like a legit business opportunity. Sex for money; money for drugs. Yada, yada. It was a clear-cut offer.

When she finished her spiel, Susie even shook my hand. I might as well have been a new employee joining an office clerical pool.

"Oh, and one more thing," she said, pausing for a moment at my open door. "We tend to get jobs after midnight, so be ready if you get a call. Don't worry. A driver will pick you up, and he'll wait for you and bring you back too."

Once Susie was gone, I had a quiet moment to think about the implications of what had just happened. I'd been nonchalant with her, but now a spasm of fear was growing inside. My imagination began jumping from one strange "what if" scenario to another. The money was extremely tempting, but I ultimately decided I wasn't yet desperate enough to assume the risks. And anyway, it wasn't likely she would call with a job. There must be plenty of other girls involved in the business, and I probably wasn't the type most johns were looking for anyway.

I was wrong. My phone rang at about 2 AM.

"OK, I have a call for you. Have you got a pen and paper?"

These words barely registered.

"I'm sound asleep," I said, still in a daze. "I'm not going anywhere tonight. Forget it."

Susie, the Madame, was indignant. She insisted I go. I held fast and told her I wouldn't. We argued for a few minutes. Then, in a rage, she hung up on me.

By this time, the fog had lifted from my mind. Although I'd convinced myself escort work wasn't for me, I began having second thoughts. You dummy. You just blew it. For a few minutes, I considered calling her back and accepting the job, but the idea didn't seem feasible. It was the middle of the night. I didn't have any dope to get high before going out. Counting it a lost cause, I went back to sleep.

The following day, all I could think about was getting high. The cravings that had stirred yesterday were now rising like a kindled fire. I'd also had a busy day at work, and I desperately needed an escape. On top of that, I'd been paid, and when I was flush with money, my nagging addiction always became stronger, as if it realized satisfaction was a step closer to reality.

Then, as if my dark spirit had been waiting for this moment, an opportunity to feed my addiction suddenly presented itself. It was the perfect offer to suit my weakness. My last salon customer said she was heading to a part of the city where one of my crack suppliers lived.

"Could you drop me off at a friend's place on your way?" I innocently asked. Not knowing my real intent, she agreed.

When I arrived at the dealer's house, Peter wasn't at home. I'd been to his place many times, so I knew he wouldn't mind if I let myself inside. He had two vicious Dobermans protecting his yard, but the dogs knew me well, and I passed them with no problem. Walking around to the back of the house, I found the hot tub running, but no one was in sight.

From the look of things, Peter must have gone out on a quick errand. I decided to make myself at home until he returned. By this time, the anticipation of scoring crack had filled me with an unbearable hunger, and I literally began to ache for relief. I hoped the warm, bubbling water would keep my mind off the pain. Stripping down to my underwear, I got into the hot tub, hoping my wait wouldn't be too long.

As I'd expected, Peter returned home shortly after. He pulled up into the drive, got out of his car, and noticed me in the tub. Although I hadn't seen him in months, his face lit up. Like a lot of the potheads and dealers in town, he knew me well. Seeing Shelly meant a party would soon follow. I was that kind of girl.

"Sorry, Peter, but I'm empty-handed tonight. In fact, I was hoping you could…"

"Then it's your lucky night, girl. I was just out for that very reason. I've plenty to share," he said, cutting me off. Peter popped into the house, grabbed his box of drug paraphernalia, and returned. His clothes came off, and he slipped into the tub.

Since I hadn't smoked for months, I got an incredible high from the first hit. Head spinning and ears ringing, I felt a power pulse through me – followed by an overwhelming sense of release. It was incredibly satisfying to have the nagging hunger abated.

About an hour later, all of the dope was gone. Peter seemed satisfied. He had no desire to score more dope. How is that possible? I wondered. How can he experience just a taste of this and so easily walk away? It worked very differently for me. I felt like a starving woman who'd only begun to eat a meal. I wanted more and more and more.

"I've got to get to bed, Shell," Peter said. "Working early tomorrow. But feel free to use the house phone – call a cab if you like."

Peter was a valuable contact, so I held back the frustration I was feeling. If I wanted to remain welcome here, I couldn't afford to push him, so I got dressed and used the phone to call a cab – but I had no intention of heading for home.

My binges always started this way. Once I fell off the wagon, the course of events was always the same. For days – sometimes weeks – I would need more and more crack to satisfy the cravings of my addiction and to bury the related sense of shame. When I left Peter's place, it was with the express purpose of finding another dealer as quickly as possible. Rather than going home, I had the cabbie take me to a shabby motel nearby. It was a nasty place, but I knew at least a few dope boys would be stationed there selling cocaine.

Four hours later, I was in the full throes of a binge. Through a bizarre circumstance, I had run into a prostitute named Shelley at the motel, and we had smoked both her crack and $200 worth of my own.

The hotel room I'd taken was oddly illustrative of what the drug lifestyle brings. It had once been clean and pleasant. Now, it was dark, filthy, and broken. The families and couples who had once used it as a vacation home had abandoned it to a much more unsavory clientele. It's once bright rooms had become gloomy with grime. The carpets were stained, the Formica tables and counters chipped, and the air musty. Thanks to our arrival, the room's stale air was now thick with smoke too.

As dawn approached, the other Shelley got up and paced the floor.

"Listen, girl," she said. "I need to get back to my man's room. He may be wondering where I am."

The television was chattering in the background. We'd spent hours watching late-night shows, getting high, and talking about our lives. The time had flown by.

"Sure. OK." I said. "I need to get going soon too."

After she left, I walked into the bathroom and was surprised by my reflection in the mirror. My face looked pale and drawn in the harsh light. There were dark circles under my eyes too. I was both wired and exhausted. The sight startled me for a moment, but it didn't deter me. In fact, I felt even more compelled to escape into oblivion. Checking my cash, I saw I had plenty to score more crack and still afford a cab ride home. Rather than leave, I decided to crash at the motel for another day.

Returning to the bed, I loaded up my pipe and took another hit, holding the smoke in my lungs for as long as I could before exhaling it. The stream of smoke was barely out of my mouth when a knock sounded on the door. I assumed Shelley had returned.

Without checking, I opened the door to two burly officers from the Broward County Sheriff's office. As I fumbled to regain my composure, they talked among themselves.

"Man, this isn't the girl we came for – the one named Shelley. Who's this one?"

My murky mind scrambled to make sense of this. Had they confused me with the prostitute who shared my name? I explained that although I had the same name, I wasn't the Shelley they were after.

"My name is spelled differently," I said

"So, do you know where the other Shelley is?" the other cop asked.

I would never snitch on a fellow addict, so I mumbled something about her leaving the motel earlier. I hoped my rambling explanation would send them off in their car to search for her. That would leave me to collect my stuff and scramble away.

"So, I really don't know where she is, but if you…"

The first officer interrupted with a goofy chuckle. He turned to his friend. "How weird is this? Have you ever arrested two people with the same name on the same day before?" The other officer snorted a laugh, shook his head, and then turned back to me. "You may not be the Shelley we came for, but you'll be going to jail with her." Both men chuckled again.

The strange circumstances, the disorienting high, and the sound of their mocking laughter suddenly made me swoon. To steady myself, I held on to the door frame and fought back an urge to puke. How would I get out of this? If they locked me up, I'd need to post bail. I couldn't possibly go to my parents for that money, and none of my addict friends would be able to help. I'd probably lose my job – perhaps my apartment too.

Knees buckling, I staggered back into the room and plopped down in a seat at the burn-pocked table where my crack pipe waited, a curl of smoke rising from its bowl.

Before I could say or do anything more, one of the cops was towering over me. He was no longer smiling. There was a new hardness in his eyes. I cried, I begged, I sulked, but the officer would have none of it. He stood me up, cuffed my hands behind my back, and guided me out of the room.

The next stop was the Broward County Jail, where I was booked, fingerprinted, and put in a cell to await arraignment. The charge was possession of cocaine and drug paraphernalia, and my bond was set at $1,000. When I asked some of my cellmates what would happen if I couldn't pay, a few of them shared their experiences. They said it was likely I would be sitting in jail for more than a month waiting for a court date. Then, I might get even more time.

This made me nauseous again. My job and apartment would be gone in a week. Being in jail for a month would be a complete disaster! Exhausted from being up all night, I collapsed on a floor mat and fell into a hard, restless sleep.

By my third day in jail, I was finally able to overcome my shame, depression, and anxiety enough to think through the few real options that remained. Still convinced I couldn't drag my parents into the situation, I made a mental list of every other person I could call. As each name and phone number entered my mind, I rejected it for one reason or another.

Then – Abracadabra!

The escort service's name literally popped into my head, and I could still recall their number from the phone book. It was a crazy long shot, but it was the most promising option I had. I'll call them and beg for help, I decided.

"Hello, is this Susie?" I asked tentatively. "This is Shelly. I called a few days ago about becoming an escort – remember?"

There was a long pause before the Madame spoke. "So, what did you get arrested for, Shelly?" she finally asked.

Rather than spin some outlandish tale of woe, I decided to approach this woman differently. I told her the truth. I spoke honestly and directly, as I might have to one of my best friends. By sharing the situation woman to woman, I hoped she would respond positively to my sincerity and need.

"Where are all your friends? Why can't they help you?" she asked. The questions had a caustic edge, but there was also a bit of compassion in her voice. When I told her I had no one I could turn to, her answer was painfully frank.

"I don't have a thousand dollars to give you, Shelly. I'm not going to be able to help you." That was it. The line went dead. My last option for escape was gone. Dejected, I slumped back to my mat and was soon asleep.

A few hours later, someone shook me awake. I was dazed and frustrated by the interruption. Why is one of the other inmates leaning over me? I wiped the sleep from my eyes, and my mind cleared.

"You're Shelly, right? You've been bonded out. Understand, girl? They're lettin' you out. The guard's been calling your name – so you better get moving."

At the cell door, an officer checked my ID tag and confirmed what the inmate had said. She opened the door and led me to a processing station where I changed back into my street clothes. No one I knew was anywhere in sight. My first thought was that my parents had found out. I looked to see if they had sent someone to pick me up. I couldn't imagine any other scenario.

Once my release was cleared, the officer handed me a folded note. She said it had been sent up from someone waiting for me downstairs. It read: Matt has come with his motorcycle to pick you up. You're going to stay with him tonight, and I will see you tomorrow.

Matt? I didn't know anyone named Matt. I racked my brain, but I couldn't recall a single friend of my family with that name. Downstairs, the mystery was explained.

"I'm Matt, Susie's boyfriend. She bailed you out, and she'll explain the payback with you tomorrow."

At first, I balked at the idea of going with this stranger, especially on a bike, but he was quick to shut down my protests. I just had a few seconds to decide, he said. I could come with him or return to the cell. Though he seemed nerdy with his thick coke-bottle glasses,

I could tell he meant what he'd said. He'd happily walk me back up and have me returned to the cell. That option was unacceptable, so I snatched up the helmet he offered.

The bike ride that followed felt like it would never end. Eventually, we reached an apartment somewhere west of Fort Lauderdale. I was unfamiliar with the neighborhood and a bit disoriented by it all. Still, there was little I could do but follow wherever he led. I'd gone this far. There was no other option. Matt parked the motorcycle, and I let him guide me into a nearby home.

The place was nothing special. It wasn't particularly odd or sinister. It wasn't warm or welcoming either. It was just a typical cracker-box apartment. After Matt strode in, he went directly to his bedroom and sat down behind a computer. Uncertain what I was supposed to do, I followed, but he barely seemed to notice. I pretended to be curious about what he was typing, but he didn't even acknowledge me. They had pulled me out of jail. Weren't they going to explain why?

Just as I was becoming frustrated enough to confront Matt, he suddenly turned toward me, catching me off guard.

"So, have you ever worked before?"

"What? You mean as an escort?" I stammered. "Well, no. But I was a stripper. And I'd date men from the club occasionally."

"Same thing," he said matter-of-factly. "Now you'll just be doing that for Susie. And believe me, she'll keep you busy."

I was shocked by the remark, but before I could respond, he continued.

"Go ahead and get undressed, and we'll have sex."

He must have read my expression because he immediately responded to my thoughts.

"Susie and I have an open relationship, and she has sex with other guys too. Besides, she'll want me to try you out. See how you are."

My street instincts kicked in. I was certain Matt was telling a lie. I'd spent a lot of time with addicts, and those experiences had helped me develop a strategy for dealing with such bluster. I shot him a disgusted look and told him where he could take his proposition. For good measure, I also said I would let Susie know what he had said.

This tactic worked perfectly. He nervously laughed off my rejection and returned to his work on the computer. Leaving him to it, I found a blanket on the couch and settled down to sleep. I kept an eye on Matt that night, but there was no more trouble from him.

The following day, I was taken to Susie's apartment for "the meeting." Thinking back on it now, elements of that day seem both mundane and profound – mundane because Susie was so nonchalant about my circumstances and profound because it was a major turning point for me. Among other things, it was the beginning of my long, strange relationship with Susie.

"I bailed you out. Now you owe me, and I expect you to work off every penny of this debt," Susie said matter-of-factly. She was so cavalier about paying off a debt with sex that it made me question my own aversion to the idea. The way she presented it, it was no big deal – hardly worthy of a second thought. Go through the motions, make money, pay off your debt. It's what anyone would do. She was so convincing, I felt awkward pushing back at all, but I did because I knew my limitations.

"I won't be able to do this unless I'm high," I said almost apologetically. It was the truth. From my previous experiences as a stripper, I knew I could only do tricks if I was able to eliminate the emotional side of the sex. Drugs put me in the state of mind I needed to perform.

Without saying a word, Susie strolled to a nearby cabinet and pulled out a crack pipe. It was nothing like the small stems I typically used. This thing was more like a bong, and it appeared to have been well used. Clearly, Susie was no amateur when it came to smoking dope.

"Take a shower. Pick out something to wear. We're about the same size, so my things should fit you."

In a strange display of multi-tasking, she then went about cooking up some cocaine while tending to her business and working on her computer. It seemed bizarre to me. She was going about these chores, as any office manager might. Only then did it sink in. Susie was an office manager. Her computer was used to keep records about the johns and tricks. Her multi-line phone was like any other business switchboard. The drugs were a necessary part of keeping the staff on the road and working – like having an office coffee machine, but on steroids.

After Susie had cooked up the dope, she broke off a piece and handed it to me.

"This is another $100 I'm putting on your tab. You'll need to work that off too – understood?"

When I took my first hit of the dope she supplied, I couldn't believe how good it tasted. The high was sweet and intense. It was nothing like the garbage I bought on the street, and I asked her about it.

"I've never smoked that street stuff. I only smoke crack I make myself," she said.

I was impressed. Having tried it her way, I never wanted to go back to street dope. High and content, I left Susie to take a shower and change. It was wonderful to be clean, and her clothes fit perfectly. I took a place on the couch and relit the crack pipe.

A few minutes later, I noticed Susie was on the phone – and that she was talking about me. The guy on the other end was undoubtedly a client. I heard her mention my name and say I was 26 years old. I was actually 32. Oddly, I was less appalled by her trying to sell me over the phone than I was about her lying about my age. I remember thinking, I hope this guy isn't pissed off when he discovers I'm older than the girl Susie described.

By the time Susie finally got off the phone, I was as high as a kite. All of my previous apprehension had literally gone up in smoke. It barely registered when she approached me with the job.

"But won't this guy be mad when I show up? You told him I was 26," I said.

"Forget about it. He's a regular of mine. Once you're there, everything will be cool. And he also wants you to bring some dope along with you," she said. "He's in a hurry, so I can't arrange a car to take you. You'll need to drive there yourself. Use my car."

I reached for the keys she offered, but she hesitated before handing them to me. It wasn't because I was stoned.

"You know, the driver usually gets twenty bucks from a girl. Just because you're doing the driving yourself doesn't mean you don't have to pay. It's my car, so I'll add the $20 to your tab."

As I started the car, I added up the money I owed Susie. My earlier fears about getting involved in prostitution seemed like a distant memory, and the idea that I would refuse these jobs struck me as ridiculous. Of course, I would go. I was in a financial hole, and doing tricks would be my way out. Beyond that, Susie was clearly a great source for dope, and maintaining those ties was one of the most important priorities in my life. Without a bit of regret, I sped off to turn my first trick for her.

Paying back Susie actually took a lot less time than I'd expected – even though I was constantly adding more to my tab by buying dope along the way. It also wasn't lost on me that I'd slipped back into my old lifestyle, but I accepted that fact without much thought. In some ways, being back in the old routine was actually comfortable for me, especially since the drugs were always there to soften the pain.

This time, the sin trap had other perks too. For example, I had begun to bond with Susie and found her friendship very satisfying. I even admired her as a businesswoman. She had a thriving operation, a nice car, fine clothes, expensive jewelry, and a steady flow of dope. She was nothing like Ray Sr. or his sons. Thank God I'd escaped their world.

Of course, no relationship based on money and drugs is without snares and difficulties. Trust is almost impossible to develop between addicts because greed and our obsession with dope influence everything we say and do. There were occasions when I felt I had a strong friendship with Susie, but at other times, I was just as convinced her kindness was a tactic to string me along and squeeze me for more drug money. In the back of my mind, I also knew I was one of her most profitable girls, seeing as many as six or seven clients a day and working stints as long as 24 hours in a row.

During these busy times, drugs were essential. Beyond making the sex tolerable for me, the dope kept me awake. Eventually, though, the intensity of it all would catch up with me, and I would crash. This cycle became routine, and before long, the routine became my lifestyle.

Wisely, Susie was careful to manage my ups and downs. She also learned to make the most of my appeal with the johns. In that way, we made an effective team, and as time passed, I gained access to her most important clients.

On one occasion, Susie joined me on one of these high profile jobs. We went to a beautiful home in Boca Raton, where I met a multi-millionaire who was also a binge crack smoker like me. When this guy got the urge, he would want to party and stay high for days on end. Susie and I provided dope and the "company" to keep his party rolling.

While on this job, I saw another of Susie's skills in action. Given a little time, she was able to shift a john's focus from sex to drugs – and I later learned this was a carefully conceived strategy used by many of the escort businesses in town.

The combination of sexual desire and addiction can be used as a powerful tool to control and exploit men. Susie and the other Madams understood both needs, and they had found ways to use prostitution to introduce and develop drug habits among their clients. In this way, the two cravings become intertwined, creating an even stronger web of entrapment.

Sex begins as the easier sell, but it has its limits. An addiction to drugs is much more powerful, and it creates an incentive for clients to call again and again and again. Eventually, some men, like the guy in Boca, even develop into profitable marks without the need for any sex at all.

For nearly two years, working this system was my life, and I served as a dutiful cog in Susie's machine. I lived with her, worked for her, and was sustained by the dope she supplied. Eventually, I became so comfortable with Susie that I thought of her as my best friend, and, like an apprentice, I watched carefully and tried to emulate her.

At that time, nothing gave either of us a hint of how terrifying both our lives would eventually become.

Chapter 8

UNSAVORY

The days turned into weeks; the weeks into months; the months into years. As time passed, my strange relationship with Susie evolved into something like the bond between sisters. We lived together, worked together, and got wasted together.

That said, we were sisters in a dysfunctional family. By that, I mean, we often experienced all of the emotional turmoil you would expect to find in that kind of household. There were joyful moments with laughs as well as terrible times characterized by jealousy, fits of anger, and conflicts over power. At times, I was so infuriated by Susie. I thought we would never speak to each other again. Then, the clashes would suddenly end.

Day-to-day, it was hard to know what to expect, and over time, this emotional pounding took a toll on us. Like sand on a surf-savaged beach, the trust in our relationship eventually eroded away, leaving nothing but hard feelings and a callousness of heart. This eventually led me to break Susie's only unbreakable rule. After a particularly vicious fight, I stormed out and went to one of her best clients for "solace."

To rationalize my actions, I thought of the trip to his house as a way of cooling off, but deep down, I knew that going to clients outside of the business was taboo with Susie. She was a master at controlling her johns, and she never let them have anything for free. The fact that I would sleep with a client outside of our business relationship would be seen as a major betrayal in her eyes.

Honestly, I understood her position. Had I done this often, my pouts could easily have crippled her business. It could have compromised her control of the sex and drug connection she had dedicated so much time and energy to forge.

A few of my previous indiscretions had already forced Susie to tap all of her skill and charisma to overcome the damage I'd done. On this particular day, my decisions and actions were "the straw that breaks the camel's back," as the saying goes.

It was a Friday, and I was driving into our condo parking lot after an appointment with a client when I noticed a man I knew leaving the complex. He was a very wealthy john, a guy Susie and I had both entertained in the past. I knew he liked me and wanted to see me, but Susie had recently shut that relationship down. He was one of her best clients, and she was locking him up for herself.

I was thrilled when he slowed his Mercedes as my car approached in the opposite lane, and we both rolled down our windows to talk.

"Shells! Great to see you!"

I smiled and encouraged him, wanting to see where it might lead.

"Hey, listen. Maybe you can give me your personal cell number, you know. We can party later – outside of this business thing," he said, cocking his head in the direction of Susie's place. "I'm still willing to pay, of course. Just bring an ounce with you. You know what I mean."

After we said our goodbyes, the gears in my head started turning. I was certain I could fool Susie and get away for a day or so. It would be risky, but this guy had big bucks and a gorgeous mansion on the Intracoastal Waterway. The place was a paradise with a huge pool, hot tubs – the works. I decided it was worth the risk.

For my plan to succeed, I needed to acquire dope quickly and, more importantly, stay off of Susie's radar. It wouldn't be easy, particularly on such short notice. I parked the car, went into the house, and headed straight for my room.

A dozen emotions were at war inside me. I was thrilled by the prospect of having a great time with this john, but I also understood the consequences. I felt pride at taking control of my own fate, but I was also guilt-ridden about sneaking around behind Susie's back. In the end, I decided to step out from under her shadow, even if it meant a betrayal of our agreements—even if it might ruin our relationship forever.

In those next two days, I enjoyed the forbidden fruit I longed for, but I also set a dangerous new phase of my life in motion. The escapade netted me a thousand bucks and a couple of exciting nights, but it also put me back on the street when I was ill-equipped to handle the situation.

Susie was waiting for me when I finally returned to her home.

"I know what you did! I know where you were!"

Susie was so furious she literally screamed over my feeble excuses. She called me horrible names, insisting I was a liar. The confrontation was nothing like our earlier fights. It quickly escalated into something much darker and more frightening than I'd ever experienced before. Terrified, I just wanted to escape.

Grabbing up my cell phone, I called for a driver, but I could barely hear what he was saying over Susie's screaming. When the car arrived, it was all I could do to grab a few clothes and rush out, her curses ringing in my ears.

"Leave then!" she yelled as I scrambled off to the car. "That'll be easy for you. But know this – it won't be so easy coming back. I've had it with you, Shelly! You're on your own!"

It didn't take long for things to go from bad to worse. Cut loose from the structure of Susie's home and business; I immediately fell back into the chaotic world of a street addict. The fight had also been traumatic, so it triggered all of my old fears. To numb the pain, I needed to get high, so the search for a dealer began. I was scouting old neighborhoods to find past contacts when a crack dealer who worked the area noticed me.

"Shelly, girl!"

I stopped short. Had someone in a passing car recognized me? It sounded like a familiar voice, but I continued walking because I didn't know the car. The driver did a U-turn and caught up with me as I was entering a gas station parking lot.

What a relief! It was Bodain, one of my favorite dealers. He told me to jump in, so I scrambled into the back of the car and we took off. Only then did I notice the driver. He was a stranger to me, and he was dressed very oddly for a friend of Bodain.

He turned and introduced himself as "CJ," and his look further confused me. He was very clean cut – almost preppy looking. He had a short, trimmed afro and wore a pair of bookish, round spectacles. He was as far from a street-tough as I could imagine.

Concerned, I gave Bodain a look. He picked up on my anxiety immediately and told me the guy was cool; a friend; I need have no worries. Since I was desperate to get high, I let it pass and tossed a hundred dollar bill into Bodain's lap.

"Whatever," I said. "You know what I want." But Bodain didn't pass back the crack as I'd expected.

"Sorry, Shells, but I'm not carrying. If you want dope, we gotta drive over to my boys' house. I can take care of you there."

I cringed. I hated going into the hood. I was always a nervous wreck there. There was always a chance we might get pulled over by raiders.

"Well, if we have too," I finally said, "but make it fast."

It was getting dark by the time we reached Bodain's part of town. CJ pulled into a parking space, and Bodain jumped out, leaving me alone in the car with his friend. Nervous and sick to get high, I stretched out on the back seat of the car to stay out of sight.

No sooner did I get settled when CJ spoke up.

"Don't freak out, but I am going to take a shot here. It'll only take a minute."

My mind raced. A shot? What the heck is he talking about? As I peeked over the back seat, CJ pulled out a syringe, tied off his arm, and began to shoot dope.

"What are you doing? Are you going to geek out on me? What are you shooting up anyway?" The words tumbled out of me. Angry, worried, and starving for a high, I felt like I was losing control.

"This is just heroin," he said as if that explained everything. "It'll be fine."

It took about thirty seconds for him to finish, and a minute or two later, he slouched in his seat as if he'd fallen asleep. Still jittery about being in the hood, I poked him and sought some reassurance he was OK.

"I'm fine – really good. Everything's great," he answered in a distant, dreamy voice.

While we waited for Bodain to return, CJ explained that he was visiting from out-of-town and had a room at a nearby Holiday Inn.

"I'm not looking for sex or anything, but I'd love to have some company if you want to join me there. We can party, you know. Who wants to get high alone?"

I thought about it for a minute and decided the invite would be good. When Bodain returned and handed me the dope, I told him I would be going on with CJ. He nodded, handed me his number in case I needed to score more later, and moved off into the night.

At the hotel, I got another dose of "the creepies" from CJ. I don't know what I'd expected, but I found the room as strange as the man. It smelled good, and everything inside was immaculate. The closet was open, and I noticed his small wardrobe of clothing was hanging in perfect order. Little price tags still hung on some of the clothes, and the shoes on the floor all looked to be top-of-the-line Italian leather.

Who is this guy? What's really going on here? My gut told me something was wrong, but my hunger for dope and companionship overwhelmed those fears. I plopped into a chair by the window, pulled out my stem, and started to smoke.

CJ opened a drawer in a nearby dresser, pulled out syringes, a spoon, a candle, and some cotton, and got to work. I watched as he poured brown powder into the spoon, added a few drops of water in it, and began to heat the concoction over a flame. This was the first time I had seen a person cook heroin. I watched intently, asking a few questions about the process as he worked.

When CJ finished, he took a belt from the closet and walked into the bathroom. I followed him, absorbed by the drama of it all. After tightening the belt around his arm, he took a shot. This time, the dope seemed to have a much greater impact. His head nodded back, his eyes turned glassy, and his lips turned up in a devilish grin. Then, he let out a deep, trembling sigh.

"Are you OK?"

"Oh, yeah," CJ answered, a little smirk still on his face. A minute later, he plopped in a chair. As his head drooped, a string of drool trailed from his lip to one shoulder.

When CJ was finally coherent again, he thanked me. I asked why.

"For not snooping through my things or robbing me while I was high," he answered, smiling.

"Look, I don't want your dope. I don't do heroin. That was a bad scene for my father," I said. "But I'm cool with staying here. I've got some money. I don't need to rob you. I'm just looking for a safe place to hang out – a place I can get high without being hassled."

CJ seemed relieved to hear this, and he began to open up. I was hungry for acceptance, so I joined in too. We talked all afternoon about our lives and our habits. Both of us had plenty of strange stories to tell. I shared with him about my adventures with Susie working as an escort, and he sympathized with me, encouraging me, and supporting my decision to leave her.

Once again, it was clear to me that CJ wasn't your typical dope head. He was soft-spoken and seemed trustworthy and kind. The truth is, my instincts had failed me. They should have thrown up a red flag, but they didn't. My little twinge of fear about CJ – the anxiety I'd felt before – was gone. It had been swallowed up in my warm, dope-induced stupor.

Finally, hours later, our physical hunger surfaced. CJ tossed me his car keys. I assumed he wanted me to make a run to a nearby fast food joint, but he had other ideas. He went to a small safe in the closet, opened it, and pulled out a stack of bills. It was like something you'd see in a movie. The cash was in banded wrappers of hundreds, fifties, and twenties. I kept my mouth shut and acted as if I hadn't noticed, but I knew he saw me look inside. CJ broke the paper band on one of the stacks of money and handed me a hundred dollar bill.

"No crap food for us," he said. "Find a place that will let you take out a steak and lobster dinner. I'm sure you're as hungry as I am."

At the door, I turned back and asked if the car he was driving was legal. I'd seen a temporary plate in the back window when I first got in. I already had a suspended license, and I didn't want to get pulled over in a stolen car. CJ reacted as if I'd told the best joke he'd heard in years.

"Yes, it's legal," he laughed. "I bought it a week ago. I'm just waiting for my new tag."

Again, the dope masked my better instincts. Rather than seeing this as another warning sign, I just shrugged, turned, and walked out.

When I returned to the room, I respectfully knocked before opening the door. I wanted to avoid alarming CJ. There was no chance of that. He was sprawled out on the bed, flying high and drooling again. I set out the food, poured each of us a drink, and roused CJ with a tug on his arm. Disoriented, he opened his eyes and checked his watch. Then, he smiled and stumbled over to the table.

We both sat quietly, devouring our meals. It felt great to have decent food in my system. I hadn't realized how hungry I'd been. I was clearing the table when CJ finally spoke.

"Shelly, why do you do this?" The question surprised me, coming from a heroin addict.

"Do what? The crack is…"

"No, no," he interrupted, "I mean, why do you resort to prostitution?"

Surprisingly, his words filled me with shame, but I didn't turn away. I looked him in the eyes.

"I do this because I'm an addict, and it's the only way I can keep myself high."

I went on to tell him a bit about my life. I shared about my family, about growing up in an amazing home with awesome, loving parents. I told him I often felt inadequate; that I could never measure up. He sat quietly, never taking his eyes off me.

When I finished, I asked CJ for his story. He sat quietly for a moment, then looked out the window and replied in a soft voice.

"My life wouldn't interest you," he said. "It's sad. Pathetic, really. Too hard to talk about."

I hadn't expected that at all. Most men I knew loved to tell you about themselves. They always had stories about some big-time score they'd made or a scam they'd pulled or something of that sort, but CJ had none of that bluster.

"What the hell. I'll tell you if you really want to know," he began. "I'm from Georgia. In those days, I lived on the streets with my wife. We were both heroin addicts, and she tricked to support our drug habit. Lots of family and friends wanted to help us, but we were in so deep – it was hopeless."

"One day, we came up with a scheme to get out of that life. To do it, we had to get big money quick, so we decided to hold up a grocery store. We planned it for weeks, saying that once we pulled off the robbery, we would use the cash to get out of the hole. We promised ourselves we'd go to detox and rehab and turn our lives around."

CJ went on to explain that his wife had a great talent for cooking and that the two of them had a dream to open a diner. He was quite a storyteller, and I ate up every word. Whenever he would try to stop, I begged for more. Eventually, he explained how the robbery went down.

"I got a gun and a ski mask to do the job. I had no bullets, but that was fine since I had no intention of firing the weapon. Using my friend's car, we drove to a local Winn Dixie, and we waited outside until the place was about to close."

According to CJ, he left his wife in the car and walked to the back of the store. There, he slipped into the rear storage area and found a staff restroom. He hid inside until the store closed, and the customers were gone.

"Once everyone cleared out, I put on the mask, took out the gun, and walked straight to the office where two people were sitting at the safe, counting money. I pointed the empty gun at them, but they obviously thought it was loaded. They stepped aside, and I took the money."

"I stuffed a bag with stacks of cash," he continued. "I took it all – everything but the coins. Then, I demanded the keys to the front door and headed straight out the way I'd come. When I got around the side of the building, my wife pulled up in the car. I jumped in the back and got out of sight while she drove away."

I sat in disbelief.

"That was it? You got away with it?"

"Yes. But that was a long time ago, Shelly. I was in my twenties then."

At this point, CJ had me hook, line and sinker. I begged him to continue.

"When we finally counted the money, we had more than $50,000," he said. "And we did what we said we would do, just as we'd planned. She and I went into a detox and then through rehab. We did it all without spending a dime of the money we'd stolen. Once we were both clean and back on our feet again, we started looking for a little diner we could buy. We found one in a small neighborhood in Savannah, and we used the cash to make a down payment. We fixed it up and turned it into a profitable business. We had the best chili in town."

CJ's story had a strange effect on me. I found it fascinating, but I was also sucked in by his simple passion to succeed. I was so hungry for self-worth that I found myself living vicariously through his experience. Finally, a "little guy" had made good!

Then, the story got even better.

According to CJ, he and his wife paid off the diner mortgage in less than a year. In the next eight years, they opened a dozen other locations. They eventually had three kids and used their newfound success to take advantage of all of the pleasures of life. They got a big house, sent their kids to private schools, and bought all of the good things they'd ever dreamed of having.

By this time, I was so emotionally affected by the story I was literally in tears. It was like a fairy tale – something any of us would wish for in life. But I also knew it would end tragically. CJ's current situation was proof of that.

"How did you lose it all," I asked, nearly sobbing. "What happened?"

"When the big money rolled in, I eventually fell back into using drugs," he explained. "I kept it secret for a while, but my wife eventually caught on. And she was furious. She demanded I go back into rehab before I ruined it all. I refused. You know how it is. I was a functional user in the beginning, but as my habit grew, I eventually lost control. In the end, even after she asked for a divorce and I knew I would lose the kids, I still couldn't stop. I couldn't give up the dope. And that's all there is."

CJ had told such a compelling tale that I could barely speak when it was over. I'd known the guy for less than 24 hours, but I felt completely tuned in to his life. In the weeks that followed, this bond would remain strong, carrying us through a blur of partying and drug use.

As I had in the past, I followed the typical pattern of a drug addict. We changed hotel rooms every few days, used a dealer we trusted for dope and did what we could to stay off the radar. The last hotel we checked into was a nice place. We stayed there three days before everything broke down.

On that last morning, I came out of the shower to find CJ sitting on the side of the bed, his head in his hands. I'd seen this kind of thing before. Sometimes addicts wear out their welcome. The party is fun, but it can all end as quickly as it begins. When I approached CJ, I expected him to ask me to hit the road.

Instead, he dropped his hands, revealing a strange, melancholy look on his face. He seemed like a child, lost and looking for solace.

Had something happened? Were we in trouble?

"Shelly, I'm completely out of cash," he said. "I don't think I can make it until next week when more money is deposited into my account. What's worse, I only have two shots of heroin left – then I'm going to start going through withdrawals. I can't take that."

"I can probably make some quick money," I said, hoping to comfort him. "I know a few really wealthy guys I can call and…"

"No!" CJ was angry. "You're not doing that – selling yourself for my drugs."

I looked back blankly. What else could we do? It was the fastest way I knew to get cash.

He sat still for a moment – then began speaking softly as if he could barely accept his own suggestion.

"There may be another way, Shelly. But don't freak out – it's just an idea. I think it could work. But you'll need to hear me out – and help with the plan."

I felt a little anxious about CJ's tone of voice but listened with curiosity. Where was this going? What could he possibly be thinking?

"Remember the story I told you about robbing that grocery store?" he asked. "It all went so easily. No one was hurt, and we never got caught."

I sat there quietly, but my stomach began to roil. Is this guy crazy? I'd never rob a person at gunpoint, much less hold up a business. For one thing, there could be disastrous consequences. Someone could get hurt.

Though these thoughts filled my mind, I was also filled with guilt. I'd spent a lot of CJ's money getting high. I'd also used his cash to eat well and to buy clothes. How could I take so much from him and not respond with help in his hour of need?

By the time CJ finished, tears were rolling down my cheeks. I was scared – really scared – but I also felt trapped. More than that, I felt obligated. I owed CJ big time. And he cares about me, I rationalized. Surely he won't involve me in something we can't handle together.

"No. Forget it, Shelly," he said timidly. "It's a crazy idea. I'm just afraid because I've got nothing else to fall back on. And if I don't get the heroin soon, I'm going to get very sick. I'm just not sure I can survive going cold turkey without methadone. Sorry, I brought it up. Really, Shelly. I'm sorry."

My heart ached, and my empathy went into overdrive. He sounded so pathetic. I looked down at the track marks on my own arms and sobbed again. I was a complete mess. Though this might put me into an even darker place, what could I do? When I spoke, I tried to sound encouraging.

"It's going to be OK, CJ," I said. "Just tell me what I need to do. I'll help you if I can."

Just like that, it happened. I couldn't believe the words coming out of my mouth, but I didn't retract them either. I just sat and listened as he began to explain the details.

Less than an hour later, we were ready to go. I'd put on a pair of shorts, a tube top, and flip-flops. It was a bizarre moment. I remember thinking, these clothes for a robbery? At least they're comfortable. After all, I won't be leaving the car. I'm just driving CJ to the store, dropping him off, and picking him up.

We drove out to the west side of the city, and during the trip, I rehearsed the plan over and over in my mind. CJ said the Winn Dixie would close at ten. It would only take a few minutes to pull off the job. Periodically, I pulled out my stem and took a hit to calm my nerves. I wanted to be as high as possible but maintain my ability to drive.

Pulling into the parking lot of the Winn Dixie, CJ turned off the engine. A parade of nameless, faceless people were coming and going from the store with their groceries, but no one was paying any attention to us. It felt to me as if someone there should be reacting to the danger we posed, but that wasn't happening. The whole situation seemed surreal.

For 20 minutes, we waited. Then, CJ unexpectedly started the car. "Forget it," he said. I was shocked. Why had he changed his mind? Did this mean we were turning back?

Although I felt confused, I was also overwhelmed with a sense of relief. It felt like the tingle of electricity, but the joy was short-lived.

"I have a better idea," he said. Without explaining, he pulled out of the grocery store parking lot and began to drive down the street. Eventually, we passed a Wendy's hamburger place.

The lights inside were dim, and we could see that chairs had been put up for the night. The only activity came from the back, where a few employees were busy cleaning up. Soon, the restaurant would close for the evening. When CJ slowed the car, I understood this would be his new target.

He drove two blocks away before pulling off the main road and into a residential area. Ironically, the first thing I noticed was a neighborhood crime watch sign. CJ pulled the car into the first apartment building's parking lot.

"OK, Shelly. Remember what I told you. You need to drive around for at least 20 minutes. Keep circling back to this point. When you see me walking up the road from the direction of the restaurant, come for me. I'll jump in the backseat. Then, you just drive on. Get the heck out of Dodge – you know what I mean."

I nodded and slid over to the driver's side.

"I have one last shot of heroin," he added. It's in the glove box, ready to go. I'll need it when I get back."

I nodded again. I didn't want to say "good luck" because the thought of encouraging him seemed ridiculous. I really wanted to drive off and leave him, but as anxious as I was, I still managed a little smile. He nodded back, then grabbed a bag of "tools" he had stashed in the back seat. Inside were a gas mask, a long coat, and a gun. He'd promised there were no bullets in the gun, and I'd made him prove that to me before we'd left the hotel.

A minute or two after he walked away, I drove out of the parking lot and down the street. I was high and twitchy with adrenaline, but I did everything I could to appear normal. I cruised the neighborhood slowly, keeping my eyes fixed on the road. It was a nice part of town and a very quiet neighborhood. The whole time, I didn't see a single person on the street.

After a few minutes of driving, I calmed down and remembered my pipe was there in the car. I deserved another hit, I decided. It would help me relax. I took a hit and felt the welcome release. I let the pipe cool and tucked it back in its hiding place between the seats. I was approaching another turn in the neighborhood, so I needed to decide which way to go.

At that moment, my eyes passed over the rearview mirror, and I realized with shock that a police cruiser had moved in behind me and was matching my speed.

I didn't panic. I didn't break. Instead, I forced myself to remain calm and kept driving. A side road was approaching. It was my way out. I took that corner, but the police car remained on my tail. Only then did I realize I had turned so many times, I'd become lost. I wasn't certain how to leave the subdivision and get back to the place where CJ had gotten out of the car.

Another side street loomed ahead, and I turned again. This time the police car did not follow. My heart skipped a beat, and I began shaking from the tension. I focused and looked for landmarks – something I could use to get my bearing and retrace my path back to the main road. My spirits soared when I finally spotted the apartment complex where CJ had parked. Then, I noticed something else. As I approached the main road, I saw men blocking my path. Some were dressed in police uniforms. Others wore SWAT gear. There were more than twenty of them waiting at the end of the street. Several had weapons pointed at me.

Though I was still fifty yards away from the roadblock, I hit the brakes. I made no move to exit the car. I just sat there in complete shock, scared beyond words.

Suddenly, everything felt like it was happening in excruciatingly slow motion. Several of the men moved toward the car, their guns still up and ready. This is it, I thought. It's all over. My mouth was open wide, and my hands were trembling on the wheel. When a loud voice suddenly sounded, I nearly jumped out of my skin.

"Turn off the car! Step out with both hands raised! We need to see your hands! Keep them open and up!"

One of the officers was using a megaphone. I turned off the car and slid out with both hands raised, fearful they might not see me clearly in the dark. If they thought I was armed, I was terrified they might shoot me. I said the only thing I could think of at the time.

"I don't have a gun. I promise." Hearing the words made me cringe. I sounded like a fool.

The cops reacted as if my words were a trigger. They immediately moved in on me.

"It's not him. It's only the girl," I heard one officer say.

They turned me around and frisked me.

"Yeah, she's just a junkie."

Down the street, lights flashed, and the cops buzzed into activity again. Tears ran down my cheeks, and the slow-motion nightmare continued. I had vague fears about them finding the crack pipe, but I'm not sure why. I was an accessory to a robbery. What would the dope matter?

Most of the officers turned and walked back to the roadblock, but a few remained with me.

"Where is he?" they asked me again and again.

When I couldn't take it anymore, I sobbed out a question.

"Do you mean CJ?"

"No. Where is Fred Hazel," the cop shot back. "Where's Hazel?"

Another cop approached and asked me to confirm my identity. Fool that I was, I used a fake name.

"You're not helping yourself, Shelly Lantz," he said. "Providing false ID – I'll be adding that to the charges against you."

My mind raced. What! How does this cop know my name? Was this some kind of trap? I couldn't make sense of what was going on.

Suddenly, coming from the darkness, three men approached. One of them was CJ. The other two, in civilian clothes, were clearly detectives. CJ was handcuffed, and the two cops guided him by his elbows. He stared at the ground, ignoring me completely.

"Is this the man who was with you, Shelly?" one asked. I mumbled a "yes."

CJ glared up at me. The voice that came out of his mouth shocked me. He sounded nothing like the man who had partied with me during the past three weeks.

"I've never seen this woman in my life. I don't know nothing about her."

I was stunned. Was CJ trying to protect me? Was he acting this part so I wouldn't go down with him?

The cop nearest to me must have read my mind because he looked me straight in the eyes, daring me to change my story and deny I knew CJ. I said nothing more. I just hung my head in shame.

As the cops escorted CJ away, he continued to insist he was innocent. They put him in the cruiser and drove away.

For the next twenty minutes, I stood and watched as the cops tore apart the car I'd been driving. They found my pipe. They found the crack I'd stashed inside. They found the heroin and syringe in the glove box. Then, they went into the trunk. That's when I learned something was seriously wrong.

Several of them began laughing. A few high-fived each other. Clearly, they'd struck gold.

I said nothing. Unable to handle it all, I began to shut down. My ears roared, and my head started spinning. I fought back overwhelming nausea. Finally, one of the officers returned from the search.

"Too bad we found you in this car instead of Hazel," he said. "Hope you can prove this vehicle isn't yours."

The words barely registered. I was overcome and disoriented – close to passing out. I asked the cop if I could sit down. He walked me over to one of the cruisers and gestured for me to sit in the back. Within minutes, I was out cold. I'm not sure if I passed out or if I succumbed to exhaustion from the stress, but either way, everything went black.

The next thing I remember was a man pulling me from the cruiser. We'd arrived at a police station, and I was brought inside for booking. From there, they put me in a cell. I went straight to the corner of the room and curled up on the concrete floor. Within a few minutes, I was out again.

I slept until the following morning when I was brought down to face a judge who explained the charges. The count included four felonies and two misdemeanors. Resisting arrest by giving a false name and possession of drug paraphernalia were misdemeanors. Grand theft auto, possession of crack cocaine, possession of heroin, and violation of probation were the felonies. While listening to the judge, I also discovered that the car trunk had contained a significant amount of heroin and crack.

Hearing this all spelled out so methodically was frightening. I couldn't even begin to imagine what would happen with my parents. They would be heartbroken, of course. Their disaster of a daughter had crashed and burned again.

Feeling shell-shocked, I returned to my cell. According to the cops, I would sit there until my trial, some 40 days away. Day by day, the time passed, but I did little more than sleep. It was the only escape I had from the shame and depression I felt inside.

Then, near the end of my wait, a visitor came. An officer brought me to a waiting room. He left, and another man entered. This guy wasn't like the cops I'd encountered. He had a gentle approach and a kind smile. He introduced himself.

"Hello, Shelly," he said. "I work for the Crime Stoppers and America's Most Wanted programs." Seeing the shock and confusion on my face, he chose his next words carefully.

Over the next hour, he explained to me exactly who CJ actually was – and why I was lucky to be alive. The man I knew as CJ, he said, was actually a wanted murderer named Fred Hazel. I listened in amazement, but everything he told me about the man fit perfectly with CJ's MO.

"Fred's pattern was to pick up destitute hookers and lull them into a false sense of security by building trust and creating dependence," the man explained. "He usually starts by getting the girl high and supplying her addiction. Once he believes he's established a strong bond of trust, he brings the woman into his scheme."

The prostitute becomes part of a robbery, he said. But, once the stolen money is in hand, the girl becomes a liability. Fred then murders this accomplice, dumps the body, and moves on.

"You," he said, "were right on track to be the next victim, and you'd probably be dead now if the police hadn't been closing in on him. You've been very lucky, Shelly."

I began to sob.

According to this man, the bust that snared me had been weeks in the making. The cops had been on Fred's trail and needed something conclusive to ensure they could nail Hazel once and for all. They had done everything by the book, and the evidence they'd gathered would guarantee a conviction.

Although I knew my own guilt, I couldn't help but be angered by this story. If it was true, the cops had let me run around with a murderer while they waited for him to attempt another robbery. When I asked the man if I had been used as bait, he skirted the issue.

By the end of it all, I couldn't help but think of God. I hadn't just been lucky. I was certain of that. This was God rescuing me again. I prayed a silent prayer of gratitude as I struggled to wrap my head around all of these details.

At that meeting, I also learned more about what had been happening with the case while I was waiting in jail. For example, the cops had dropped the charges for auto theft. They'd discovered I had nothing to do with the car. It was also unlikely I'd take the stand in the case against Fred. Hazel had been wanted in several states where other evidence and testimonies were available, so they didn't need me to get a conviction.

Near the end of our time together, my visitor said something I'd never expected to hear.

"Shelly, I believe God has his hand of protection on your life. I just feel I should pray for you. Would that be OK?"

I encouraged him to go on, and I hung my head and cried while this man I barely knew prayed for me. His prayer wasn't long, but it was delivered with sincere compassion. All I could do was sob and accept the peace that entered the room with his words.

When he finished, he sat quietly while I struggled to regain my composure. Once he saw I would be OK, he stood.

"I'll try to come and visit you again, Shelly," he said. "I'm sure you realize your parents will be contacted at some point. Perhaps you should call them before that happens. Let them know how you are."

"Yes," I said softly, "and thank you."

With that, he gave a little nod and was gone. The officer who had brought me to the room returned, and I was taken back to my cell. As I climbed into bed, the strange revelations shot off in my mind like fireworks.

CJ had duped me. He was a murderer. He'd killed women like me before. My fear of him had been justified, but I'd ignored my instincts. How could I have been so stupid! Once again, God had used an arrest to pull me out of a dangerous situation. Being caught had seemed like a disaster, but it had actually saved my life.

As these thoughts subsided, I probed my soul, looking for some kind of answer. Did God really know my heart? Had He seen my repulsion when CJ suggested the robbery? Did He have mercy on me because He knew I was desperate for a way out?

After four and a half weeks, the justice system finally ran its course, and the time came for the authorities to disclose their findings, to formalize their charges, and to set my trial date. When I heard their conclusions, I was shocked again.

Almost everything in the case against me had been dropped, except for the possession and violation of probation charge. I couldn't believe it. A couple of days later, I met with a public defender. He said the prosecution wanted to give me six months jail time. My jaw dropped again! Only six months? Considering the fact that my arrest had occurred while I was on probation, this seemed unbelievably lenient. I jumped on the offer immediately.

My spirit soaring from the good news, I made all kinds of promises to myself and to God. Things would change. This latest brush with disaster – possibly even death – was finally the push I'd needed, I assured myself.

This time would be different. This time, I would get my life together and turn things around!

Knowing the future, God must have shaken His head and grieved when He heard those words. He knew that in my own power, I could do nothing. I was an addict, and He knew how prideful and stubborn I'd remained.

Chapter 9

UNAWARE

Even though I'd been through an incredible scare with CJ, it didn't take me long to fall back into my old routines. By this time, I had surrendered to the devil's most powerful lie: there is no way out, and if there is no way out, why bother to change?

It was now 2003, and by this point, I felt as if I had been branded by society. I really couldn't argue about the labels it had for me either. Addict. Prostitute. Loser. Lost cause.

Even knowing this, I grieved, not because I felt the condemnation I experienced was undeserved, but because I still held on to the childhood dreams every little girl embraces. In spite of my horrid history, I still secretly wanted what any normal woman wants: a husband who adored me; a couple of sweet kids I could cherish; a cozy house with a white picket fence.

To keep my sanity in the face of this pain, it eventually became necessary for me to challenge those dreams by framing them as lies. Real love didn't exist. There was no such thing as a happy or normal life. These were just the fairy tales only the gullible chased after – and I was no fool.

I also began to challenge the myth of recovery, scoffing at the success stories I'd heard. Such things, I told myself, never really happen. No addict can ever be cured. No one ever really finds contentment and peace. There is no way out, I'd convinced myself to believe, so there was no longer a reason to try.

That said, my experiences with CJ did make me more streetwise – and more paranoid. I'd learned the value of staying "off the radar," and to avoid the scrutiny of the police, so I became much more careful about where I went and who I saw in public. For example, rather than blithely waltzing into bad neighborhoods to buy dope and hang out with friends as I had in earlier days, I now bought my crack through inconspicuous channels and stayed away from my least stable friends. The tricks I took were also handled as discreetly as possible, but I did continue in the trade because it paid the bills and supplied my dope.

One evening, the phone rang, and I was surprised to hear the voice of an old friend. It was Diane, a favorite roommate of mine from several years earlier. We had lost touch, and I missed her company. Like Susie, who had introduced me to turning tricks, Diane was someone I had come to rely on and trust. Hearing her voice was a wonderful release from all the trauma and tension I'd recently experienced. Warm memories of better times flooded into my mind.

One thing led to another, and Diane and I soon reconnected. She was going through troubles with an old boyfriend, and I helped her break free. During the time we spent together, I also discovered what she had been doing while we'd been apart. Diane had found a "business partner" in South America who was helping her make big money without having to resort to tricks on the street.

She claimed she had a contact in Brazil who had involved her in some operation overseas. It was easy money – $10,000, she said – and the work had been no trouble at all. She also swore no trick was involved. Based on the dope she had on hand and the clothes and jewelry she was wearing, the story sounded legit.

"I sure hope you intend to let me in on this," I laughed, gawking at her jewelry and dress. "I'm sick of turning tricks. I'd love something better."

Ask the devil for a favor, and he's quick to grant it. A few days later, I got a call from Eric, Diane's Brazilian business partner.

"I'd like to meet, Shelly," he said. "I'll be up in Fort Lauderdale next week. Will that work for you?"

His aggressiveness surprised me, but it didn't scare me off. I asked him why he wanted to meet.

"I like to talk to people face to face," he said. "That way, we can get to know each other a little better. Then, I can explain what Diane and I have going."

I almost gasped out loud. Things were moving so quickly! My heart pounded, but I was also very aware of the stakes, and the memory of Diane's nice things danced in my head. I had to be careful not to let this opportunity slip out of my hands. It might represent a very big score.

"Do you have a passport, Shelly?"

Too eager to please, I fumbled through my response.

"I'm legal. I mean … I have a driver's license and a birth certificate. I'm sure we can work something out."

Eric undoubtedly sensed the excitement in my voice, and he probably grinned on the other end of the line. Show the devil your weakness, and he'll happily exploit it.

Days passed, but nothing happened. Eric had ended our call cordially, saying he would get back to me to arrange a meeting at a nearby hotel, but that second call had never come, and I ached to know why he wasn't confirming. I wondered if it might have been because of something I'd said. When Diane finally stopped by, I probed for more information. Was Eric for real? What had she really done for him to earn ten grand? Why had he set up a plan and not followed through?

Diane tried to dodge these questions at first, but I eventually wore her down.

"If I tell you, Shelly, you'll have to promise it won't go anywhere else." She was clearly uncomfortable talking about her business without Eric present. "Here's what happened. Eric had me carry a suitcase from Brazil to Spain. It was full of bank securities. You know – surety bonds."

Huh? I could have guessed at a hundred schemes, and I would never have considered this.

"How much was involved?" I asked, still trying to understand the angle.

"I have no idea. I just carry the bag. Eric said the securities were sewn into the lining."

I knew moving large amounts of money without reporting it when entering a country was illegal, but I never realized there was cash to be made by smuggling it through.

"I got $10,000 for the job. It was the easiest money I ever made. I spent $1,000 of it on this suit!" Diane said, getting caught up in my own excitement about the scheme. Eyes wide, I hoped she didn't see me gulp down my shock. This really was easy money – and I wanted in.

Diane went on to explain that Eric was actually a middleman for another contact who lived in São Paulo, Brazil. Diane had only met the guy a couple of times, but she felt certain he was a key player in organized crime – possibly in the Mafia.

"How do you know these guys aren't having you transport drugs?" I asked.

Diane scoffed at the idea.

"These guys hate drugs," she said. "You'll see that if you meet them. They're really nice men – good, clean-cut, family-man types. I'm sure what they are doing is illegal, but it's all about moving money. Drugs aren't part of the picture."

"How did you come to meet them? Did one of them call you for a trick?"

She harrumphed at this.

"No way! Eric is happily married. He has four kids. It wasn't anything like that," she said. "We just met and got to talking. He helped me get a passport. When I went down to Brazil on his invitation, I didn't even see much of him. A few other guys showed me around. They took me shopping, and I went to a salon and had my hair and nails done. It was like a vacation – but they insisted I stay off dope.

That's what I mean about the drugs. They didn't want me to have anything to do with them."

At the time, this made strange sense to me. I never suspected Eric might have an ulterior motive.

"In the end, all I had to do was carry a suitcase – a big 55-pound Samsonite bag – over to Madrid and then on to Turkey," Diane said. "There was nothing to it. I flew first class and was treated like royalty. When I landed, I went to a hotel we'd set up as a contact point. Eric met me there, and I shopped for a few more days. Then, I flew back home. I'm guessing Eric will want you to do the same thing."

Now, more than ever, I ached for Eric to call me back.

Day by day, the time slowly passed, and my life continued on its tedious course. After fantasizing about Eric and his easy money with Diane, facing "real life" felt like drudgery. Every day I turned tricks, bought dope, and got high. I was able to keep ahead of my bills for a while, but eventually, the tricks slowed down, and I got behind.

At that point, I began another terrible downward spiral. I would stay in my room for a week at a time, just smoking, eating, and sleeping. Eventually, I fell so far behind on my rent that warning notices started showing up on my door. Even this threat of eviction didn't shock me out of my stupor. In fact, it fed my depression, and I continued my destructive behaviors until a final notice eviction was delivered. Get out, it said, or be thrown out by the police.

Though I had been through this many times before, I was angry at myself for being so weak. Why had it come to this again? Why couldn't I find a way out? I needed the kind of big break Diane had arranged with Eric. In my frustration and desperation, I gave the devil the final key to my soul.

The phone rang, and from the number, I could see it was Eric.

I snatched up the receiver, ready to take whatever he offered. I barely got out my "hello." I didn't want to sound as anxious as I felt, but my hands were shaking with nervous energy.

"Hey, Shelly – this is Eric."

I gulped something in reply.

"I'm going to be visiting a friend in the Fort Lauderdale area this week, and I thought it would be a good time for us to meet," he explained. I could barely contain myself. I had been teetering at the brink of a precipice, and in the nick of time, Eric was arriving to pull me back.

"That would be great," I said. I felt like a drowning woman scrambling to take hold of an outstretched hand.

He seemed unfazed by this eagerness, though in hindsight, I wonder if he didn't sense my desperation. Men like Eric often do. Consciously or subconsciously, they find and exploit a person's weaknesses. Perhaps it's the instinct of a predator. But no fear of being exploited entered my mind at the time. I was just overwhelmed and grateful for a way out of my financial collapse.

After we made a few arrangements, and I hung up, I felt only euphoria. I literally jumped up and down, screeching, "This is it! This is it!" And nothing in the days that followed brought me down or gave me any reason for pause. Eric, as far as I was concerned, was a hero who had saved the day.

A week later, we met for the first time. Having only known Eric by his voice, I was a bit surprised when I opened the door. He was of average height, a bit husky with silver-grey hair, cut in a surfer style. For a man of his young age, the silver hair seemed strange, but it did give him a strong, distinguished look. He wore very expensive clothing too. When he reached out and shook my hand, it all felt very business-like – as if I was meeting a banker or a company president.

My thoughts flashed back to what Diane had said. Eric is a real gentleman. A clean-cut, family-man type. It seemed true. I motioned him inside, and we sat down to talk. After a few pleasantries, he dropped a bombshell.

"So, Shelly, are you willing to clean up your act and get off the dope?"

I was a little high at the time, and I probably blushed. It was a shock to hear the question put so bluntly.

"How did you know?"

"Diane told me."

The air spilled out of me in a deep sigh. Had Diane ruined this for me? Was he here to tell me that I was out of the picture? I wasn't certain what to say. Again, he seemed unfazed.

"This job involves traveling overseas. You'll also have to do that, of course. So are you willing to do those things? Can you stay clean, and will you be able to travel? Tell me straight up one way or the other. If we're going to work together, we need to be a hundred percent honest with each other. I'm not going to fly to Europe with you if you're high or carrying drugs on you. If that's the case, forget it. The men I work with hate drugs and don't approve of anyone who uses them," he explained.

The comments took me down the path Eric hoped I would take. I thought, if these guys hate drugs, they're clearly not trying to use me as a mule to carry dope for them. This really must be an operation to transport paper. And Eric looks to be that kind of guy too. He's clearly a businessman. Not on the up and up, possibly, but just working some kind of business scam.

So I told him exactly what he wanted to hear.

"I can do this, Eric. I need a break like this. I've been wanting to clean myself up – and I'll make it happen. The travel isn't an issue either. In fact, I love the idea. All of this is perfect for me, and I won't let you down."

He sat in silence for a moment. I could hear my own breathing and felt the anticipation building. He let the delay work for him, like a fisherman, waiting a beat before setting the hook.

"Okay, Shelly. Then, let's talk about getting you a passport so you can travel." The pattern that followed was perfect. He never strayed from his all-business approach. I can still hear his orders: You need to have this and that, you need to go here and there, you need to expedite your passport paperwork – yada, yada, yada. His direct, no-nonsense style fueled my enthusiasm, and when he left my room, I danced again, thinking I must be the luckiest girl in the world.

*   *   *

Eric was right on time for our trip to the Miami passport office. Paperwork in hand, I followed him down to his rental car, and we headed off. Before we had been on the road for five minutes, I drifted off to sleep, only to be jarred awake a few moments later by a shove to my shoulder.

"Come on, Shelly, this isn't a joy ride. We've got things to do. You need to stay focused."

I could hear something new in his voice – a bit of frustration; or perhaps resentment. It got my attention because I desperately wanted this bond transporting thing to work out. The last thing I needed was Eric second-guessing himself about choosing me for the job. He knew I was a hardcore addict. Perhaps, he was wondering if I was stoned, and he'd made a bad decision by involving me at all.

I used my fear to refocus my attention and keep on task. When we reached the office, I dutifully got in line. The clockwork routines of going from station to station seemed to ease Eric's mind. He helped me fill out the forms and work through the process. By the time we finished and sat down for lunch, he seemed much less agitated, and I also breathed a sigh of relief.

Before two o'clock, we were back on the road again, heading home. When we pulled into the hotel I was living in after the eviction; he told me to sit tight. He would call me tomorrow and let me know the details of our travel plans.

"Get some rest – and pull yourself together," he said. "This is serious business, Shelly. I'm offering you a real opportunity. Don't blow it."

As soon as I got back up to my room, I retrieved my dope and got high. I also called a few clients. I needed the tricks to make some fast money. There was no way I was leaving for Brazil in two days without a supply of crack for the road.

That night I saw as many clients as I could, smoking crack to keep me awake as I went from one trick to the next. Finally, around four AM on the day of our departure, I knew I needed to start getting ready. There were clothes to be packed and arrangements to be made. I'd been up for more than forty-eight hours with no sleep, and I was exhausted. I had to smoke heavily just to keep my eyes open.

Around 8:30 in the morning, my cell phone rang. Eric was on the other end.

"You're ready, right? I'm on my way over."

I got my bags together and checked out of my room. This was it!

A car arrived, Eric got out, and we put my bags in the trunk. When he glanced at me, I saw him roll his eyes. He knew I'd blown it and gotten high, but he didn't say anything until I was settled in the car.

"Why, Shelly? You said you'd lay off the dope. You look terrible. Why couldn't you stay off that stuff and get some rest like I told you to?" he said, shaking his head. "Well, it's a long flight. Hopefully, you can sleep on the plane."

When we got to the airport, my fatigue and exhaustion took over. We had to wait in a long line, and my legs ached. I could barely keep my eyes open and almost fell asleep standing up. When I would start to sway, Eric would nudge me. I could tell he was embarrassed by my condition, but I didn't have the energy to care. All I could think about was getting on the plane and going to sleep.

When we finally boarded, I was overjoyed to see plenty of open spots, and after we lifted off, I immediately moved to a place where I could stretch across three seats to sleep. As soon as my head was down, I was out like a light. I woke up hours later when a flight attendant asked me to sit up and fasten my seat belt for our landing.

The hotel Eric had chosen in São Paulo was beautiful. When he unloaded my suitcase, I was surprised to see his bags remained in the car.

"Aren't you staying here with me?"

"No, I'm flying on to Europe in a few hours. Don't worry. You'll be fine. I'm leaving you money, and your room is paid for through the week." His expression hardened. "But listen, Shelly. Whatever you do, don't get busted. Smoke whatever crap you have left – then sleep it off. When I get back in a week, I'll take you shopping. After that, you'll meet my contact here. From this point on, you better pull it together.

I mean it!"

After Eric left me with one of his associates for safekeeping, my best intentions of following his orders literally went up in smoke. In fact, I'd barely gotten checked into the hotel room before I'd begun strategizing ways to score more crack. I was well cared for, taken shopping for beautiful clothes, and sent to salons for hair and nails, but I still could not keep my addictions under control.

This led to a confrontation a few days later. It was handled calmly by Eric's people, but the outcome devastated me.

"You're being sent back to the U.S. today, Shelly. This hasn't worked out."

The message was delivered with excuses about "things not coming together," but I could read between the lines. I had been told to stay clean, and I'd dropped the ball. They were saying I couldn't be trusted.

During the ride to the airport, the door I assumed had been slammed shut suddenly reopened unexpectedly. It was an emotional rollercoaster to go from seeing the situation as a disaster to one offering new hope.

"We do have an idea to run by you, Shelly. We think you could be a good recruiter for us. We need to bring in a few more girls who can help us move this paper. But they can't have drug issues. They need to be clean. Would you be interested in doing that for us? We'd be willing to pay you a referral fee for every girl we accept."

This idea seemed like a godsend, much more appealing than the idea of carrying the briefcases myself. All I would need to do to score now was find a few girlfriends I could bring in to the scheme. Even before the plane took off for home, I knew exactly who I would call.

*   *   *

Three weeks later, Susie and I were on a Lufthansa flight headed back to São Paulo. I still couldn't believe how little it had taken to persuade her to come with me. Susie's escort business had been slowing down, and she had some serious debts she needed to pay. After we talked it over, she came to the same conclusion I had – working for Eric would be easy money and a perfect option for paying off her bills.

The trip mirrored my earlier visit to Brazil. Eric's people shuttled us around and helped us prepare for the next leg of our international travel. We checked into a beautiful hotel, had a great dinner, and settled in for the night. I'd been a nervous wreck about involving Susie, but everything went extremely well.

The next morning, I was up early. I showered and dressed long before our contact arrived to pick us up. At 10 sharp, there was a knock on the door. Jimmy, Eric's key contact in Brazil, asked if we'd let him in. I opened the door, and he stalked inside, carrying a large black suitcase. He ignored Susie and focused his attention on me.

"Here's the deal, Shelly. We're sending you to Turkey with this suitcase," he said matter-of-factly.

"What? I asked, surprised by his curtness. "What's in that thing?"

"It's just chocolates, coffee, and some clothes."

"Can I see that for myself?"

"You don't trust me?" Jimmy said. He didn't seem angry – just a little put out by having to deal with my suspicions. Rolling his eyes, he pulled out a small key and opened the case. Inside were men's clothes, several boxes of chocolates, and a few bags of coffee, just as he'd said.

I felt a bit embarrassed for challenging him, so I mumbled something about wanting to be prepared with answers if they asked questions before opening the case at the airport. Jimmy ignored me and continued.

"When you go through customs in Turkey, you need to watch everything that happens; listen to everything they say. Then, after you get through, call me on the cell and tell me how it all went. Do you understand, Shelly?"

"What about Susie?" I asked. "Will she be with me?'

"Don't worry about her. She's coming along after. I can't say exactly when."

Reaching into his bag, Jimmy pulled out a thick wad of cash and handed it to me.

"When you call me to tell me what happened with the customs people, I'll tell you which hotel you should go to. Just take a cab, check into the place, and stay there until I contact you again."

I was a little surprised by how quickly things were moving along, but I kept my focus on Jimmy, listening carefully to every word he said. I'd blown it before, and I didn't want to be sent home again.

Jimmy reached into his pocket, pulled out a little flip phone, and handed it to me. "Only use this phone to call me. Never call me from your own phone. Understand?"

I nodded, took the phone, and started getting my things together. Susie sat quietly. She'd been watching us closely but hadn't said a word. When everything was ready, I went to her and gave her a big hug.

"I guess you'll be okay, right?"

Susie, always in control, seemed much less anxious about the whole plan than I did.

"Sure, I'll be fine," she said as we parted ways.

On the way to the airport, a strange sense of inevitability overwhelmed me. Whatever was in motion – whatever was going to happen – was now underway, and there was no turning back. I felt a little uneasy about it, but more for Susie's sake than for mine. To escape this troubling feeling, I succumbed to my weariness. That allowed me to sleep through the entire flight to Turkey.

When I arrived at the airport there, the concourse was deserted. Going through customs was a breeze too. The customs people didn't even check my bags. They just stamped my passport and let me through. Once I was on the other side, I settled on a bench, pulled out Jimmy's flip phone, and called the number I'd been given. It rang a few times before an automated voice kicked in with a message. It said the number I'd called was no longer a working line. Then it hung up on me. My stomach turned, and I immediately called the number again, but I got the same recording. Another call. The same message again.

I sat in stunned silence. So, was this it? Had I been screwed? Was the whole trip some kind of scam? I couldn't figure out what Eric's angle might have been. I took out the money Jimmy had given me and counted it. It was $265, and that was all I had.

Eventually, confusion and embarrassment were replaced by slow, burning anger. I got my bags and began walking through the airport, tears flowing. I felt both rage and despair. What was I going to do in a foreign country with just $265 to my name and nowhere to go?

Someone tapped my shoulder, and I flinched. I turned to discover an elderly man had approached me. He asked me something in a language I couldn't understand. I was still dazed, but out of desperation for any kind of assistance, I replied.

"I'm sorry, but I don't speak Turkish. I'm an American." The old man's next words were in perfect English.

"I see. Well, can I help you?"

This brought a huge surge of relief. I explained my problem. I told the guy about my failed attempts to reach a friend. In recounting what had happened, I was overwhelmed, and the tears came again.

"No, don't cry. You'll be okay. Perhaps the problem is with the phone. Let's go to my office. We can try calling him from there."

I tried to relax, but I couldn't recover my nerves. My stomach felt tied in knots. We went to a small office nearby, and the old man dialed Jimmy's number on his desk phone. Seconds later, he began speaking in another language I couldn't understand. It sounded different from the dialect he'd used when he talked to me the first time. From the tone of the conversation, the old man sounded like he was speaking to a long lost friend. He talked, laughed a couple of times, then handed me the phone.

I almost sobbed again when I heard Jimmy's voice.

"I'm sorry, Shelly. There must have been a problem with that phone, but I'm glad you found this guy to help. He says he'll take care of you. Just do what he says, okay? He's going to take you to the Best Western Suites in downtown Istanbul. When you get there, have something to eat and wait."

I was so glad to have escaped a potential disaster, I could barely speak. I told Jimmy I would do exactly as he said and hung up the phone.

Less than an hour later, I was checked in to the hotel. I ate a room service steak dinner, climbed into bed, and was soon fast asleep. It had been mid-morning when my plane arrived, but I slept through that day and woke up early in the evening. I was so disoriented it took me a few minutes to realize where I was. That night and next day felt like a dream. I ate and slept without any connection to the normal pace of life outside the hotel. A case of jet lag, I suppose.

The next night, the phone rang with an ear-shattering sound, and I lurched awake, heart pounding. I scrambled out of bed to stop the terrible racket, but when I picked up the receiver, it was to another blasting sound. Someone with a thick accent was calling my name.

"Ms. Shelly?"

"Yes, this is Shelly," I mumbled, barely awake.

"There is a Ms. Susanna down here in the lobby, and she wants…"

Interrupting him mid-sentence, I confirmed I knew who she was, and I told him to send her right up. Thank God, I thought, Susie made it and this nightmare trip is nearly over.

I wanted to make myself presentable before she arrived, so I rushed into the bathroom to wash my face and brush my hair. Having been sleeping only in underwear and a T-shirt, I considered getting dressed, but I decided there wouldn't be time before she arrived. Susie should be opening the door any second, so rather than change my clothes, I just sat on the bed to wait.

Five minutes passed. Then ten. I started to get nervous. Had the clerk sent her to the wrong room? Was she tied up with something else at the front desk?

I cracked open the door of my room and peered down the hall. Just then, a ding sounded from the elevator, and I was certain she'd arrived. But Susie didn't step into the hall. Instead, a group of men in business suits exited the elevator. Their earnestness struck me as peculiar – and disturbing.

What followed confirmed my worst fears. Entering the hall behind the men in suits were six more people dressed head-to-toe in camouflage gear with combat boots and Uzi machine guns. I was in shock. It was like living out the daydream I'd conjured up at the all-white house of the Ohio drug dealer my father had visited. But this SWAT team drug bust was real – a full-scale police action, not some imaginary movie scene.

Feeling like I'd been kicked in the gut, I slowly moved away from the door, shuffling back until my legs struck the mattress of the bed. Wide-eyed, I stared at the door. There was nowhere to run, no-where to hide, so my mind conjured up a terrible series of imaginary outcomes. In one, they broke through the door, rushing at me and screaming for blood. In another, I was shoved to the ground, brutally restrained, and handcuffed. Even worse, I imagined being shot. It was stupid, perhaps, but a sequence of these frightening scenes played in my mind.

Within the next few seconds, there was a strange sound, like roll-ing thunder. It went on for a few moments, then stopped. I suddenly understood – it had been the men running down the hall toward my room – and the thunder had stopped just outside my door.

What was next? Would bullets explode through the door? This was Turkey, so I had no idea what to expect. I might even die. Deep grief overwhelmed me. Have I seen my parents for the last time?

In fear, my eyes dropped to the ground. When I dared to look up, I saw the door opening, and I prepared for the worst. The soldiers armed with the Uzi machine guns pushed through first. They were all young – little more than boys – but their expressions were serious, showing no sign of mercy. Another terrible thought surfaced then. They probably hope I'll resist. They probably want an opportunity to shoot me.

The last person to enter was a woman. She was a soft, round-faced girl with curly black hair, and she had none of the ferocity of the men. I still did not move. My hands were flat against my legs. Feeling an overwhelming sense of shame, my eyes dropped back to the floor, and tears began to flow down my face. I could hear the sound of moving uniforms and metal clicks as the men lowered their weapons.

The woman soldier approached me and reached for my hand. She said something in Turkish, and the men turned around. She smiled slightly and addressed me gently.

"You must get dressed, please."

Tears still flowing, I mumbled a "yes" and turned to pick up old slacks and a top I had tossed on the floor the night before. She joined me in the bathroom and shut the door. As I took off my T-shirt and put on the pants and shirt, she carefully watched every move I made. Once I was dressed, I went for the hairbrush and she grabbed my hand. Only when she was convinced what I'd been reaching for was harmless did she step back and allow me to finish.

I brushed my hair in a trance. The woman looking back at me from the mirror seemed cast in stone. Nothing in my eyes revealed any spark of life. It was the face of a lost soul. I was completely undone.

This was no U.S. drug bust, and I understood that. I was thousands of miles from home. I had no lawyer, and it was unlikely I'd receive one. There would be no bail. No friends to comfort me. No rescue from home. When I set the hairbrush down, I knew I would be going away to somewhere horrible – perhaps forever.

I glanced over at the woman soldier. Our eyes met in the mirror. She was so young, so pretty. The men had seemed hard and dangerous, but her face communicated none of their maliciousness. I could tell she pitied me. Her eyes said it all. She knows your life is over. She knows what you're about to face.

"You'll have to come with us now." Her expression was full of compassion as she guided me out of the bathroom.

Surrounded by the soldiers, I was escorted out of the hotel. Two walked in front, one paced me on each side, and two walked behind me. All kept their weapons at the ready. My heart thumped furiously. It was so loud, I felt certain they could all hear it pounding, but strangely, I felt nothing inside. There was none of the "fight or flight" panic I'd experienced during past arrests. This was different. It was more of an out-of-body experience, the way I'd felt after the drug overdose in Texas. I was present in the flesh, but not literally there. I could tell my heart was pounding, but I felt no physical pain or fear.

From the hotel, I was quickly escorted to a car in the parking lot. They never handcuffed me. They just put me in the backseat with a soldier on each side. The mustached men in business suits piled into the police cars too. In the car I had entered, one took the wheel, and the other sat on the front passenger side. They were much more animated than the soldiers had been. They shouted to each other in Turkish, laughing and chattering like excited schoolboys on a field trip. All the while, I sat in silence.

We drove for what seemed like hours, but in all honesty, I can't really say how long the trip actually took or exactly where we went. I was stunned during the whole journey. I had no idea where they were taking me, but I assumed it would be to some kind of prison.

At one point, we passed a location, and something bubbled up from my memory. I remembered both that building and one we had passed a few minutes before. It made me realize we were on a path back to the airport. In fact, I felt certain we were now very close.

As we turned a street corner, these suspicions were confirmed. There had been a "business-as-usual" feeling about the places we'd driven through earlier, but this street was very different. I saw signs of chaos and activity ahead. There were tons of cars, media vehicles, and police cruisers with flashing lights. Lots of other people who probably lived in the area were out there too, and most were looking this way and that, hoping to see what all of the fuss was about.

I could imagine the questions buzzing around the scene. Didn't you hear? Some stupid American girl just committed the crime of the century. Based on how many TV stations and reporters were on the scene, I had to believe I'd done something extraordinary.

People began pushing in close to get a glimpse inside the car, and my guts churned. My God – what was in that suitcase! It must have been something horrific to elicit this kind of attention. Then, a terrible thought entered my mind. Where was Susie? Please, God, I prayed, don't let her be dead. It couldn't be that, could it? Was that why all the reporters were here?

When the car finally stopped, one of the soldiers pulled out a towel and placed it over my head. Then, we exited the car.

I could see little, but my mind was still slammed with sensations. Brilliant red and blue police lights bounced everywhere. Voices – yelling, hooting, and shouting orders – assaulted my ears. There were odd smells and strange languages too. The police tugged me one way, then another. Suddenly, the world had become overwhelmingly chaotic. One moment we were running as a group. The next, we were crammed together in some building's doorway, as dozens of reporters threw undecipherable questions at me.

A door flew open, and I was pushed inside. Once it was closed, the sounds abruptly stopped. Someone lifted the towel from my head, and the female soldier faced me. Even she seemed rattled by all of the chaos outside.

"Please follow us," she said in a commanding tone of voice.

I complied, of course. The walk was full of twists and turns as we went up halls and down corridors. Most of the rooms we passed were simple and bleak looking – basically concrete cells containing a single long table and a few chairs. Finally, I saw Susie and my heart leapt with relief. She was lying on a couch in one of the rooms. When she noticed me, she feebly reached out a hand. That image will forever be etched in my mind. Her face was swollen and red. Her eyes – barely slits – were disfigured from crying. My spirit ached for her, and I knew it was all my fault. God, I thought, Susie has a little girl – just five years old. This can't be happening to her. She must be terrified.

I could see Susie had been through a horrible interrogation, and I was sure I'd be next. We bypassed her room and walked beyond two others before I reached my destination.

The room I entered was empty except for a large suitcase open on the floor. I stared slack-jawed at what it contained – dozens of odd packets; bundles coated in some kind of wax. Each was tied with string. The stack looked like a disorderly pile of brown paperback books.

Slowly, I turned to face a mustachioed man standing nearby. My expression must have communicated my confusion and shock.

"Do you know what that is?" he asked.

"No, sir," I mumbled.

"It's cocaine, Miss. Twenty-five kilos, in fact. You and your friend tried to smuggle it in, and I can assure you, you will pay for that. Do you hear me? Do you understand?"

I never answered. I had nothing to say. What we had done was quite clear to me now. I understood completely – and he had made himself equally clear. We would pay.

Chapter 10

UNEXPECTED

We'd been told we would pay for what we'd done, and I could guess what that meant. Susie and I had taken part in a historically significant crime on that day in 2004, so I expected we'd be sentenced to an equally epic punishment. I'd heard we were being moved from the jail to a new facility to await sentencing, and the news left me with mixed feelings.

Traveling into the unknown was stressful, but part of me was also relieved to be leaving the jail because I couldn't imagine anything worse. At the very least, the next place would have a shower, I assumed. Three days without bathing had been awful, and my own stink had become sickening to me. It had even begun invading my dreams, leading to the last night's fitful sleep.

Finally, a guard approached and motioned for me to get up and follow him out. As they had before, the jailers gave me access to my belongings, and I pulled out shoes, socks, a hairbrush, toothbrush, and toothpaste. I was pawing through these items when the sound of Susie's soft voice came from the doorway behind me. My throat tightened, and my heart skipped a beat. I had to summon all of my courage to face her.

The poor girl was a mess. Susie's eyes looked glazed, and her expression was blank. Hugging her, I tried to reassure her our move would be a good thing, but from the look on her face, I could tell she didn't believe me. It made my heart ache to see how lost and hopeless she'd become. My own arrest seemed just, but her punishment troubled me. I felt as if I had betrayed her and her daughter. Both would suffer now, and it was all my fault.

After collecting up our few possessions, the guard escorted us downstairs to a waiting car. There, I saw Eric for the first time since the night of my arrest. It was a terribly awkward moment, and I shuffled around nervously while the guards organized themselves. Two men got into the vehicle's front seats, and Susie and Eric joined a young guard sitting in the back.

I was told I would need to sit on the young guy's lap, and the group chuckled. My cheeks burned with humiliation, and I could sense the guards delighted in my embarrassment. Rather than give them further satisfaction by hesitating, I quickly complied, sitting sideways on the man's lap so I could face Eric and Susie. The young guard rubbed my leg where the others couldn't see, but he pulled his hand away when I glared at him.

The car left the jail parking lot and was soon speeding down a major highway. We drove for what felt like hours, with only the guard's incomprehensible chatter to break up the monotony of the ride. It was an incredible relief when we finally pulled off the highway and entered a town. Passing through several narrow side streets, we eventually stopped at a huge building. Several police were walking nearby, so I assumed this was our destination – and the place looked awful.

Susie was mortified, and it pained me to see the fear in her eyes. She also began breathing in gasps, and I worried she might begin hyperventilating. Please, God, I begged, don't let this place be worse than that horrible jail. Drawn into Susie's panic, my heart began pounding too –but this stop was for Eric. The guards quickly removed him and reorganized us in the car. The transfer was so abrupt; it felt as if Eric had been dropped through a trap door. There one moment, gone the next.

Within a minute or two, we were speeding on again, and for the first time since we'd left the jail, Susie spoke to me in a whispered tone.

"Poor Eric. That was a terrible place."

I understood the sentiment, but deep down, my greater concern was still for us and for our fate. After all, why should we expect our destination to be any better?

The second leg of our drive was much shorter, and I was relieved to have a seat to myself. We were approaching the city of Istanbul, and its surrounding neighborhoods looked promising. They were nothing like the dingy town where Eric was left behind. For the first time in days, I could see trees and gardens. The buildings also seemed more modern.

As we took a corner, our destination loomed ahead, and I was surprised by its appearance. The building's walls were nicely painted, and there were no barbed wire fences or heavy, unsightly barricades surrounding the property. Quite the opposite, in fact. The building looked clean and welcoming as if it had recently been renovated for the benefit of visiting guests.

I felt a flicker of hope, and it grew stronger when we were taken inside. In the first building we entered, two young guards sat at a desk chatting and drinking tea. They smiled and greeted us, motioning for us to take seats nearby. As they asked a few simple questions, another woman entered with a tray. It held a few small cups of chai and a stack of sugar cubes on a little lace doily. When they offered the drinks to us, Susie and I exchanged a confused look. It was a surreal moment.

Once we finished the tea, a guard took us to another building. There, we discovered the luggage the police had confiscated from our flight. As we stood watching, an officer went through every item in each suitcase, separating the things we would be allowed to keep from those the police would put into storage. I had packed modestly, so my case contained only a few pairs of jeans, t-shirts, a couple of pairs of shorts, and some pajamas. There were very few items they withheld from me. Susie had more in her luggage, including a laptop, an expensive camera, and some jewelry. They withheld all those things but assured her she could reclaim them upon her release.

Susie didn't hide her skepticism. She had already noticed two of her packed items were missing – a carton of cigarettes and an expensive bottle of perfume she'd purchased in Brazil.

"Might as well kiss that stuff goodbye," she muttered, rolling her eyes. "I'll never see any of it again."

Moving through the checkpoint, we entered the secured grounds of the prison, and it struck me as a little walled city within the city. The place was surprisingly busy, with inmates walking around pretty freely. They came and went from what I assumed were freestanding cell blocks. Eventually, we arrived at what appeared to be a little house within the grounds.

As we entered, a group of women who'd been eating snacks and chatting immediately dropped their conversations and looked up. It was as if a blaring TV show had suddenly been switched off. The abrupt silence was awkward, but there was little we could do but stare back into their shocked faces. Finally, the guard spoke, and I picked up a word I recognized – banyo. This was music to my ears. As I understood it, banyo meant bath or shower – something I craved with every ounce of my being.

Responding to the guard's remarks, a young Turkish woman rose and motioned for us to follow her into an adjoining room. It contained an old tub with a simple faucet. Any other time I might have asked about the availability of a shower, but reeking as I did, I didn't hesitate to accept the woman's offer. At that moment, all I wanted was to shed my nasty clothes and wash my stinking body. Then I remembered Susie. She was in even worse shape, so I stepped aside and let her go first.

Susie's medical condition and her nights on the hard jail floor had taken their toll. She winced as I helped her undress, and once the clothes dropped away, I could see she had lost weight. For three days, we had only been given bread, olives, and water. From her appearance, I wondered if she had even eaten the little we'd been given.

The tap would only produce cold water, but Susie didn't seem to care. Like a weak, compliant child, she squatted down in the tub, and I poured water over her fragile body. Next, I positioned her head under the faucet so I could rinse her hair. A young woman standing near-by noticed and approached with a container of shampoo. She smiled shyly and held the bottle out to me. Though she couldn't speak English, the girl had found a way to be helpful, and I was very grateful.

After Susie finished, I took my turn. The sensation of washing the grime away was so overwhelming it almost felt like a spiritual experience. We both left the bath with buoyed spirits and got more uplifting news in the next room. Dinner was being served!

I nearly cried when I saw the fresh loaves of bread and steaming bowls of vegetable stew, and we plopped down on the cement floor to gulp down these meals. Within a few minutes, the fog in my head began to lift. It was as if every cell in my body had become a sponge, eagerly absorbing the nutrition we'd been deprived of for days. This energy pushed through my chest, arms, and legs, and I felt wonder-fully reenergized.

Susie and I had no idea what would happen next. We hadn't yet been assigned a place in the prison, so we assumed someone would collect us and take us to a cell. As we waited, we decided to show our gratitude by taking our bowls and glasses to the sink and carefully washing and returning them. Nearly an hour passed before a female guard showed up, calling out for "Shelly from America" and "Susie from America." We didn't know it then, but those descriptive names would be used throughout our incarceration at Pasakapisi Prison.

As we'd supposed, the guard was there to take us deeper inside the place – quite possibly to another dingy cell with metal bars. She guided us through passageways and down corridors until we reached a set of steps. These led to a huge metal door that she unlocked with a key. The heavyset woman inside greeted the guard in Turkish. With less fanfare, she simply motioned for us to enter – and the door was closed behind us.

"My name is Asiah. I'm the kosh leader," the big woman said in good English. "You need to pay attention now – you understand? You must obey everything I tell you."

It was easy to see why Asiah had been chosen to lead. Her size, posture, and tone of voice were commanding. Taking her at her word, I listened carefully as she explained she was from Germany and was, like us, serving time as a prisoner.

Asiah next introduced us to the places we were allowed to enter, the areas we would now call home. Taking us through the grounds, she stopped in a huge empty space. This, she said, was the recreation area where we could walk and exercise. It had no roof, and the surrounding walls were so high that all you could see was the open sky above. Looking up, I felt like an ant at the bottom of a teacup. I knew there was a world beyond those walls. I'd seen it. But those people and buildings already seemed distant. I wondered to myself – years from now, will I even remember what the outside world looked like?

Leaving that recreation area, we walked through an open door and downstairs to a large room containing seven metal-frame bunk beds. The lower beds were easily accessible, but the top bunks were nearly seven feet off the floor. I was surprised to see each bed had a new mattress.

The next room Asiah showed us was filled with lockers, long rectangular tables, a big double-tub sink, a refrigerator, and a couple of hot plates holding coffee pots.

"This is where you will eat your meals from now on," she said, "and tomorrow you'll be given one of those lockers. You can buy a lock for it at the canteen. They sell almost everything you'll need there – hygiene products, bedding, a pillow. They also have lots of snacks, but you must have your own money for those things, of course."

Turning on her heel, Asiah marched back into the bunk room and through another door leading into a communal bathroom.

"Those are the showers. We have hot water, but only for a few hours in the morning and evening," she explained. I understood the point. Come to the bathroom on time or live with the consequences – an ice-cold shower. Peeking inside the dank room, we saw a few women lined up, towels in hand, waiting to shower.

As we reentered the bunk room, Asiah approached a couple of girls sprawled on beds. She spoke to them in Turkish, and they quickly cleared their things from one of the bunks.

"You two will have to sleep on a single bed until another bed opens up," she said. Her scowl told us there'd be no debate about it. Susie and I nodded submissively and quickly claimed the cleared bed. When Asiah left us, we sat down to gather our thoughts.

Our bunk had no sheets or pillows, and we had nothing of any use or value. After sitting there for a few minutes, I decided it was silly of us to stay put.

"We may as well see what else is going on," I said. "I don't know about you, but I'm a little surprised by this place. It's not nearly as bad as I expected."

Susie agreed. "The walls look like they were just painted, and this mattress is almost new. Even the floors look like they were tiled just a few weeks ago," she said. "Do you think the rest of the place is as nice, or did we just happen to land in a new part of the prison?"

Before I could reply, a woman lying on a nearby bed spoke to us. She'd been knitting but had set the work aside. She asked who we were and where we were from. She told us her name was Janet, and she was from England. There were only a few women in our kosh who could speak understandable English, so we were immediately attracted to her.

Janet asked if we had any money. Susie and I both had a little, but we hadn't thought much of it since we'd been told the canteen would be closed until morning. Janet offered us cigarettes and snacks, a pillow, and a set of sheets.

"Tomorrow, when the canteen opens, buy your own stuff and return mine," she said. I waited for the other shoe to drop. I expected her to demand exorbitant interest on this loan, but she never asked for more. Having served a stint in a U.S. prison, I was very familiar with the usury practiced by prisoners. Everyone I'd met in a U.S. prison was always scheming to make money or better their position. If you borrowed a sheet of paper, you were expected to return two. The women in Turkey were different. They seemed to look out for each other. It operated more like a sorority than the snake pit I'd expected.

After our encounter with Janet, a few other women came up, shook our hands, and told us their names. It didn't take long to learn our cell block was considered the "Foreigners' Kosh." All the women housed there were from somewhere outside of Turkey – citizens from about 12 different countries in all. Like me, they were now strangers in a strange land.

It had been a very emotional day, so Susie and I turned in for the night. The next morning, I woke early, determined to do some exploring. When I tried to rouse Susie, she pushed me away, telling me she felt sick and needed more sleep. From the nearby kitchen, I could hear the rattle of pots and pans, so I knew the other girls were already up and preparing for the day. I decided to join them.

That morning, one of my goals was to visit the canteen, and that trip gave me a chance to walk through most of the prison. I discovered its grounds were not nearly as extensive as I'd first thought. There were six different cell blocks for Turkish women, each marked by a letter of the alphabet, "A" through "F." Blocks "E" and "F" were for people who were HIV positive and carried the Hepatitis C virus. These prisoners, I learned, were deliberately quarantined from the rest of us for their safety. Their weakened immune systems would have made them susceptible to any illnesses the rest of us carried. In addition to the Turkish blocks, there was the one "Foreign Kosh" where Susie and I had been placed.

To reach the prison store, I eventually had to travel down a walkway lined by beggars – poor Turkish inmates who squatted along one bordering wall with their hands out. It grieved me to see these women. Most were very old and incredibly frail. As I passed, they cried out for help. Many had no teeth, and their arms were skin and bones. They reminded me of the desperate outcasts of India or the lepers described in the Bible, and my heart broke for them.

Seeing poor, old women in this position was a cultural shock, but it also opened my heart. Prior to the encounter, I'd rarely thought twice about people in need, but these women stirred something deep inside me. I would remember them later when reading the passage in Matthew 25, where Jesus speaks of helping "the least of these" – saying that serving them is like ministering directly to him.

The second cultural shock I experienced while in prison came later that night, shortly after the girls settled down and the lights were turned out. I was drifting off to sleep when I heard a howling noise from somewhere beyond our block's walls. It sounded like injured dogs wailing, or the noises insane people make in horror movies. I sat bolt upright, and Janet noticed my eyes go wide with fear.

"No worries, Shelly," she whispered. "The Turkish women are just cutting themselves. They live like animals in those other blocks. When they feel hopeless, they cut themselves. You'll have to get used to it. It happens almost every night."

An involuntary shiver pulsed through me, and I slipped back under my covers, but just then, another woman howled, and I found I could no longer contain my pent up emotions. They had to be released, and I sobbed uncontrollably. Janet's word – hopeless – resurfaced in my mind. Deep down, I knew it also applied to me. Like those wailing women, I was broken, hurting, and alone. How long would I remain a captive? Would my family try to help me, or had they finally abandoned me completely? What must my parents be feeling? Anger? Disgust? On that horrific night, as these thoughts assailed me, the distant howls seemed like the terrible echoes of my own soul's pain.

Eventually, I cried myself to sleep, but that night brought me little rest. I frequently woke, so the time trudged on, a seemingly endless nightmare. Each time I would stir from my fitful sleep, I would cry again until weariness reclaimed me. It was a horrible cycle, repeating over and over again.

When dawn finally came, my eyes were so swollen I could hardly open them. Desperate to escape the ghosts of the previous night, I grabbed a towel and ran to the showers, where I stood under the water for a very long time. My emotions were still raw, but the physical cleansing felt wonderful. Had it not been for the hard cry and the catharsis of the shower, I'm not sure I would have made it through those first days in prison. Perhaps God knew I needed a traumatic break from my painful past before I could build something new.

During the next few weeks, I spent most of my time watching the women around me and listening to their chatter. There really wasn't much else to do in the prison. I could have watched Turkish soaps on a snowy TV, but the drama playing out around me was much more interesting. In fact, I was enthralled by the way the women from so many different countries were interacting, getting their points across in spite of the language barriers we faced.

I also spent a lot of time in bed, staring at the ceiling and reflecting on my life. For the first time in a long time, I was completely sober, and this clarity of mind was an unexpected blessing. For years, life had been a wild ride on a runaway merry-go-round. Now, thanks to my incarceration, I'd been flung off the dark carnival ride and was free of its chaotic twists and turns. For the first time, life was moving slowly enough for me to think.

Entering this slower-paced world also gave me more time to talk to God. Those prayers were often intense. In the past, drugs had numbed my feelings – just as I'd intended – but now my emotions were very real and were clearly defined. In prayerful contemplation, I could explore their full range, from happiness to sadness. More often than not, I found myself feeling shame or remorse.

Shame had always been the most powerful emotion controlling my life. Now seen clearly through my sobriety, it made my heart cry out to God for help. But I didn't beg Him to remove me from my situation. Even then, I understood my jail time was part of His will. All I wanted from God was reassurance – to know He was still with me; to know He would use this situation for some greater good. I knew my own bad choices had put me in prison, and I saw no injustice in my incarceration. In fact, part of me understood prison could be good for me and that it might be the means through which God would save me.

By this time, I'd heard terrible stories about the guys who'd organized my smuggling trip to Turkey, and I considered it a miracle I was still alive. Susie and I had been mules for the Moroccan and Lebanese mafia. If Susie had made it through with the drugs she'd been carrying, they probably would have shot us at the motel meeting point. They'd have taken the drugs and left our dead bodies behind. That or we would simply have disappeared. I was grateful God had protected us.

With each passing day, I became more and more convinced of God's goodness in my situation, and I eventually began to pray for a Bible. My prayer was simple. Please, Father, I need a Bible. I'd never called God "Father" before, but something in my newfound gratitude toward Him allowed me to accept this new intimacy. Father seemed right. It seemed natural, and I began to see my request for the Bible as a child's plea for a father's embrace, a full surrender to His power and love.

When I finally reached this point, God answered.

It was very hot on the day the Bible arrived. During the sweltering summer months of the year, temperatures in the prison would get up to 105 degrees, and the women in the blocks would strip down to their underwear – even go topless – anything to find relief. Our prison only had female guards, so no one cared about the nudity. It was our only escape from the brutal summer heat, so we took it.

That day, I'd retreated to my bed to daydream and listen to the girls' chatter. Earlier that morning, I'd prayed for the Bible as usual. I'd also mentioned my plea to a few other prisoners, and they'd laughed at my pipedream. Turkey has a mostly Muslim population, so Bibles are uncommon, and most of the girls doubted I'd be able to keep such a book even if I could obtain one. Still, I prayed.

On that afternoon, as I was becoming drowsy from the heat in the room, I heard someone enter our block.

"Shelly from America!"

I sat up immediately and discovered a guard standing in the middle of the room. She was holding a book. When she saw me sit up, she gestured for me to come forward. Confused, I looked around the room. Had I heard correctly? I'd never received anything before. Was the guard really delivering something to me?

Growing impatient, the guard called me over again, so I crawled from the upper bunk and rushed to her side.

"This is for you," she said.

I opened my mouth, but before I could speak, she waved me off dismissively, pushed the book into my hands, and marched out of the room. I was stunned and stood frozen in shock. Then, realizing I might be attracting unwanted attention, I tucked the book under an arm, walked to my bunk, and crawled back up into my space.

The other girls had become quiet, and several were watching. I knew they expected me to explain the strange gift, but rather than encourage them I acted as if the delivery was trivial. Without any fanfare, I casually pushed the book aside and lay back down as if I intended to sleep. Only when I felt I could investigate the package without attracting any attention did I examine it. The book was a beautiful, leather-bound Bible. Life Application Study Bible was printed on its cover. Still in shock, I stared at the words, reading them over and over again. My eyes began to burn, and a few tears rolled down my cheeks. Eventually, unable to contain my emotions, I wept openly.

Since the arrest, I hadn't spoken to my family. No one else would know I was in Turkey. How could this have happened? After racking my mind for possible solutions to the mystery, I had no choice but to conclude the Bible had come from God. It was a miracle.

At that moment, Susie entered the room. Approaching the bed, she saw the book and my strange expression – a combination of tearful joy and bewilderment.

"What is that? Where did you get the book?" she asked. Still afraid of attracting attention, I answered in an excited whisper.

"You're not going to believe this. I've been praying every day for a Bible and look God heard me." I tipped the book so she could see its cover.

Susie stood in disbelief. Before she could speak, Angelica, a new Russian prisoner with a decent grasp of English, approached us.

"How did you get that Bible?" she asked. "That's not allowed here. The guards will take it away from you."

"A guard gave it to me!" I said, and Angelica's eyes widened with surprise. She retreated and didn't challenge me further. Feeling giddy, I held the Bible tight to my chest, determined not to let it out of my sight for a minute.

"Good for you, Shelly," Susie whispered. "You finally got the Bible you prayed for. So, who is it from?"

"I have no idea," I told her. "I'm almost afraid to open it."

Susie laughed at my silliness and slipped into her bunk for an afternoon nap. Alone with my thoughts again, I couldn't stop thinking about God. He had done it! He had heard my prayers and had cared enough to answer them. God wanted me to have His Word. I was convinced of it.

Sitting up cross-legged, I set the Bible on my lap. The book wasn't new, but it was in great condition. Silver foil letters stood out on its dark blue leather binding. I reread the cover again, this time memorizing the shape of every letter until I could visualize the words perfectly in my mind's eye. God, I promise I'll read it, I prayed. I want to learn everything in it!

Having grown up around church people, I knew the Bible was God's word. In fact, I'd even memorized a few passages at points in my life, but the importance of those scriptures had never sunk in or made much sense to me. That was the past; this would be different, I assured myself. Sitting there on my bed, in that amazing moment, I felt certain I'd been given the Bible so God could speak to me, and I promised Him I was ready to listen.

As I considered what I hoped to learn, several spiritual questions came to mind. Each began with why. Why was I alive? Why had God continued to pursue me? Why was I so resistant to change? These were the answers I would seek.

Deep down, I also wondered why God was reaching out to me at all. For most of my adult years, I had been incredibly selfish and obstinate. Surely, I didn't deserve a good life or God's mercy, so why was

He bothering with me? As these why questions swirled in my mind, something in my soul told me the feelings of worthlessness that had dogged me were a lie. Though I didn't yet understand why, God did care. He did love me. And, most surprising of all, He was actively fashioning a better life for me – even now, after my latest failures.

A still small voice in my soul surfaced to reassure me. Shelly, reading this book will answer all of your questions.

Bolstered by this strange feeling of encouragement, I opened the Bible and began to examine it very slowly, studying each page as if even the layout of the text held importance and meaning. Chills ran up my spine, and I was overcome with an exhilarating sense of purpose. It was as if God had thrown out a literal lifeline to pull me from an abyss, and I was giddy with the realization this rescue was underway.

Turning another page, I was shocked to discover a folded letter tucked inside the Bible. My heart leapt. Would this solve the mystery of who had sent the book? I felt certain the letter was intended for me, and I opened it, feeling as if something profound was in store. At that moment, it felt as if time stopped and everything else in the room had faded away.

Hi Mom. I hope you receive this letter because we have so much to share with you.

Mom? I reeled momentarily with confusion and disappointment. Was this Bible actually meant for someone else? Had it been delivered by mistake? I read on.

We are finally settled in our barracks here in Istanbul. Barbara and I are really comfortable here and feel safe. But the reason I am writing you is to tell you about the Bible studies we are holding with other soldiers in our barracks. Each day, the studies are growing, and we feel blessed things are coming together so well.

Mom, I wanted to ask – have you heard about the two American girls that were busted for drug smuggling here in Istanbul? They're being held in the Turkish prison. We have been following their arrest story here in the news. We are so heartbroken for these girls.

Shocked, I paused to get my bearings. The letter seemed to have been written by an American soldier and his wife. Feeling lightheaded, I struggled to make sense of their words. According to the letter, the couple had been stationed somewhere nearby and had been following our story on the news. Somehow, they had learned about our transfer to this prison. The idea seemed inconceivable.

The letter went on to explain how the couple had prayed for Susie and me every day. They had prayed for our safety and that we would somehow find God. They said they knew God loved us and had a purpose for our lives. Their goal was to help by opening a door for us to experience God through the Bible.

As I read the letter, tears of joy came, but so did a pang of shame. These were soldiers. They had selflessly chosen to serve their country though it took them away from their families – possibly even their children. How could such noble people show concern for Susie and me? Every cell in my body screamed, "You don't deserve their compassion! This couple obviously doesn't realize how many people you've used and hurt. They don't know how rotten you are. They may think you're a victim, but you are guilty as charged, Shelly! You're undeserving! You should be suffering this fate!"

Each of these rebukes smashed against me with the impact of a tidal wave, and I felt myself slipping off the lifeline. Perhaps I only deserve to sink back into the depths of my sin, I thought. Maybe that is just and right. Still holding the Bible tight, I could feel the cold darkness of condemnation growing inside me.

Then, unexpectedly, something the soldier had written took hold of my flailing soul. It gave me something stable to grab in the tempestuous sea of my shame. The soldier and his wife had known of my guilt, but they'd still shown compassion. They believed this Bible could save me, and that gave me the strength I needed to take hold of God's lifeline again.

The still, small voice spoke to me from within. Shelly, you need to accept this undeserved mercy. You need to open your heart to the love expressed through this gift. Soft as the words were, they rose up powerfully in my soul and shouted down the condemnation.

The couple's letter had not been a summons demanding I account for my mistakes or a verdict demanding I pay for my wrongs. Theirs had been sweet words – more of a love letter, as if written by God Himself. Suddenly, I understood. The Bible gifted to me was a reflection of the compassion and selflessness Christ had shown in dying for the lost and sinful. Even now, even after all my failures, Jesus had not abandoned me. In fact, He was showing me He would go to the ends of the earth to rescue me.

Overwhelmed by this realization, I began to cry. But these were tears of joy, and as I read on, the rest of the letter explained everything, confirming my hopes.

Mom, we are going to try to smuggle a Bible in to these girls. If they have God's word, perhaps it will speak to them and encourage them and give them hope. Please pray for us and these women. Pray they will get our Bible.

At the end of the letter, the soldier promised to share any news of his success or failure. He said he and his wife loved and missed their mother. The closing section was very touching, and I sat in silence for a very long time, absorbing the weight of it all.

Eventually, tucking the letter back into the Bible, I climbed down from my bunk and looked for Angelica. When I found her, I asked her how a person might smuggle stuff into the prison.

"Shelly, I'm sure people smuggle things in here all the time – drugs, food, whatever. All it would take is money," she said. "These guards are dirt poor. They probably don't care what gets smuggled in as long as they can make a few bucks in the process. You'd just need to get the right guard to help you – someone who's happy to take the money and doesn't want whatever she's being asked to deliver."

The rest of that day, I sat in bed reading the couple's letter over and over again. I wanted to remember every word. The sacrifice they'd made for me was incredible, and I would never forget it. One day, I hoped I could thank them face to face. I was deeply grateful for the risks they had taken and for the prayers they had offered on our behalf. It still seemed miraculous to me that a stranger would care enough about Susie or me to make such sacrifices. Did such people really exist in the world? I'd never sacrificed anything for anyone. To encounter this kind of selflessness stunned me.

As the hours passed, I went on a rollercoaster ride of emotions, laughing one moment and crying the next. The deep, spiritual impact of my circumstances dredged up everything. I was reliving terrible situations in my life, as well as remembering past blessings and deliverance. It was like wrestling through time with the many ghosts of my past.

When I felt overwhelmed or some past failure tried to drag me down, I would repent, read scripture, and find a reason for hope. Eventually, the promises in His Word chased away the last nagging demons of doubt. Through the Bible, His power overcame my weaknesses. His bounty filled my emptiness. His encouragement brightened my darkness, and through this journey of mind and soul, I became convinced God had chosen me, loved me, and would remain faithful to me.

The experience also felt like a new birth. It was as if my very nature had been changed for the better, and over time, I became convinced this "new me" was real. I'd enjoyed a momentary escape from my addictions before, only to return to my old lifestyle again, but this felt different. This time, my mindset had been changed, and a new sense of purpose was taking root in my soul.

Though I found the idea of making radical changes in my life daunting, I was also excited about the new opportunities God was setting before me. I was hungry for God, and I was finally ready to focus on Him alone. From now on, I pledged, everything I do will be guided by the Lord. I will trust only God to direct my path, and I will only move forward with Him at my side.

In the weeks that followed, I faithfully read my Bible each day. I would devour a chapter, sit for hours digesting its lessons, and then return for more. Years earlier, having to spend even an hour in the Bible would have filled me with dread. I'd found it incredibly boring, confusing, or both. Now, its messages were incredibly energizing. For the first time in my life, optimism began to take root in my heart, and my spirit soared to heights I'd never experienced before. Reading the Bible was like finding a gateway to a heavenly place where God had placed treasures forged specifically for me.

Of course, every day from that point forward wasn't euphoric. Even a wonderful new relationship with God will have its earthbound moments, and I experienced more than a few of those dry periods too. In fact, there were occasions when I would wake up in the morning, grab my Bible, and feel nothing. At those times, I would wonder if the joy had only been a dream, and I was now returning to the hard realities of my old life. I would still reach out to God, but I simply couldn't tap into the same energy I'd experienced before. On the worst days, the ghosts of past insecurities would haunt me again too. Depressed, I would lie on my bed, stare at the grimy ceiling and ask, "God, where are you today? Have I done something wrong?"

I soon learned God uses times like those too. In His hands, every human experience, satisfying or not, becomes a teachable moment. On one doubt-filled day, I went to the canteen with a group of girls from my kosh. When we rounded a corner, I noticed a cluster of women sitting on the stairs into a nearby building. A little Filipino woman in the group stood up as we approached. She searched our faces, and her expression changed when she made eye contact with me.

"Excuse me. Are you Shelly – the girl from America?"

I was so shocked to hear her speak English; I couldn't help but stop. I was also surprised she knew my name. I was certain we hadn't met before, and that made me wary. Instead of identifying myself, I asked her why she was looking for Shelly.

"I need to find her. I've heard about her, and I want to speak to her."

I was still suspicious, but I was also curious, so I admitted I was Shelly. Her eyes lit up, and her face broke into a wide, excited smile. I'll never forget that expression of pure joy. Before I could say another word, she reached up, threw her arms around me, and praised God, saying, "I prayed God would help me find you!"

The little woman's embrace sent a charge running through me like the tingle of electricity. I also felt a powerful connection with her – like the kinship enjoyed by family members – and then I understood why. She and I were sisters in Christ! After hearing my cries of depression, God had orchestrated this meeting, bringing me to this specific place and person for support.

I took a seat next to the little woman. She said her name was Jane – short for Janelle. I smiled and told her my name was Shelly, short for Shelly. We both giggled, giddy with an excitement neither of us fully understood. Jane explained that she had only been in prison for a short time. Though she was from the Philippines, she had been placed in a block with Turkish women, perhaps because she had lived in Turkey for many years.

As Jane explained it, she had come to Turkey in hopes of finding a better life but had encountered only hardships. She had slaved away her youth in hard, menial labor, sending a significant portion of the money she earned back to the Philippines to support her children. After losing that job, she'd made poor choices, eventually turning to drug smuggling as a means of survival. Unlike me, Jane had never been a drug addict, and her life had not been marked by a consistent struggle with sexual sins. Rather, she'd been a strong believer in God since her childhood and had only recently engaged in crime to escape a desperate situation. I could tell she loved her children deeply and desperately wanted them to have a better life.

Stopping to speak to Jane, I may have missed my visit to the canteen, but I did return to the spiritual mountain top. Thanks to her enthusiasm and faith, my depression and self-doubt disappeared. I told Jane how happy I was she'd sought me out. I'd been feeling lost and alone, and her fellowship had blessed me and refocused my mind and spirit on God.

Through Jane, I also learned Susie and I had become celebrities in the prison. I found this very odd, but I knew it was true. The Turkish inmates saw all foreigners as special people, and as the first Americans to be incarcerated at the prison, Susie and I were considered particularly significant. Of course, I knew nothing could be further from the truth. I was just another woman. We prisoners were the same. We'd been stripped of every rank and privilege and now held everything in common. The prison had served as the great equalizer, taking our freedom regardless of our home country or cultural background.

From a spiritual point of view, this equality among sisters made perfect sense. In fact, it began to shape my new impression of the world. It helped me see all people as God's creation, made in His image. Rich or poor, American or Turkish, we were all part of the same family.

Meeting Jane also made me see mankind's shared journey as a beautiful thing. Jane and I were part of the same incredible search for Purpose and Truth. Millions had walked this path before us, and millions more would follow in the centuries ahead. Seeing Jane as a fellow traveler on this exciting journey, I was eager to get to know her and share our lives as friends.

"I've been coming to these stairs all week," she told me. "I knew you would eventually go to the canteen, and I was hoping to find you and speak to you." Like me, Jane felt our meeting was important and that our connection had been forged by God.

In the weeks that followed, Jane supported me in my Christian walk, but there were other ways God helped me stay the course too. In fact, God moments seemed to blossom all around me in those wonderful days. My Bible reading might feel unproductive one day, but an unexpected blessing would pop up the next. I would turn a corner and suddenly see or hear the Lord encouraging me through some person or circumstance. Through these "God moments," I was continually renewed and energized.

In fact, I would wake each day in a state of anticipation, feeling as if God and I were playing a game of spiritual hide and seek. The minute my feet hit the ground, I would be on high alert, looking and listening for some sign of Him. When He would show up – and He always did – it was like a beautiful surprise, like discovering a hidden treasure. This made my relationship with God an exciting adventure, more thrilling than any drug I had ever taken, and more satisfying than any relationship I'd ever had. Only those who have known such joy, peace, and satisfaction can understand the pleasures of those moments. Falling in love is probably the closest thing to it.

In those wonderful, euphoric days with God, all of the fear I'd been carrying for years completely disappeared. I also lost my sense of dread and all my worries about the future. I felt surrounded by a force that could protect me fully and completely. I was in a God bubble. It was the most amazing feeling to know I was being protected by the very Creator of the universe!

During this time, I also discovered God's many promises in the Bible, and I trusted in every one of them. I no longer fretted about getting out of the prison. In fact, I began to see the value of my incarceration. In a very real way, prison had become a safe haven for me, a place free of the temptations that had plagued me so often in the outside world. Eventually, even my tormenting nightmares – usually about searching for drugs and getting high – also went away. Rather than wake in a cold sweat, I would find myself quoting scripture in my dreams!

Eventually, the outside world and its snares lost their power to control me, and I gained a liberating understanding of God's perspective and of eternity. The Bible describes this world as insignificant compared to the things of God, and it warns us that our mortal bodies are destined to become dust. Only the spirit is eternal. Only God and the things of God live on. For the first time, I truly understood the folly of pursuing possessions, self-gratification, and worldly power. These things are superficial. Fading smoke. Unimportant. Only God is real. Only living in His presence and being taught by His Spirit can ground us and satisfy us.

As winter arrived, God confirmed my faith with a miracle. It came at a mundane moment when I least expected it, but it proved to me that God was my protector and that I remained His child.

You may think of Turkey as a tropical place – and it does have brutally hot summers – but the country can also become very cold in winter. When the night winds would blow, they would penetrate the prison blocks and chill our beds. There was no glass in the building's windows, only bars, so the girls had become adept at fashioning cardboard panels to provide some protection from the elements. Breaking down old boxes, we would shape the cardstock into rectangles and jam them into the window openings. My high corner bed was near a window, and we often used it as a makeshift ladder to accomplish this job.

On the day of the miracle, Susie handed me a cardboard panel, and, standing on my bed, I reached out toward the window. As I pushed the panel into place, my foot slipped, and I shifted my weight to compensate, losing my balance completely. I fell sideways from the high bed.

Susie lunged forward but failed to reach me, and the women in the cell block gasped. For a horrible moment that seemed to last forever, I tumbled in space. In that slow-motion drop, I imagined my head breaking open as it struck the cement below, and a pulse of fear shot through me.

When the impact came, it was punctuated by screaming. Then, someone shouted for a guard. I'm sure they expected broken bones, a huge gash in my head, and blood to flow, and I'd imagined the same, so the outcome shocked everyone.

Laying there, I remained completely still. The girls surrounded me, eyes wide. But I felt nothing. There was no pain, just the pounding of my heart echoing in my ears. I finally gathered my wits enough to speak.

"I think I'm OK. Nothing's wrong."

When I tried to sit up, the girls all yelled for me to lie still. "The guards are coming." one said. "They'll know what to do."

"Really, I'm OK," I said, "Just help me up."

The girls were stunned, but I slowly pushed myself up and got to my feet. I'd been shocked by the abruptness of the fall, but I hadn't been hurt at all. There wasn't even a scratch. The girls stared at me in disbelief, shaking their heads. A few patted me on the back, saying I was very lucky to have been uninjured after such a terrible fall.

Once things calmed down, and the girls returned to their bunks, a woman in my kosh approached. She was Bulgarian and had brought a friend to translate. She took me to the kitchen and told me what she had seen.

"Shelly, the reason you weren't hurt was because an angel caught you and set you down on the ground," she explained through the translator.

Susie and I were skeptical, but the Bulgarian woman insisted the story was true.

"I saw it with my own eyes," she said, smiling ear to ear. "It was as if your fall went into slow motion, and I saw a huge hand underneath you. It cushioned your fall."

Although I didn't know the woman's language, I knew she was a believer. I'd seen her praying. She was as attuned to the spirit of God as I was, and I had no reason to doubt her. For the next hour, we all just sat in awe, discussing the miraculous nature of the rescue.

Another "God moment" came later in the form of a letter.

Shortly after I'd received the Bible, I had written letters to my parents to tell them about my encounters with God, but I had never received any mail back. The U.S. consulate rep visited at one point and showed me an email from my family saying they hadn't received any mail from me. Upset by this, I joined a few of the other prisoners in appealing to the director of the prison about our problems with the mail system.

One day, a guard came and announced a mail delivery. I was ecstatic when my name was called, and I rushed forward to see who had written to me. I was shocked to discover the letter was from my grandmother, Lottie. I'd never had a very close relationship with my dad's mother, but I was still thrilled to be reading something from home.

Jumping into my bed, I eagerly tore open the envelope. Her words brought me to tears. The letter was beautiful, inspiring, and encouraging. It was filled with wonderful passages of Scripture, expressing God's promises. It was as if Grandma Lottie had read my mind, knew my heart, and was confirming everything I'd been feeling.

Through that letter, I learned wonderful things about Grandma Lottie I'd never known. She told me she had been praying for me since the day I was born. She shared her deep love for the Lord and said she felt certain He would guide me safely out of my situation. As I grew to know Grandma Lottie through these words, amazing healing began to take place. God was at work, bringing restoration to my family. I also learned to appreciate a grandmother's love for her grandchild – and I gained new insights into the power of prayer. Even more than the miracle rescue from my fall, this beautiful letter renewed my soul and left me in a state of awe over what God could accomplish in a willing heart.

Chapter 11

UNWORTHY

In the following weeks, my walk with God intensified as I drew on energy from the purest of sources – His Word. I loved reading the Bible, and my time in scripture quickly developed into a wonderful, daily routine. Like an automatic alarm clock, God would wake me before dawn to sit with Him. Those quiet mornings, when all the other girls were still sleeping, became my favorite time to read the Bible. The world seemed so peaceful, and my time with God so intimate.

In the hours before lunch, I spent as much time as possible in prayer and Bible reading. Sometimes, my prayer took the form of contemplation, and I would simply sit quietly, waiting on God to speak to my heart. When He did, I would absorb His attention and love.

This love was returned too. Through prayer and expressing my affection for the Lord, I gained an even greater sense of security in our relationship. His satisfaction and encouragement shattered all of my old fears, finally unmasking them as the terrible, draining lies they had been. This was an incredibly liberating experience. Finally, my old nature was being changed from the inside out. Never again would I feel unworthy of God's love. Never again would self-loathing draw me back into the darkness.

I had embraced God, and I would hold on tightly.

This exciting healing was paralleled by profound changes in my family life too. Like clockwork, letters from my Grandma would arrive about every 10 days. I waited eagerly for my name to be called at the mail deliveries, and I couldn't wait to open each new letter and hear what Grandma had to say – even though these letters would sometimes challenge me.

Grandma Lottie was an amazing woman, and her spiritual insights had always impressed me, but I also respected her for being honest and never sugarcoating anything. As a woman of principle, she believed Christian values should never be twisted or soft peddled to coddle or justify.

For example, there were times my letters to her would include gossip or mean-spirited comments about one of the other girls in the prison. In those cases, I expected Grandma Lottie to sympathize with me, supporting my position, but instead, she would soberly correct me or share passages of scripture rebuking me for my negative comments or actions. Because she carefully backed up what she wrote with references from God's word, it was impossible for me to reject her points. Even when anger would rise up in me, the Holy Spirit quickly calmed me down, ministering to my heart and opening my eyes to His truth. Eventually, my feelings – and my behaviors – began to change.

A strange mystery also surfaced during this time. While Grandma Lottie's letters came regularly, my mother's mail never arrived. Emails from the consulate would mention how my mom was writing me weekly, but the envelopes were never delivered. When my name was called, the letter would always be from Grandma Lottie.

At first, I didn't understand why this was happening, but eventually, I saw the hand of God in it. I think he was keeping my mother from corresponding with me because He knew I had developed a very codependent relationship with her, and mom's messages might conflict with the work He was doing in my life. My mother is an amazing woman and would give her own life for mine, but I'm convinced there was something in her letters God felt would hinder my healing at this time and in this place.

Throughout my life, mom and dad had always been there to bail me out and make things right, but in Turkey, this dynamic had changed. I was finally being forced to face hard truths, deal with the circumstances of my sin, and look elsewhere for support – specifically to the Word of God.

This realization also forced me to confront my abuse of relationships, particularly my manipulation of my mom and dad. Alone and in prison, there was plenty of time to think about those things and to see the error of my ways. I now understood the pain I had caused and the financial burdens I had created. I had been the source of so much stress, so much suffering. I begged God to forgive me and prayed the Lord would allow me to mend the relationships I had so callously broken. I began to pray for my parents each day, asking God to bless them and heal their hearts, removing any pain I had caused.

In those months, with no other person to guide me, I also asked God to help me study the Bible. It seemed logical to me to begin at the beginning, so I started in Genesis and moved forward from there, reading chapter after chapter. I began each of these sessions by praying for God to speak to me and open my eyes to His truth.

"Father, help me understand these stories and how they relate to me," I would ask – but to be honest, I still found the reading daunting at times. Many of the chapters were very hard for me to understand, possibly because I approached everything very literally, but I persevered in spite of this, purposing in my heart not to stop, even when I wasn't certain what God was communicating through the stories I was reading.

It took about two months for me to get through the entire Bible, and when I finished, I spent some time assessing what I'd learned. I found the experience included both low and high points. Certain scriptures had jumped out at me and really spoken to my heart, but most of those were passages I had already heard while growing up. Other stories seemed odd or irrelevant, and I wasn't sure what to make of them. Clearly, learning truth and understanding God would take more than one reading of the Bible, I decided, so I committed to starting all over again. But this time, my approach would be different. Rather than treat the Bible as a book of history, I would embrace its supernatural origin and treat it like a personal encounter with God himself.

"God, will you help me?" I remember asking. "I want to know you, and I need your guidance to really understand your Word and how it applies to me."

This approach led me to read the Bible with my deepest personal questions in mind. Why had I been created? What was the reason for my life? Most important of all, I wanted to know why God had pursued and protected me through the years. As I read the Bible through again, I pretended God was sitting beside me, sharing stories from scripture like a father might share family history with a beloved daughter, intending each incident to communicate a moral or message beyond the names, places, and events themselves.

I also asked God to clear my mind of everything I'd heard in the past. I wanted to approach Him afresh, with no preconceived notions of who He was or how He operated. Growing up, I'd heard different pastors explain what God loved or hated, how He should be worshiped, and about what it meant to be holy. I was determined to set all of that aside and let the Bible alone reveal the character and attributes of God.

"Holy Spirit, teach me. I want Jesus to be my shepherd – the only voice I follow." That was my daily prayer and the desire of my heart.

While I set out to explore personal questions, I found my reading and prayer time with God actually led me to focus less on myself and my own circumstances. I had every reason to wonder about the impact of my impending prison sentence, but instead, I found myself drawn into a love of the Lord that wrapped me in warmth and peace. Over time, my personal fate began to matter less and less because I was convinced God was in control, and whatever He planned for me would be best. I would be His forever, so I didn't have to worry about anything anymore.

As my fears of the future faded, so too did my regrets about the past. Just a few years earlier, the "what ifs" of life had held incredible power over me. They'd haunted me, stained my identity, and destroyed the joys of life. More than any of the men or women who had abused me, they had been the oppressor in my life, pounding me with feelings of guilt and inadequacy. Through my encounter with God, their power had been offset by unconditional love. I could trust Him with everything – the good, the bad, and the ugly – present and past.

By the time the date of our criminal trial arrived, I was no longer praying to God for my release and return to America. Instead, I was asking Him for the courage to tell the truth, and accept my fate. I prayed the Holy Spirit would speak through me, so everyone involved in the case would encounter God as I had.

The U.S. consulate representatives came to visit us a few days before the trial. They were kind but never promised anything positive. I suppose they didn't want to give us any false hope. In fact, their intent was probably the opposite – to make sure we understood the worst-case scenarios. Over and over, they would remind us of the seriousness of our crime. They would tell us the Turkish authorities might want to make examples of us and suggest we should be prepared for a lengthy sentence, possibly twenty-five years or more.

No matter what they told us, I felt a perfect peace in those moments, convinced whatever happened would be God's will and in my best interest. If He felt I needed to remain in prison for twenty-five years or more, I was certain He would have a purpose for it, and I would ultimately be blessed as a result. I felt no fear, and this baffled me. It was so different from my reactions when I'd been jailed in America. In those cases, I'd been a complete wreck, overwhelmed with anxiety even to the point of becoming physically sick. I felt none of that now.

In fact, as the time for our sentencing drew closer, what I felt was excitement. How would God use that moment? Who would be involved? I felt certain God was working out something amazing on my behalf, and whatever it was, it would be an incredible blessing. The Lord knew everything about me from beginning to end, and I had told Him through prayer I never wanted to return to the selfish, painful life I'd known before. Surely, God would honor that cry of my heart.

At about this same time, the hospital finally scheduled the surgery for the treatment of my cyst. Different inmates approached me with warnings not to let the Turkish doctors operate on me. "You'll have no idea what they are doing to you while you're out and under the knife," they would say, or "They'll cut you up, and you'll never be the same." I knew this talk wasn't of God – it was the enemy trying to put fear into my heart – so I rejected their counsel, telling them I had accepted the diagnosis and was glad to be free of the problem before it developed into ovarian cancer.

When the fateful day for the surgery arrived, I remained strong. I'd been to the hospital dozens of times, had been poked and prodded, and seen so many different doctors I felt numb to the whole process. Never in my life had I been tested so much for a surgery.

Still, I can't say I fully understood what was going on. During the hospital visits, most of the doctors and nurses had not spoken to me. When I would ask questions, they answered in Turkish or shook their heads. Only when I got back to the prison would the doctor there give me any feedback on what had happened or what was being planned. Even up to the day before my procedure, I still had no idea who exactly would perform the surgery!

While I was effectively ignorant of the medical points of my case, I did become an expert in one thing – waiting. In fact, everything in my prison life revolved around waiting, and I believe God had good reasons for teaching me this lesson. I had never been patient about anything, and many of my life's problems could be traced back to that root weakness. Selfishness is bad enough, but self-absorption fueled by an impatient spirit is often both self-destructive and dangerous to others.

A nurse led me to an unfamiliar room and had me sit on a hospital bed, telling me someone named "Surfeon" would soon be in to see me. Surprisingly, she spoke perfect English, and this made me feel much more confident. Please, God, let the doctor speak English too. I also hoped I would finally be able to ask some specific questions about the procedure!

A few minutes later, the door opened and a handsome man in a white coat entered. He smiled warmly and put out his hand, which I shook tentatively.

"Hello Shelly, I see you are American," he said and began the normal routine of checking my pulse and listening to my heart. I sat quietly as he asked me questions about my previous health problems and the surgeries other doctors had performed on me. He listened politely and then shared his plan to remove my ovary. In the process of showing me where the incision would be, he gasped at the long scar below my belly button.

"Wow! Who botched this earlier surgery?" he asked.

I'd always been very insecure about that scar. For one thing, it reminded me of one of the worst experiences in my life. I had to go to a county hospital, and the anesthesiologist had not given me enough sedatives to keep me asleep through the entire procedure. I had regained consciousness while they were stapling me up, and hearing the loud sound of the machine, I'd become terrified and floundered on the table, screaming for help. They'd put me out completely at that point, but the damage had been done, and the day after I was released, three staples came out in the night. I had to be rushed back to the hospital. They re-stapled the open area, but the incision was no longer straight, and the procedure had produced this horrible scar.

"I promise you that will never happen here," the young doctor assured me. "You are in great hands now, Shelly. I don't want you to be afraid. I've scheduled your surgery for nine AM tomorrow morning, and I'm sure it will go flawlessly. We do many of these surgeries. Once I remove your ovary, I'll have it tested right away and pray it is benign."

Had he said pray? I wondered if he was Christian. Before I could inquire, he asked me why I was in prison. I now felt completely comfortable with the man, so I shared a bit about my life story. I explained

I had been an addict, had gotten involved with bad people, and had smuggled drugs into the country under their direction. He sat quietly and listened, making direct eye contact with me the entire time. When I finished, he reached over and placed a hand on my shoulder.

"That was your past, Shelly. Now you can look toward a new future. I pray it works out well for you – that you can be home with your family soon," he said.

I thanked him for his kind words, and he followed up with another question.

"Have you ever had a child?"

"No," I said. "I did have two abortions."

As I lowered my head in shame, he comforted me again.

"That too is in the past. We can't change what has happened before, but we can change our future, Shelly. All it takes is making the right choices from now on – and I hope you will."

I told him the doctor who performed my earlier surgery had said I'd never be able to conceive, but Dr. Surfeon didn't seem convinced. Instead, He said he would confirm my true condition during the surgery the next day.

When he left the room, I felt elated. He'd shown so much personal concern for my health and peace of mind. I hadn't experienced anything like it before, and it helped ease my anxiety about the surgery and my eventual recovery, both physically and emotionally.

The next morning I was up early. I packed a little bag of belongings, and Susie gave me a hug. Some of the other girls came by and wished me well too. I wasn't afraid. I was happy. Finally, this daunting health problem would be addressed, and I could find out what my future risks would be.

In the van ride to the hospital, I was accompanied by three guards. They had the usual Uzi guns with them, but I noticed they each carried a stack of magazines as well, and I wondered why. When we reached the hospital, I was taken to a very plain room on the first floor. It had an open, unscreened window and was very primitive compared to the hospital rooms I'd had in the U.S.

The guards waited outside while I changed into my examination gown. As I looked out of the open window, a thought occurred to me – somebody could jump right out of this place and run. Fortunately, a nurse entered the room before I could do anything stupid, and when she left, the guards entered.

As I got into the bed and pulled up the sheet, one of the men shackled my feet to the bed frame. Then they pulled up chairs and opened their magazines. I'd brought a good book, so I settled in to read too. The weather was beautiful, and I could feel a fresh breeze washing in through the open window. Within an hour, I'd fallen asleep.

I slept like a baby for some time, and when I woke, drowsy thoughts drifted through my mind. Would I eventually be taken to a more sterile room, or was the whole hospital this primitive? There were bugs flying in through the open windows. What if a gnat gets inside me while I'm on the operating table?

A nurse roused me with a tap on the shoulder. Handing me a pill and a glass of water, she told me this medication would relax me. "They'll be here in fifteen minutes," she said. "This is your chance to use the bathroom and freshen up."

I wanted a shower, but I knew that would be impossible. The three guards were still in the room. One was asleep in his chair, his head back and his mouth wide open. Another was lying across the other twin bed in the room, his Uzi next to him. The third guard was staring right at me. I smiled at him and, using improvised sign language, indicated I needed to use the toilet. He unlocked the chains on my ankles, helped me out of bed, and motioned for me to join him. He took me down the hall and waited outside while I entered a little bathroom.

Well, this is it, I thought. In the privacy of that odd sanctuary, I prayed silently, asking God to protect me and to guide the doctor's hands. Afterward, I felt certain the Lord would help me get through the surgery safe and sound. When we returned to the room, two male nurses were standing at my door with a gurney. I climbed aboard, a little lightheaded from the meds but calm and ready to see an end to my months of pain.

Two of the guards followed the gurney down the hall. The other stayed back. Thankfully, they didn't shackle my feet again. As we took elevators up and down and passed through hallway after hallway, nurses stopped here and there, grabbing paperwork or discussing things in a language I couldn't understand. Finally, we reached our destination – a room with a strange window in the middle of its far wall. I'd never seen anything like it in a U.S. hospital.

The nurses rolled my gurney to a point where my feet were facing the window, and the guard pressed a button near the panel. The window opened up, and before I knew it, the flat of my bed was sliding right through the opening and into another room beyond. What I experienced next shocked me. The room I'd entered was ice cold, and its walls were all made of some kind of sterile metal. The nurses that had pulled me through to the other side were all dressed in green scrubs with nets covering their hair and masks over their mouths. They all snapped into action, moving quickly to begin the procedure. Unlike the room I'd started in, this place smelled of antiseptic and was impeccably clean. I felt a big surge of relief. It seemed I was in capable hands after all.

I thought this room might be where the surgeries were performed, but the nurse pushed the gurney on through another open door, and I was suddenly in an even larger space with high vaulted ceilings. Before me, the entire wall, top to bottom, was made of crystal clear glass, and the natural scenery beyond showcased a beautiful mountain vista. I stared in disbelief. None of this seemed real.

At that moment, my surgeon entered, a smile on his face. He walked up and asked me what I thought of the room. I laughed and told him I had never seen such amazing scenery in my life. My next thought was macabre – might they do this so people who die will have one last beautiful image in their mind.

"Shelly, I am the chief of surgery at this hospital, and I want to reassure you that you are going to be just fine," he said. "Lay back and relax."

As I reclined, the doctor started giving orders to the others in the room. A mask was placed over my mouth, and I was told to start counting backward from ten. I barely remember even saying ten. My next memory was of a soft slapping on my cheek. I opened my eyes and saw the doctor standing over me.

"Hello again, Shelly from America. You're alive, and I have good news for you," he said, laughing. "You can have babies! I took your cyst out with no problems. It was all contained and benign. I'll stop in to see you tomorrow."

That was it. I fell back to sleep.

I struggled with some pain that night, but the next morning dawned on another surprising experience. One of the guards woke me and unlocked the shackle on my leg, motioning for me to sit up. Was I going back to prison so soon? I hadn't seen the doctor yet.

Unaware of my unspoken questions, the guard took my arm and made me stand. It hurt a bit, but I understood movement was import-ant to my recovery, so I complied. I stretched a bit, and he walked me to the bathroom, holding me tightly by the arm as one might guide a sick child. He spoke softly, too, clearly trying to reassure and comfort me. I felt a little embarrassed – perhaps because I still believed such kindness was undeserved.

Soon after we returned to the room, the surgeon walked in, as energized and upbeat as ever.

"I have something I want you to see, Shelly from America."

The guards left the room.

"I know the world may portray us differently, but I want you to know that the Turkish people are good. We are a compassionate peo-ple."

Why was he saying this to me?

"I wanted to do this for you," he said with a smile, and reaching down, he took the bandage off my abdomen. I stared in disbelief. The ugly, lopsided scar tissue of the botched surgery I'd had in the U.S. was completely gone. He had removed it, straightened the skin, and performed the plastic surgery necessary to correct those imperfections. Itty bitty stitches had been made in a beautiful, thin line. The wound looked as if it was almost healed. There was no swelling or dried blood. Unable to help myself – I burst out crying.

"Why did you do this for me?" I sobbed. "I can't pay for this. I'm a prisoner – a stranger in your country."

"Shelly from America, I felt called to do this," he said, the smile still in his eyes. "I didn't want you to have to live the rest of your life with that horrible, ugly scar. You're a beautiful young girl. You have your whole life ahead of you."

"From now on, please do what you know is right," he added. Sitting on the bed, he put his arm around me while I cried, and I felt God surrounding us at that moment. I understood the whole experience as an object lesson. No matter how bad your life has been, God can offer restoration if you are willing to live for him.

After my tears stopped, I thanked Dr. Surfeon over and over again. I told him that if I ever got back to my country, I would tell others about the wonderful Turkish people I had met. Not all who follow Islam seek to destroy. I already knew that because many of the Islamic women in the prison modeled only a loving behavior. They had been some of the kindest, most generous people I'd ever met. They loved God, just like me.

I was back at the prison dorm the following day, and I felt amazing. I was healing very fast, and the positive news from the doctor had given me a new lease on life. I felt like a whole woman again.

Unfortunately, the cares of the world eventually intruded on this happy time. That bad news came in a letter from Grandma Lottie. In it, she explained that a close family friend of ours, David Hoskins, was in the hospital facing a serious medical problem. I'd grown up knowing the Hoskins family, so the news hit me hard. I also knew David's parents, Bob and Hazel Hoskins. They had been missionaries for many years, at one point starting a U.S. ministry called OneHope.

Grandma said that David had been born with only one kidney, and it was failing, threatening his life. At the same time, he was also suffering from retinal detachment in both eyes. I felt so bad for David, I immediately began praying for him, asking God to heal him completely.

"Please send them someone who can help by donating a kidney for him," I begged.

As I sat quietly in prayer, God spoke. He said, "Shelly, you will be that donor."

I opened my eyes and looked around. Had anyone else heard the voice? I closed my eyes, and God spoke into my heart again. "Shelly, you will be David's kidney donor."

The idea was crazy. I couldn't possibly be the one to donate a kidney to David. I was in a prison halfway around the world. It was unlikely I would ever be free again, and even if I did return to America, how could my alcohol and drug-ravaged organs be of any use to anyone.

The voice came a third time – "Shelly, you will be the donor."

Surely, I thought, this wish must be coming from my own mind, but nothing in my spirit confirmed that view. I contemplated the words again and saw they could only have one source. The message had to have been from God.

I crawled down from my bunk and told Susie what I had heard. She laughed at me.

"You don't know if you'll ever get home, but it is sweet of you to want the best for him," she said. "If God wants to help him, it'll need to happen in some other way."

Yes, I thought. She's right. By the time I get back – if I ever get back – David will probably have found another donor.

Crawling back into my bunk, I got paper and a pen and wrote to my Grandma. I shared the usual things about the awesome ways God had blessed me, gave details about my daily walk, and the like. I also mentioned I was praying for David and asked my Grandma to tell him so. In closing, I told her about God speaking to me three times, telling me I was going to donate my kidney to help him in his hour of need.

As usual, Grandma wrote back. Most of the letter was written to catch me up on family news, but she did mention my prayer for David at the end of the letter. "Shelly, you are kind to offer David your kidney, and I will tell him if I see him at church, but I think your focus should be on getting well and returning home to us," she said.

I knew what she'd written was reasonable and right. This was just her way of saying that the voice had come from my own mind – because I was so eager to help.

As the days went on, my relationship with God continued to grow and blossom. I felt complete in Him and through Him. I slept well at night, at peace with myself and my maker. God was in control, and I was convinced He would show Susie and me how much He loved us as we continued on and faced the challenges of our trial date.

Chapter 12

UNFETTERED

The trial was a test of my faith.

The process took many months, and each time we were needed in court, we would be handcuffed for transport. It always seemed like overkill to me, but six guards were involved, and they would escort us out of the prison at the business end of an Uzi. It was about a forty-five-minute drive from the prison to the downtown Istanbul courthouse, and when we arrived, we would sit in the sweltering hot truck for another hour, waiting to enter the courtroom.

When we would finally leave the vehicle, it was to face an angry mob of protesters with handheld signs, some claiming we were terrorists. The guards would rush us past this group and into the courthouse. There we would sit on long benches waiting for our names to be called.

Every few months or so, it was the same drill. Each time, we would be shackled for the trip to the courthouse, we would be "greeted" by protesters, and we would endure a long wait for the proceedings. After all of this, we would be brought before a small group of judges – men in their sixties wearing what looked like choir robes.

During those encounters, representatives from the U.S. consulate were always present, smiling as if to reassure us they'd support us in any way they could. The first time they brought us into the courtroom, we also saw Eric. Though it had been six months since we'd parted, this wasn't a surprise. We knew he'd taken part in the same crime we committed, and we'd expected he would participate in our trial. Still, we were shocked by how much he had changed. Eric had become thin, haggard-looking, and fragile. We almost didn't recognize him when he nodded at us and took his seat.

Seeing Eric was unsettling, but it wasn't as disturbing as the trial process. That felt like a waking nightmare. During the long courtroom sessions, as people spoke back and forth in a language we didn't understand, all we could do was shrug our shoulders. Having no money for our own lawyer, we had no advocate in the courtroom, and the language barrier made it impossible for us to speak up for ourselves. This left us feeling lost, alone, and confused.

At a few points in these long, bewildering sessions, our names would be called, and we would stand up to answer questions with the help of a translator. "What is your name? Where do you live? Why did you come to Turkey?"

Susie and I would always answer honestly. We knew if we lied, things would only get worse.

My deepening relationship with God also influenced this decision. I knew my future was in the Lord's hands, so rather than use deception to get out of trouble as I might have in the past, I resigned myself to pray God would touch the hearts of the judges. My hope was that the Lord would give us favor through their merciful decision, so I would sit quietly and wait on Him.

Eric took a very different tact. He retained a powerful and expensive Turkish lawyer and fought the system head-on. I must say, seeing his lawyer in action challenged my resolve. The man was a bulldog, arguing aggressively with the prosecutor and judges. There were times this made us feel like lambs in a slaughterhouse. For all we knew, Eric's lawyer was arranging lenient treatment for him at our expense. It was incredibly frustrating – and frightening – to have no idea what was being said, but there was no other course we could take. We simply stood when called upon, took the judges' questions over and over again, and answered them as honestly as we could.

There were also a few occasions when one or more of the judges appeared to fall asleep during our questioning, and I remember becoming angry with them for being so cavalier about our fate. How dare they fall asleep when our lives depended on their deliberations! Then, as quickly as the anger came upon me, I would feel the Holy Spirit rush in to speak to my heart and calm my emotions. Be calm. Trust God. You don't control this anymore. Turn this over to the Lord.

For a year-and-a-half, they took Susie and me to the courthouse every three months, and each time, we would return to Pasakapisi prison at the end of the session with no clearer idea of where the case was heading.

As time passed, I surrendered more and more of my life and my fate to God. I didn't do this with the hope I would miraculously be delivered from punishment. I fully expected to receive a harsh sentence. I surrendered to Him because I believed by accepting my fate – no matter how terrible it might be – I could honor God through my faith and obedience. That said, I did pray He would help me cope with the long sentence that was coming. I also believed God would use the experience for my ultimate benefit. It may seem odd, but this was my interpretation of God's promise in Jeremiah 29:11.

I still feel that way. I still believe accepting and surrendering to one's circumstances is essential to finding real peace in life. No matter what happens or how a situation feels to me in a given moment, I stand on the belief that God will remain at my side and will use my experiences to bless me in the long run. Back then, I could have seen my prison sentence as a form of divine justice and punishment, but instead, I thought of it as part of God's plan to restore me, and I set my mind on finding silver linings in any unexpected blessing it might provide.

For example, I saw benefits in my incarceration. In prison, I was safe, sober, and clean for the first time in many years. I was able to think more clearly, and I had discovered an inner peace.

Yes, my body was captive, but all was well with my soul. It was ironic, but I was happier in prison than I'd ever been through most of my prior adult life.

Susie also seemed to accept what was happening, but I could see it was harder for her. Her young daughter was back in America, and her heart ached for the girl every day. I remember hearing her cry about that at night, and it broke my heart.

My family was far away too, but I knew my parents and grandmother believed in and trusted God, so it lessened my pain. I felt certain I'd see them again someday, and until then, I knew they were receiving my letters. From those notes, they would know I was safe. They could see my life had drastically changed. Learning I had finally come to know God would bring peace to their hearts; I felt sure.

When the day of our sentencing arrived after all those courtroom visits, I remember feeling both a tingle of anticipation and a sense of peace. With the proceedings ending, I knew sentencing would come next, but I had lost my fear of the trial's outcome. In fact, it felt as if God's grace was pouring in and through me as I was escorted into the courtroom on that last day.

Susie and I took seats facing four judges. Eric was on the other side of the room, and about a dozen other people were scattered on benches behind us. I wondered who they might be. I assumed most had followed our trial in the media and now wanted to see how the story would end. Leyla, our representative from the consulate, was in her usual seat too, and she smiled and waved to us, though her face communicated very little hope or assurance.

Next, I looked over at Eric, and when our eyes met, he nodded at me. By this time, I'd been warned whatever sentence he received would likely fall on me too since we were both charged with the same crime. Susie had been arrested for cocaine trafficking, but Eric and I had been accused of conspiracy to smuggle drugs. As the judges saw it, we had planned the crime, while Susie was just a hireling who had carried out our scheme.

Since this was the trial's last session, we were given a chance to share our final comments directly with the judges. I told them how sorry I was for what I had done. I admitted to having committed a terrible crime, and I told them my addiction to drugs and my selfishness had been my downfall. Then, I explained how God had opened my eyes and changed my life. I concluded by asking them to show mercy on us by giving us a sentence that would allow us to see our families again someday.

As I finished, feeling as if my fate was now in these four men's hands, I heard God whisper into my soul – "They are not your judges, Shelly. I am. What happens here is for me to decide. I hold the earthly king's heart in my hands."

Once Susie and Eric concluded their personal pleas, we were all escorted into a cell just outside the courtroom. It was a very dark place – damp and gloomy – and it added to our sense of foreboding. Susie and Eric plopped down on the long benches set against the walls of the room, but I found I couldn't sit, so I paced back and forth instead.

After about twenty minutes, the door opened, and a man led us back into the courtroom. It was frighteningly quiet inside, with only a couple of people whispering in the room. We took our seats, and just as my nerves were settling, I was shaken again as a huge printer in the room roared to life, loudly spewing out reams of documents. The translator collected three sets of these papers into piles, and everyone's attention shifted to the judges. One of them spoke, and the translator asked all three of us to stand. This was the moment of truth – our sentencing. When the judge spoke again, the translator turned toward Susie.

"You have been sentenced to seven-and-a-half years and have been given a $12,500 fine. If you or a family member is not able to pay the fine, your prison term will be extended in lieu of the fine."

Susie and I had been holding hands to comfort each other, and I could feel her body begin to shake. My own spirits had been lifted by this news, so I wondered if her reaction was one of excited joy rather than fear. We had been told we'd receive between twenty-five years to life, so getting sentenced to less than ten years seemed like an incredible blessing to me.

The judge spoke again, and the translator walked over to Eric. She translated, explaining that he would be incarcerated for fifteen years. Now, I felt my knees getting weak. I prayed, God keep me strong. Please don't let me fall apart in front of everyone.

As the judge continued, I prepared myself for the same sentence Eric had received. I was still holding hands with Susie when the translator turned to me – and repeated the punishment Susie had been given. I, too, would serve a seven-and-a-half-year sentence and be given a $12,500 fine!

I looked to Leyla for reassurance and saw complete shock on her face. Susie turned and hugged me. Though I was overjoyed, I could see the news still troubled Susie, and I suddenly realized why. She had done the math in her head and had calculated how old her daughter would be when she got out. This realization burned in her eyes, and I felt her pain. Susie's daughter would grow up while her mother was in prison. What a terrible thing for both mother and child to endure!

Without any more fanfare, the trial ended, and the guards escorted us back to the truck for our return trip to the prison. Some protesters still lined our path, but they no longer displayed any signs. Once Susie and I were safely inside the vehicle, we talked about the sentence and thanked God for the mercy the court had shown us. We understood the severity of our crime and believed the punishment would have been much greater if we had been sentenced by a U.S. court. The Turkish authorities had actually been extremely lenient on us, we believed.

In time, some of the concern and pain faded from Susie's face. We even laughed a little as we celebrated "God's ways" and talked about the anticipation that would be building back at the Pasakapisi prison. Most of the women in our cell block were awaiting trials for trafficking drugs, so the outcome of our case was on everyone's minds. They would be desperate to learn every detail about our fate.

As we considered this, we realized not everyone would be happy about our relatively short sentences. We knew of three Bulgarian sisters who had taken part in a much less significant crime and had been given twelve-year sentences. Surely, they would be angry about the favoritism the court had shown us. It made my heart heavy to think our "good news" might make them feel bad, and I decided I would not make a big deal about our lucky break when we returned to the prison, hoping it would lessen the jealousy or disappointment the others might feel.

That plan never materialized. As we approached our cell block, the door opened wide, and a room full of girls stood before us, their eyes wide with curiosity. The Russian girl named Angelica could hardly contain herself.

"So – what sentence did you receive?"

There was no way to keep our good fortune a secret, so we explained the situation, and Angelica translated our description of the events for the women in the cell block who didn't speak English. To my surprise, all of our cellmates were thrilled. Showing no jealousy, they flocked in to hug us, smile, and share words of encouragement. I still felt a twinge of guilt, so I accepted this kindness humbly and quickly slipped away to my bed to write to my family with the good news.

* * *

About four weeks after our sentencing, Leyla from the U.S. consulate visited us at the prison. When we entered the meeting room, she jumped to her feet and hugged us. Afterward, she gave me a bag of Hershey Kisses and offered Susie a package of Almond Joys. We mumbled our thanks as we stuffed our mouths full of the treasured candies.

"I was shocked by that sentence! Did you ever think you'd be going home to your families in less than eighteen months? You must be thrilled!"

Susie and I had been so focused on the treats we'd been given that Leyla's comment didn't register immediately. When it finally did, we looked at each other blankly, and she saw the confusion on our faces.

"Didn't anyone tell you? There's a lot of overcrowding in the Turkish prisons, so those convicted of crimes are only required to serve thirty-five percent of their sentence. And based on how long you've already served, you only have seventeen months left – as long as the fine is paid."

We were slack-jawed.

"If you don't pay the fine, though, you'll have to serve a slightly longer period in lieu of that," she added. "But, if the $12,500 is paid, you'll be going home in seventeen months!"

After digesting this unexpected news, Susie and I let out a yelp and hugged each other. Home again in just seventeen short months! We could hardly believe it. Laughing and re-energized, we thanked Leyla and rushed back to our cell block to share this news with the others.

I was on cloud nine for the next few days, but eventually, the ramifications of this news dawned on me. What would I do when I returned to America? Where would I go? Would my parents help me get back on my feet as they had so many times before, or would I end up in some kind of transitional halfway house before I could start over?

Every time thoughts like this challenged my spirit; I would turn to God to help me overcome my anxieties. I'd learned focusing on Him could keep me from drifting back into dark emotional places, so I relied on regular prayer to stay grounded through the months that followed. I am in His hands, and He is in control of everything. That's what I kept telling myself.

One afternoon, these convictions were challenged by an unexpected event. I was in bed reading my Bible when a group of guards entered our cellblock with a clipboard, and one of them began yelling something I couldn't understand. Then, my name was mentioned. Flustered, Susie and I rushed to track down a translator. Fortunately, Angelica, the young Russian girl, had heard the announcement, and she understood what was happening. She told us the guards were ordering us to pack up all of our clothing immediately. We were being transferred to another prison.

"They say you're only allowed to take your clothing and hygiene items," she explained. "Nothing else."

By this time, Susie and I had amassed a collection of books. They'd come from family members and friends back in America. We'd cherished them, and some had been read over and over again. Since these would have to be left behind, we offered them to the few other girls in the block who spoke English, and they were very grateful to us.

Then, as I began packing my clothes, I noticed the Bible on my bed and realized I would have to leave it behind too. Tears welled up in my eyes. This particular Bible held incredible significance to me. For example, seeing it there on the bed brought up emotional memories of the soldiers who had delivered it to me in the prison. What a touching sacrifice they had made! There were many personal notes in the margins too. Because I'd always expected to keep the Bible as a memento of my conversion experience, the thought of leaving it behind was overwhelming.

No matter what, I resolved, I wouldn't allow the prison guards to confiscate and destroy it.

Hunting down an old plastic bag, I carefully wrapped up the Bible, climbed to the top of my bunk, and pulled back the corner of the mattress facing the wall. As I slid the precious package into this hiding place, I begged God to protect it.

"Please, please, Lord, make sure this Bible gets into the right person's hands. Pass it on to someone who will be blessed by it."

I knew this was unlikely because very few of the inmates could speak or read English.

"And let it be someone who can read it," I added.

Eventually, all of the girls being transferred were called out to the transports. This was a bittersweet moment, and there were many hugs and shared good wishes. Susie and I had known most of these women for nearly two years, and as strange as it sounds, the Pasakapisi prison had become something of a home to us.

By this time, we had also heard about our destination – the Bilecik prison – and some of the girls were clearly frightened by what awaited us. The place, about a four-hour drive outside of Istanbul, was in a mountainous region we knew very little about. We'd also heard Bilecik prison had been established to incarcerate men. Only a couple of cell blocks there had been modified for women. According to the whispered rumors, many of the men kept there were from Iraq, and one girl had also told us that even the drive there would be very scary because we would need to travel on narrow roads along frightening cliffs with no protective railings.

"You can't even see the bottom of those ravines!" one girl had said. "God help you if the bus goes over the embankment."

I glanced over at Susie and saw her eyes filling with tears. Susie had always found comfort in routines, and change never sat well with her. I, on the other hand, was always up for new experiences, and I thought of the move as a new adventure – something to make our life a bit more exciting. Bilecik prison would give us a chance to meet new people and have a change of scenery, I told myself. There was nothing to fear.

This pep talk worked until I saw the guards loading our belongings on the transport. Only then did I realize we would never see Pasakapisi again. This had been my place of sobriety. Though a prison, Pasakapisi had literally liberated me from the drugs and behaviors that had controlled so much of my life. I had finally found God there, too, growing in Christ within the prison's walls.

So many miracles. So many memories.

As it happened, there was little time left for reminiscing. Guards shackled our hands and feet to the metal bars in front of the seats, and the vehicle was underway. The ride was rough, and we were tossed around mercilessly, so it didn't take long for an aching back to demand all of my attention. I'd gotten aboard hoping to enjoy the trip beyond our prison walls, but I was soon praying for a chance to get out of that uncomfortable vehicle.

When the transport finally stopped, it was at a scary, isolated building in a rural area – nothing like the prison complex I'd expected. The place looked abandoned, and parts of the building were literally falling apart. My heart was pounding, and I began to panic. Could this really be our destination? Something seemed very wrong, and I had to struggle to control my fear.

After about thirty minutes, our driver climbed back into the van and started the engine. Thank God –we were leaving. Still, the experience rattled me, and I began to regret my earlier longings for a change of scenery. God, I prayed, please don't take me out of the frying pan and throw me into a fire!

The next part of the journey took us through the mountains my friend had warned us about, and all of her dreadful descriptions of those treacherous roads now seemed understated. We were traveling very fast and taking dangerous curves at terrifying speeds. At points, I felt as if the bus was hanging over a bottomless trench, and my shackles felt like a death sentence.

My stomach also rebelled, and I turned away from the window to pray. Susie saw the look on my face and yelled at the driver to slow down. I could see fear in her eyes too. After she shouted, an unnatural silence fell over us. Minutes before, the girls had been chattering and laughing. Now, the few that could still speak also began begging God for help.

Something about this suddenly struck me as ironic – and silly. Just a few hours before, I'd professed God loved me and was in complete control. Now, I was reacting like He might dump me off a mountainside. How could I be convinced God had plans to bless my life one moment and fear He would let me die the next? I was deeply convicted by this spiritual hypocrisy and decided to fully embrace God's sovereign control of all things. This simple but profound decision buoyed my spirit, and I began calming the other girls down, reassuring them we would get through the mountain pass unharmed.

Soon after, our destination came into view. The place dwarfed Pasakapisi in size, but it had none of that prison's character. Pasakapisi had been a renovated hunting lodge. It had also been painted pink, so it had never appeared very imposing. Bilecik prison, on the other hand, was massive, hard-edged, and very ominous looking. The buildings were daunting, the high walls seemed impenetrable, and the Uzi-toting soldiers patrolling the ramparts were clearly very serious about their jobs. As our van climbed the last winding road toward the place, I also saw two tall watchtowers and shuddered at the thought of constantly being under the eye of armed men once we were inside.

As a large gate rolled open and our vehicle entered the compound, I could only pray we would be safe, and our living conditions would be tolerable.

*   *   *

As God had done before, He took care of me in Bilecik prison.

While a much less hospitable environment, in some ways, Bilecik was actually an improvement over Pasakapisi. For example, Bilecik's facilities included a recently completed gym, and we were allowed to make use of it four days a week. There was also a sports field, and we spent a lot of time there too. Those activities filled our free time and made our stay there go much more quickly.

The transfer to Bilecik also produced a couple of interesting "God moments."

The first was a surprising encounter. One day, while guards were leading a group of the girls to the gym, we went down a hallway in the men's section of the prison. Around one corner, a few of the men's cellblocks came into view, and some of the guys began to congregate near us. They reached through the bars and yelled out to us in languages we didn't understand. The guards kept us moving along, but I suddenly heard a familiar voice call out my name. When I turned, there was Eric waving to me through a gap in the bars. I smiled and waved back, happy to see he was close by and still alive.

After the trial's conclusion, I had heard some frightening news about Eric from my family, and I'd begun to wonder about his fate. In their letters, my parents had told me Eric had been beaten up several times by Iraqi prisoners. I'd also heard he'd been stabbed and that some of his bones had been broken in these altercations. It grieved me to think he had been treated so much differently than Susie and me, and as we left that section of the prison, I prayed things would improve for him. Years later, I found out God answered that prayer.

The other "God moment" involved something so mundane it may seem laughable, but it had a profound impact on me at the time. It happened during my last weeks at the prison, just as my release date was approaching.

As I've said, I spent a lot of time in the prison gym and on the sports field. One day, as I was going through my possessions – deciding what I would take back to America and what I would leave behind – I picked up my sneakers. These were shoes my parents had sent to me nearly three years earlier, and while they'd gotten less rigorous use at Pasakapisi, I'd worn them regularly at Bilecik, putting them through a real workout on our exercise days.

I'd expected to dump them when I departed because I'd assumed they would be too worn out to be of much use, but as I examined them, I was shocked by their condition. I hadn't noticed it earlier, but I now saw the shoes looked brand new, including the soles.

Immediately, a story from scripture popped into my mind. I remembered how God had blessed the children of Israel after their exodus from Egypt. Though they had traveled in the wilderness for forty years, the Lord had kept their shoes and clothing from wearing out. Laugh if you like, but I am convinced God preserved those sneakers through my entire prison "wilderness" experience.

In fact, I believe God guarded my well-being throughout those difficult years. He always provided me with the things I really needed, and He never let me down.

I even received a replacement Bible! It came from my grandmother along with some devotionals just ten days after I arrived at Bilecik, and as I had at Pasakapisi, I continued to read it and talk with God every day. These moments were very real and very intimate for me, as if I was sharing the key points of my day with a best friend. And as He had before, God also spoke back, revealing revelations of His truth that continually ministered to my heart.

Although it would have been tempting to share these spiritual lessons with others at the prison, I ultimately came to believe most of the things God was revealing to me were specifically for me and tailored to my situation. That's one reason I now believe so strongly in individual Bible study and devotion. While there are definitely universal spiritual truths the Lord wants to share with everyone, I think there are also specific and deeply personal lessons He wants each of us to learn. Those who limit their relationship with God to a series of church sermons and never read the Bible deprive themselves of that important blessing!

I also believe God welcomes specific questions from us. In fact, I think He longs to reveal all Truth to us, but we need to be patient and willing to spend time in the Word for that revelation to come. For me, this process would usually begin with a thought in my mind or a desire of my heart. I would share it with God, but without any expectation an answer would come immediately. Then, as I was praying or reading my Bible later, His response would appear suddenly, almost leaping off the page. The connection between question and revelation would be obvious then, and it would touch my spirit in an undeniable way. In those moments, I would often smile, sit back, and just rest in God's love and peace.

Eventually, I developed a complete trust in God to teach me, lead me and guide me, just as Isaiah 45:3 promises – I will give you hidden treasures, riches stored in secret places, so that you will know that I am the Lord, the God of Israel, who summons you by name.

That's not to say I lived free of human fears and failings after my spiritual conversion. For example, during my last weeks at Bilecik, I began to fall prey to serious doubts – but they had nothing to do with God's sovereignty or kindness. My fears centered on my own weaknesses. There were days when I would fret about my return to the U.S. and the unknown challenges the transition would bring. Would I be able to maintain my strong relationship with God? Would I be tempted to return to that horrible life of sin and drugs? Could I repair all the damage I'd done in my relationship with my Mom and Dad?

My parents had always been supportive, but I'd put them through many years of addiction and craziness. I couldn't help but be haunted by my Dad's last words to me as I left for South America. "Shelly, if something happens to you overseas and you do something illegal, we won't be there to bail you out."

To fight back these fears, I continually went back to God's Word and tried to keep His promises in mind day and night.

One day, with my release date fast approaching, I finally made a phone call home. My folks got on the line, and I told them I would be released in two months. There was complete silence on the other end of the line, and my heart sank.

"You'll need a plane ticket," my dad said. "It's the only way you can get back to the states. We can take care of that."

They were kind words, but his tone was restrained.

"Do you know where you'll go when you return? Have you thought about that?"

At that question, I fought back a twinge of anger and had to calm myself down. I understood their position, but the words still stung.

"I've trusted God to this point. I'm going to keep trusting him. He'll prepare the way and show me where to go and what to do," I said.

Those words seem to break the tension between us, and my dad's familiar gentleness returned.

"Yes, we'll deal with it when the time comes."

My last weeks at Bilecik went faster than I expected, and the day finally arrived for my release. It was Susie's release date too. I packed my few remaining belongings in a suitcase – the same suitcase I'd carried when I was arrested – and I prepared my spirit for the next stage of my life.

That day was like a dream. Although a prison representative joined us on the bus from Bilecik prison to Istanbul, our shackles were gone, and we finally felt free.

When we arrived at the deportation holding area, we were processed through the system one last time. This deportation facility was very different from the prison we'd left behind. It was in the center of a residential neighborhood with open windows that overlooked a cluster of many houses. It was strange to experience such an open environment after years of confinement, and it added to our sense of freedom.

At the deportation center, we learned that Susie's parents had gotten her airline ticket right away, but my departure was being held up for three days for a clearance I'd not yet received. I was happy for Susie but also a bit anxious about her leaving me. We had been inseparable for the past three years. Losing her companionship at this critical point, frightened me a bit, but there was no other option for us. She would be leaving. I would need to stay.

I did make one new friend while I waited for my flight clearance. After spending a night in a simple room, I was taken to meet the director for the center, a Turkish man named Hanifi. When we met, he asked about my experiences, and I told him my unvarnished story, including all of the details of my crime. He was kind, never seemed judgmental about my arrest, and showed no hostility when he learned about my Christian faith. I could tell he had a tender heart and truly cared about people. It was the same kind of openness I'd found in many of the Turkish women I'd met while in prison, and it changed a lot of my views about the people in the Middle East. In America, the news often characterized Islamic people as angry and intolerant, but my experiences contradicted that stereotype – at least in the places I'd visited.

After my three-day wait ended, I was picked up for my trip to the airport. Hanifi came by and said farewell. It was odd, but I felt like I was losing a close friend even though we had only known each other for a few days. I think God was in that too because years later, I was overwhelmed to open my Facebook to find a friend request from Hanifi and we are still in contact to this day.

When I left the detention center, it was with an escort. The two men said they would remain with me until I picked up my e-ticket. They spoke perfect English and said I would be taken to flight attendants who would be informed of my status. I would need to do as they said. I must sit in a designated area of the plane, and I could not be left alone until the flight landed.

"Once you land, you'll be escorted to customs and handed over to Interpol for processing on to the U.S.," they said. "What happens from there will be up to them."

This revelation startled me. Was it possible I might be arrested again in America? Thankfully, I was told all U.S. indictments against me had been dropped because the prosecutors in America felt I had endured enough while incarcerated in Turkey. Little did they know how wonderful the experience had actually been! How could they have suspected my years in Turkey had led to my redemption and salvation!

I was upset about the conditions on my travel, but I dutifully followed one of the young men to the airline counter, where he spoke to the attendant there. Smiling, she printed off my e-ticket, and I continued on to the gate. A long line had already formed for boarding, and I joined it.

As we waited, my escort struck up a conversation with me. He asked me what I had done to be arrested and sentenced to prison. I told him the truth – I had been an addict for more than twenty years and had conspired to bring drugs into Turkey. I told him about my regrets and explained the lessons I'd learned in prison, including the details about my conversion. He responded kindly but bluntly.

"So, you are a Christian now?"

A momentary fear swept through me, but it faded quickly, and I answered confidently, "Yes, I am." Then, I told him how blessed I felt that God had been with me through my ordeal. To my surprise, he smiled and told me he was a follower of the Islamic faith. Then he addressed me by name.

"Shelly, please never do this again," he said. "Please don't bring drugs into my country."

With a renewed twinge of shame, I again said how sorry I was for what I had done, and he surprised me by handing me my ticket and passport.

"I'm going to leave you here – allow you to fly back as a regular civilian," he said. "I think you've had enough to deal with. Are you OK with that?"

Standing there in disbelief, I nodded "yes."

Without another word, he put a hand on my shoulder, gave it a little squeeze, and walked away.

I looked back just in time to see him turn, look directly at me and salute me like American soldiers do. I smiled and waved back.

I'm completely free now, I thought. I'm not going to have a babysitter on this flight, after all. Showing my ticket to the stewardess at the door of the plane, I boarded with a big smile.

I was finally on my way home.

Chapter 13

UNFINISHED

My flight home was exhilarating.

For one thing, I was excited about being reunited with my family in America. But there was much more to it than that. I had undergone an amazing personal transformation in Turkey, and, in many ways, I was returning home an entirely different person. I'd left America as a slave to drugs, but I was coming back a liberated child of God. Before the trip to Turkey, my soul had been plagued by darkness, fear, and self-loathing. Now, I had a clean body and a clear mind.

Finally, at peace with myself and God, I felt ready to soar like a bird.

With the years in Turkey replaying in my mind, I marveled at the many miracles that had taken place there. God had revealed so much of Himself to me and had guided me through so many challenging circumstances. He had met me in my weakness, spoken to my heart, and taught me His liberating truth!

In that moment of reflection, I found myself asking, "Will it always be like this, Father? Can I expect this awesome relationship with you to continue year after year?"

As you might expect, Satan butted in with his own twisted answers. As a creature of lies, he loves to turn our innocent questions against us just as he twisted Eve's curiosity about a forbidden tree into a reason to doubt God and, ultimately, into a temptation to sin. I'd learned his game well during my incarceration, so I knew exactly how to defeat him. I took the dark thoughts captive with the Word of God. In this case, I relied on, "The Lord will never leave me or forsake me."

Satan must have hated the fact that I now knew the Lord deep in my soul and understood the full extent of His love, grace, and mercy. I could be confident God had not rescued me from my hellish addictions only to destroy me once I returned home, and that truth would continue to provide me with another defense against the devil and his lies.

As I considered all of these things, I suddenly remembered the plan God had revealed to me – how my return home would lead to me helping David by providing him with the kidney donation he so desperately needed. With this pleasant thought in my mind, I drifted off to sleep.

*   *   *

An hour out of Miami, my excitement about the homecoming returned. I'd been told to expect a welcoming committee that included my mom and dad, my sister Kim and her husband Kevin, and their two children, Nikki and Jessie, and I couldn't wait to see them all. I was also eager to talk to my grandmother, but I'd been told she would be waiting back at my parent's house. During my twenties, I'd been so self-absorbed I'd had little time for any of my family members, but now, I couldn't wait to sit at my grandmother's feet and share my experiences with her. I knew she was excited to see me too. She'd written to me regularly and faithfully while I was in prison, and those letters had been a lifeline to me, brightening my darkest hours. She'd also been a spiritual guide when I needed it most.

The pilot's voice suddenly broke in on my thoughts.

"We are making our final approach into Miami International Airport."

The words sent a tingle down my spine, and my heart began beating wildly. This was it! I'd been numb on drugs for so long I found it hard to contain the raw emotions welling up inside. What would it be like to face my parents as this new creation, this child of God? Would the changes in my life be obvious to them? Would they see the transformation that had taken place, or would they still have doubts – expecting the old me to arrive on this plane? I reminded myself God was in control, and whatever took place, He would bring about the best for me.

When the plane landed, I grabbed my small suitcase from the overhead bin and eagerly joined the line of exiting passengers. It felt odd to have been away for so long but have so little luggage. In fact, my suitcase held very little. The most important possession inside was a box containing correspondence I'd received from my family members. I had kept every letter, intending to bring them home and read them all again. Possessions mattered far less to me than the family connections those letters represented.

Still thankful there had been no police or airline escort on the flight, I followed the crowd to customs like any other passenger. Standing in that line, a funny thought entered my mind. During the years I'd spent in prison, I hadn't had a normal haircut. A friend of mine named Samara had offered occasional trims, but my hair had grown down to the middle of my back. The time spent in the Bilecik prison had also been very good for my health. I'd been exercising more and dieting for almost the entire eighteen months I'd been incarcerated there, and I'd lost more than forty pounds as a result. My skin had bronzed in the summertime sun too. My family may not see my spiritual transformation, but I'll certainly look very different on the outside, I thought.

I walked up to the customs counter and handed my passport to the attendant.

"Welcome back to America," he said, stamping my passport and motioning me through. Though his actions were routine, the experience was incredibly emotional for me.

I next followed the crowd through a walkway and toward a transparent wall separating arriving passengers from the waiting public.

Holding my breath, I scanned the crowd behind the glass for a recognizable face. There – I saw my mom and dad! There were my sister, her husband and my two nieces too! All were smiling from ear to ear, and I broke down in tears. Pushing on through the doors, I ran into my mom and dad's arms.

The other surged in, and the group embrace overwhelmed me. That moment was wonderful, but the sweetest words came from my dad.

"Let's go home."

Like Dorothy waking after her trials in the Land of Oz – finally safe and among friends – I felt an incredible sense of relief and a deep appreciation for all of the people I had ignored before. This wonderful sense of family unity washed over me again when Grandma Lottie greeted us at the door. It was delightful to hug her, finally understanding her value after all my troubled years. Her smile warmed me like the sun, and we held hands as she walked me into the living room.

In the hours that followed, I shared my stories, and they caught me up on all kinds of family news. Eventually, when we were all worn out from talking, my sister and her family got ready to go. I hugged her again and shed a few more tears as they drove away. My grandmother saw this as an opportunity for me to have some private time with my parents, so she retreated to her room too. Once she was gone, the house became very quiet. I was at a loss for words, so I sat patiently, waiting for my parents to share their thoughts. It was my mother who broke the silence.

"We're so happy to have you back, Shelly. We want you to know we love you, and this is your home. We're not going to send you anywhere. We believe God has done an amazing work in your life, and we don't want you to worry about anything – where you will go, where you will live, or about getting a job. We just want you to rest and relax. We'll all wait and see what God will do next."

I sat there in disbelief. My parents had always been quick to offer up a long list of suggestions and plans, and I expected them to handle this situation in the same way. Instead of trying to solve my problems or challenging me to offer up my own solutions, they seemed to be putting their faith and trust completely in God alone.

At that point, my father showed me how he could close off a portion of the family room to create a simple bedroom for me.

"I hope this will do. We plan to buy you a dresser once you've settled in, but for now, we've cleared out the hall closet so you can use that space for hanging up your clothes."

I was overjoyed that they were taking this approach, and I thanked them over and over again.

"I know God will show me what He wants for me next," I said, hoping to confirm their faith. "He didn't bring me this far – rescue me out of that horrible life – just to leave me now."

That first night at home was surreal. I knew I had been changed by my encounter with God, but I hadn't expected to see the same kind of awakening in my parents, yet there were clear signs of some kind of transformation. Their serenity in the Lord was something I'd never seen before, and in words and actions, they were forgiving and loving. I had always sensed an underlying legalistic tone in their religious walk, but now they were expressing the kind of spiritual confidence I also felt, and I thanked God for it.

A couple of days after my return to Florida, my Uncle Bill called and spoke to my mother about a potential job for me. He had just sold an alarm company he'd owned for many years, and he asked if my mother and I would help him get things in order before the new owners took over. Though it was a short-term project, I loved the idea of working with my mom, and we accepted his offer.

As the weekend approached, my parents asked me if I would come to church with them. I was eager for us to attend church as a family, and we went together in high spirits. Soon after I sat down in the sanctuary, a finger tapped on my shoulder. I turned, and there was David, my friend of many years, the man who needed a kidney transplant. We hugged and began chatting. I briefly told him about my time in Turkey, and he shared a few stories about his recent visit to Russia. Then, I told David how God had spoken to me about his need for a kidney. David began to laugh.

"You're so kind, Shelly, and I appreciate your thoughtfulness, but do you really think I want your kidney after all the drugs you've taken through the years?"

I knew David was only teasing me, but there was also a lot of truth to what he said, and we both began laughing.

"There's really no need anyway," he added. "Someone else came forward, and we've already started the process down at Jackson Memorial Hospital in Miami."

I was glad for his news, but I again felt that stirring in my spirit – Shelly, you will be the kidney donor David needs. As crazy as it seemed, especially in light of my drug use, I continued to believe the Lord's prophesy. Somehow, I would still be involved in David's medical case, for his sake, and for mine.

Before I could express this, David changed the subject.

"Shelly, what are your plans? Have you thought about a job? Where will you work?

I told David about my uncle's offer and expressed my gratitude to God for the opportunity it had provided.

"Well, I have a job for you to consider once you finish working with your uncle. We need a front desk clerk in our building if you're interested. It's a full-time schedule, and you can get health benefits too."

This was stunning news. I hadn't worked a traditional job in nearly twenty years, so I'd expected the gap in my resume and my criminal background to make finding a position nearly impossible. Now, I was being offered a second job opportunity, and I knew with certainty this was a gift from God.

On the drive home, I shared this amazing news with my folks.

"The job is a blessing, but what will I do about clothes. I definitely can't work at the front desk position with the wardrobe I have."

"Shelly, that's not a problem. While we were working for Uncle Bill, I saved my paychecks for you, thinking you could use the extra help getting things started," my mother said. "My friend Chari also has three bags of clothes. She thought you might have a use for them."

Once again, I couldn't help but see the hand of God in this circumstance. He had a plan and was helping me take my first steps down the right path. Days later, I went through the clothing Chari had offered, found a use for almost all of it, and marveled at God's love again.

That night, as I lay in bed, I thanked the Lord over and over for His faithfulness, and the promise in Deuteronomy 30:3 came to mind. It says God will restore your fortunes and have compassion on you and gather you again from all the nations where he scattered you. Even if you have been banished to the most distant land under the heavens, from there, the Lord your God will gather you and bring you back.

While in prison, I'd read this passage and had relied on its promise. Now, God recalled that memory to show me that His Word never returns void. The passage had been just as true during my years as an addict, but I'd been ignorant of the blessed assurance it offered because I had not read the Bible or lived by what it taught. Only now, because of my deeper relationship with God, could I see His hand in the events of my life, and it thrilled me to have this new perspective.

I started work at The Forum for Global Missions the following week. The building housed a group of Christian organizations and served as a lodging facility for visiting missionaries. It was owned by OneHope Ministries, a mission founded by David's parents. One-Hope occupied part of the building and leased the remaining sections to a group of churches and charities.

I loved my job and found living with my folks was awesome too. There had been times years earlier when I couldn't be in the same room with my mother without fighting with her about something, but now I couldn't wait to get home after work to spend time with my family. The house had become a wonderful home, filled with God's presence and peace.

I spent many evenings with my grandma too. I loved to hear her stories about when my mom and dad were young. Together, we also watched several videos shot during those days. We laughed a lot, but there were also times I would cry. I'd missed out on so many of the wonderful family experiences I might have enjoyed. It was heartbreaking, but I also felt God understood this pain and was using my grandmother to help me rediscover my heritage and history – blessings I'd lost in the years I was strung out on drugs and living a life separate from God.

*   *   *

Months after my return, my mother and I were sitting in the kitchen when another God moment came. I will never forget that day. The phone rang, and when I picked it up, I heard a "hello" I recognized immediately by its accent.

"Samara!"

Samara had been a very close friend in prison, and I knew from letters we'd exchanged since my return that she was nearing her release date. She was calling me from the same deportation center I'd stayed in just before my flight home.

"I am free, Shelly! I am free!"

We laughed and did a bit of catching up. Then, Samara changed the subject.

"Shelly, hold on the line – there's a woman here named Miriam, and she wants to talk to you."

Miriam? I couldn't remember anyone named Miriam at the prison.

The woman who got on the phone had a very thick accent.

"Hello, Shelly from America."

I hadn't heard that name in some time. It was what the guards and soldiers had always called me. Could this be a guard?

"My name is Miriam, and I'm from Somalia. I was arrested and brought to Pasakapisi prison to await my sentencing."

Her next words rocked me to my soul.

"I prayed for a Bible to read, and one day, while taking my mattress down to turn it around, I saw a package underneath. I opened it and found a Bible – your Bible. Inside, it said Shelly from America."

Chills ran down my spine, and the hairs on my arms stood on end. At that moment, deep in my soul, I heard God say – see Shelly, I heard your prayer.

As Miriam thanked me again and again, I knew it was really God who had provided the blessing in answer to her prayer. I told her how happy I was she'd found the Bible and explained that when I'd hidden it, I'd prayed God would put it in the right person's hands.

Samara got back on the phone, and I asked her how Miriam happened to be at the deportation center. Had they worked out these arrangements ahead of time?

"No, Miriam was standing behind me in the line, just waiting to use the phone," she said. "As we were standing there, we got to talking, and I told her I was calling a friend who had been released from prison. I told her your name was Shelly and that you were from America."

I couldn't believe my ears. God had orchestrated Samara's chance meeting with Miriam to inform me of this miraculously answered prayer! I could hardly wait to share this wonderful news with my family. It was incredible to see God showing up in so many of my life's circumstances.

My job at The Forum developed into a tremendous blessing too. I made friends quickly, and many people encouraged me to share my conversion story. I loved talking about those experiences because they glorified God. My hope was that the stories would encourage others to look for and share "God moments" in their lives too.

The fact that I was transitioning back into a normal work life in a Christian environment was such a godsend! I'm not even sure I could have found a job in the secular world at that time. I was a former drug addict and had a criminal record. Both would have been major roadblocks to getting even an interview at most places – but among God's people, I found only compassion and encouragement. In fact, the Lord used those people and my transparency to open new doors for ministry. For example, when a local church learned about my incarceration in Turkey, they suggested I consider taking part in a local prison ministry.

I loved going into the jails and sharing my life story with the girls there. My own hardships and experiences made me relatable, and the young women really seemed to take my suggestions to heart. I felt like this might be a special calling for me, and it gave me a wonderful new sense of purpose in life.

About the same time, I discovered The XXX Church out of Las Vegas and saw a fit there too. Their mission was to help people fighting porn addictions, and it included outreaches to men and women caught up in the sex industry. They were set up at a porn convention in Miami and were looking for volunteer help. I went to the pre-event training and met a woman there named Julie. She also had a booth at the convention under the name, Beauty From Ashes Ministries.

Never having heard of this program before, I told Julie I'd been a stripper for many years and understood the culture. At the end of the convention, Julie invited me up to Ft. Myers, where they based their operations, and she asked if I would pray about getting involved in her outreach. Old emotions welled up immediately.

"I will never step foot in a strip club again!"

"Be careful about saying never," Julie challenged. "Say never to God, and you may find that's exactly where God sends you next."

I shook my head, but I also agreed to pray about her offer. I understood the point of her mission, but that part of my life had produced so much heartache, I couldn't see myself ministering to strippers – and I honestly felt I would be more effective in prison ministry anyway.

A few weeks later, Julie called me while I was on a lunch break.

"Shelly, I was praying today, and God brought you to mind. I thought I should give you a call to see if you would be interested in coming over for a training."

"I really haven't thought about it, Julie – but I have to tell you, I don't feel God calling me to join your outreach."

Julie was very sweet about accepting my answer, but she clearly felt otherwise.

"OK," she said, "but please keep your heart open to the idea and listen for what God wants. Sometimes we come to conclusions about what God wants for us, but those things are really what we want for ourselves."

This wasn't something I wanted to hear, but I accepted Julie's suggestion as graciously as I could, hung up, and thought about her words. Could God really want me to return to the strip clubs and serve the girls there? I did give it some thought, but I eventually set the opportunity aside.

The following Saturday, I set out on my next assignment with the prison ministry – a visit that would allow me to share my testimony with women in one of the area's larger facilities. Arriving with my team from the church, I hit a roadblock. At the entry point, my license was checked, and the guards discovered a red flag on my record. The stigma of my arrest in Turkey had followed me home, and I was told I couldn't join the group inside.

My pride hurt, I fled to my car. I was sitting there crying when my cell phone rang. It was Julie on the line, and I was shocked she'd called at that very moment. When I told her how I had been turned away at the prison gate, she had an immediate and compelling response.

"Shelly, perhaps God is trying to show you he has something new for you. Go home, pack a suitcase, and join us in our outreach to the strip clubs this weekend."

I did go home, threw some clothes in a case, and headed up to Ft. Myers – nervous, but also a bit excited by the prospect. Though I'd fought the idea before, I now believed God was leading me to this opportunity for a reason. Even if it didn't develop into a long-term mission for me, I sensed he would use the experience to serve Him in some special way.

Some may believe this simple view of obedience lacks a proper level of prayer and discernment, but I have found God sometimes demands an immediate response in faith. When we are aligned with Him through His Word, we can expect this kind of spiritual leading at a moment's notice, and we should be prepared for those opportunities.

In this particular case, I also believe God used these experiences to teach me the real essence of sacrifice in ministry. I think pride had begun to creep into my decision making, and God wanted to keep selfish ambitions from poisoning my life. Going into prison ministry started as my plan for serving God, but it had quickly become more about getting positive feedback for the things I was doing. When we try to take the glory for ourselves, God is quick to show us our true motives and to reset our path if we are off course. God did that to me, not because He was angry at me, but because He loved me enough to show me how a destructive pride was beginning to taint my life.

As if to confirm His love, the night I joined Julie's outreach was life-transforming for me.

The Beauty from Ashes team had been ministering to women for more than six years. Once a month, Julie and her team would take thoughtfully prepared meals and gifts into the dressing rooms of the strip clubs. Their goal was to love on the girls working there – to show them they had value and were worthy of respect. Experiencing Julie and her team's unconditional compassion for these weary, broken women opened up my eyes to the power of love. It taught me a more effective way to reach people with the Gospel and to restore lost hope.

I'll never forget that first night of service. After a time of prayer, the three of us packed up our food supplies and gifts, and we drove to a strip club, much like the places I had worked in years earlier. Julie had developed a friendship with the manager of the club, earning enough trust to get through the door. That night, he even helped us move our folding tables, food, and gifts into the girls' dressing room.

When the young women saw Julie come in, they rushed over and threw their arms around her. There was a clear bond of love between them. While they chatted excitedly, our little team organized the tables of food and gifts.

Uncertain how I should proceed, I sat next to a girl who was flat ironing her hair. I tried to start a conversation, but I could tell she wasn't the least bit interested in what I had to say. Then, the Holy Spirit prompted me – just be quiet, listen, and learn. I got the message loud and clear, stepped away, and watched how Julie and her friend Annie interacted with the women.

What I saw surprised me. Julie and Annie never talked about themselves. They focused entirely on the girls they were there to serve. If I had to describe their approach in a few words, I would say they became conduits of God's love. They let His compassion flow through them and into the girls.

The young women, starved for the compassion of an uncondemning friend, eagerly shared their innermost feelings, venting about the pain and injustices they felt had befallen them. As each finished, Julie would hug the girl, love on her, and ask if she wanted prayer. The prayers they offered were warm and encouraging, and the girls hung on every word. It was a powerful, intimate time of sharing, and Julie handled it with honesty, maturity, and grace.

As I watched all of this, the Holy Spirit spoke to my soul again. *Shelly, this is ministry. It is not about you. Ministry allows me to work in and through your life. At times, it means you offer an ear for people who simply need someone who will listen.*

This made total sense to me, and I saw how it glorified God rather than serving one's own ego. I felt incredibly blessed to have watched and learned from those two special women that night, and by the evening's end, I was on a spiritual high. I sensed this was the mission God had for me – at least in this season of my life – and I made a year commitment to join Julie as part of Beauty from Ashes Ministries. From then on, I looked forward to the day we would serve each month.

* * *

Though many positive things continued to fall into place with my job, ministry opportunities, and family relationships, I'll highlight only one other key event here – God's prophetic promise that I would help my friend David in his hour of need. Although David had laughed off the idea I would play a role in his kidney transplant; God had other plans.

I occasionally saw David at work, and I was getting updates on his situation. It had been almost six months since I'd told him my "God story" at church, and there hadn't been any real progress on his treatment. Every time the doctors would get close to setting a date for the transplant, something would come up, causing them to reschedule. I could see how disillusioned David was becoming. He couldn't stand the waiting game, and I felt for him. He'd been on kidney dialysis for more than four years at that point, and his health was clearly failing.

Now and then, I would remind David I should get tested because I was supposed to be his kidney donor, but he continued to laugh the suggestion off.

"David, I'm not just asking for your sake. I really want to know the results myself. I want to know if I was out of my mind when I heard God tell me this would happen." No matter how I positioned it, he still didn't take me seriously.

Finally, there was a day of reckoning. David stopped by the reception desk and asked me to pray for him. He and the guy who'd agreed to be the kidney donor were leaving the office for a final medical test, and the surgery would follow three days later. After he was gone, I sat alone behind the desk, my soul aching. I must have been wrong. God must not have been behind that prophetic word. I was sad about it but tried to laugh it off. I would simply pray all would go well for David and his friend.

Later that afternoon, as I was checking in a guest, David walked past the front desk, a look of shock and disappointment on his face. I called out to him and asked what had happened.

"Terrible news. They've postponed the surgery for eight more months."

"Why?" I was shocked now too.

"The last test didn't go well."

"David," I pleaded, "please let me get tested. You need me. And I want to know if God has actually called me to do this."

For the first time, David seemed open to the idea.

"Are you sure, Shelly? You've been through a lot, and with all the drugs you did in the past—do you really think your body could handle this?

"If God is in this, then it will all work out," I told him. "I believe in His plan. Now, let's see how He accomplishes it."

The next day, David and I took off for the Miami hospital. I remember how excited I was – until the lab guy had to draw more than a dozen vials of blood! They were also a little surprised to hear I wasn't a family member. That's typically the better option for transplants, but they didn't discourage me. The test results were what mattered, they said, and they promised to call us when the numbers were in.

Two days later, my cell phone rang. It was the hospital, and my heart was pounding as I answered it.

"Shelly, you're a perfect match," a woman said, "and we want to get the ball rolling as soon as possible. We need you to come back to the hospital right away."

Normally, transplant testing would go on for six to eight months, but David was having serious medical issues, so they needed to shorten the schedule dramatically.

When I went down to the hospital on the following day, I was asked if I would submit to an interview. They told me this was done with all donors. The doctors would ask me questions about my life, my medical background, and what had inspired me to donate my kidney. It seemed like a reasonable request, so I complied.

There were three doctors involved, and each had a clipboard and pen. Taking notes, they started with routine things – my full name, age, and the usual stuff. Then the questions became more intimate. First, they asked about my relationship with David. I said our parents had been longtime friends, and David and I had known each other since we were teens.

Then, things got more serious.

"We need to ask you some very personal questions about your past," one of the doctors said.

"It's very important you're completely honest with us."

"Have you ever used drugs before?"

When I said I had, their pleasant expressions dropped.

"What kind of drugs?"

"Well, I used cocaine and crack for about twenty-five years, on and off – but honestly, I've done almost every drug you can think of. Cocaine was just my drug of choice."

The startled doctors looked at each other.

"I know that doesn't sound good, but I believe I am very healthy. And I'm convinced I'm supposed to give my kidney to David."

All three doctors set their pens down.

"Exactly why, do you believe that?" one asked.

"Well, when I was in prison…"

"You were in prison?!" a doctor interrupted.

"Um, yes. I got out in 2007. I was in Turkey and…"

"You were in a Turkish prison?!"

I could tell the conversation wasn't going well.

Finally, and without too many other interruptions, I was able to share the full story. I covered my years in prostitution, my drug use, and my Christian conversion during my time in prison. Although the doctors had been a bit restless at the start of my interview, these details were so unusual that they displayed rapt attention through most of the tale.

"Three times, God spoke to my heart, telling me I would be the kidney donor that David needed," I concluded. "I know all this may sound silly to you, but I really need to know if what God told me will come to pass. I need to know all of this wasn't just a trick of my own imagination."

After a long pause, one of the doctors spoke up.

"OK, Shelly – I say, let's do it. Let's see if that really was God's voice." And the others agreed.

I grinned from ear to ear, and my heart soared. Already, God was working through these circumstances, I believed, and He would be glorified if the doctors confirmed my kidney was healthy enough to serve as a match. The doctors told me I would need to submit to three weeks of tests and that those results alone would establish my suitability as a potential donor for David.

The following weeks were filled with all kinds of appointments. Each time I took a new test, I used the opportunity to evangelize, telling the tech or doctor about God's revelation and my excitement about meeting David's need. By now, I had complete confidence God's plan was on track, and I put my fate fully in His hands. As if to honor my obedience and faith, the results of each test showed perfect scores. My decision to help was confirmed time after time after time.

Finally, I was taken to an MRI for a comprehensive examination of my entire body. According to the doctors, this would expose any problems with organ functions. I was injected with a solution and placed into the machine for about 20 minutes of scanning. When the test was over, I saw the three doctors had all come to review the results, and I felt my only pang of concern – not because I feared for the health of my kidneys, but because I knew the test might reveal cancer or some other malady that might put my own long-term health at risk.

Those fears evaporated when I saw the three doctors exchange smiles.

Before I could speak to any of them, the tech came over to unhook me from the machine, leaned over, and – probably against hospital rules – whispered the good news.

"Girlfriend, you have the two biggest, most beautiful kidneys I've ever seen! All your bodily functions are perfect," he said. "There's no reason to hold up this transplant."

I knew it! Overwhelmed with joy, I smiled at the tech, feeling as if his words were a direct message from God – an exclamation point on the prophecy I had heard so many years before.

Later, I had a chance to share this joy with some of the doctors and hospital staff involved in the transplant. It was just before the surgery. Although David and I had different medical teams working on the actual operation, there was a time after surgery prep when we were both together in one room.

As we were waiting to be taken to the operating room, a group of doctors and nurses arrived and began to form a large circle around the two of us. There were about twenty people, and as I examined their faces, I noticed that they represented many different nationalities. All held hands. Bob, David's father, had been a missionary for most of his life, and after praying over David and me, he asked for God to bless the doctors and nurses. It was a beautiful prayer, and it seemed to unify and rally everyone in the room. Even other patients nearby bowed their heads to join in. I felt like I was in heaven; honored and blessed.

The surgery, as you've probably guessed by now, came off without a hitch, and my recovery went very smoothly as well. Once again, God was faithful, and I felt incredibly blessed to have been an instrument in His hands to provide hope and comfort to someone else in need.

In the years since, other ministry opportunities have opened up, and many other wonderful things have happened to me – but I've experienced the trials and hardships we all face in life as well. Subsequent years have brought good and bad, but I've never lost the important connection to God I established in the Turkish prison, and I'm confident I never will.

Although I wouldn't wish my life journey on anyone, I do know that others are already in that difficult place, walking at least parts of my walk and fighting many of the same demons I have faced. There are parents like mine too, and I've met many of them as I've shared my testimony in one place or another. I know they suffer as much as their wayward children do. Some even wonder if God has forsaken them – if their sons and daughters will ever break from their addictions and return home.

My ultimate hope is that by sharing the often horrific twists and turns of my own life, I can demonstrate that no matter how far down a path of sin a person goes, there's no place beyond God's reach and no point at which He gives up on lost souls.

In those times when all is dark, and you're mired in chaos and sin, it can be hard to imagine you'll ever have anything close to a normal life again.

During the bleakest parts of my own journey, I'd experienced this overwhelming sense of despair. Hope was always fleeting because every time something positive buoyed my spirits, a condemning memory of some past mistake or weakness would be right there to bring me back down. The deceptions I'd used on my parents, clawing through the dumpster for the dope Larry had tossed, my years in prostitution; these and so many other past failings reminded me I was foolish, unworthy, and unredeemable.

Eventually, I lost all of the optimism I'd had as a young girl.

Had you met me in jail or a crack house or the strip club in those darkest years, you probably wouldn't have suspected I'd had childhood dreams at all. You might even have laughed to learn I'd once wished my life would lead to a loving marriage, a little house with a white picket fence, and a chance to ride horses under an open sky – but deep inside, that's who I was.

My interest in horses started when I was twelve, and a neighborhood friend brought her mare to a school function and invited us all to take a ride. The animal was beautiful, and as I got up into the saddle, I was careful to show no fear, in hopes this girl would see my joyful confidence and invite me to ride with her again. She did, and we rode many times on the weekends that followed until her family finally sold the horse and moved on.

Even after I could no longer ride with her, I cherished the idea horses might play some part in my own life too, and even in my wayward adult years, these childhood fantasies would resurface when I drove by a pasture and saw horses running and at play. These hopes of mine were shattered by the time I was arrested in Turkey, of course – but I shouldn't have been so quick to abandon them because, with God, all things are possible.

Beginning with my conversion experience in prison, God began a process to restore my life and my dreams.

This restoration began with my own family, and I am deeply grateful for that gift. Relationships are often destroyed in situations like mine, and shame and anger are just two of the cruel tools Satan uses to keep family members apart. The ties to my parents and siblings could easily have been forever severed by my fall and terrible selfishness, but God saw to it that some thread of connection remained. It was strengthened by the letters my grandmother wrote to me while I was in prison, and it was restored further when I returned home.

That said, the transition wasn't without its trials. By the time I got back to South Florida, life had moved on for my extended family, and most of my aunts, uncles, and cousins were no longer living in the area. My sister had also moved to Colorado, so she seemed a world away. To be honest, I was a little scared. I felt my relationship with Christ was strong, but I also knew my nature and was fearful of the many temptations I might face.

Fortunately, my mother and father had relocated within the state, and I could see them regularly. We would have get-togethers occasionally, and my lunches with mom kept me up to date on family news. During that time, my mother became my best friend, something I'd never believed possible when I was struggling through the dark years of my addictions.

When they eventually left the urban parts of South Florida looking for a simpler life, I considered doing something similar myself. I knew this would be a healthier option for me too. As if in answer to prayer, a friend I met shared just such an opportunity with me. She told me about a small house being built about a forty-five-minute drive from Lady Lake, Florida, the place where my parents had retired. The house she described was tiny, but I was on my own, so I really didn't need a lot of space, and I felt the choice would also help me keep costs down.

I knew South Florida very well, so moving to a more rural part of the state would be new for me, but something about it felt right in my soul, so I decided to embrace it as a fresh start. Whatever awaited me there would be part of God's plan, I felt certain, and my faith in that was comforting.

The little home ended up being perfect. My little dog Liberty seemed to love it too. Robert, who had built the house and would be my landlord, also helped make the transition a pleasure. His easy-going personality and helpfulness eased all my fears. He made all the changes I needed in the house and helped me settle in.

Before long, I had a new job and was spending a lot of time over in The Villages, the community where my folks now lived. I also began a wonderful friendship with Robert. We started spending time together, having cookouts, and sharing stories about our lives. He was very easy to talk to and was an amazing listener too. I hadn't seen it yet, but God was beginning a new work in my life, removing more and more of my painful past and replacing those dark things with bright and wholesome pieces drawn from my childhood dreams.

Robert seemed genuinely concerned about me and my daily life, but what moved my heart most was his faith in God. He had known the Lord for many years, and when I would share stories about my past addictions, prison time, and other hardships with him, his eyes would fill with tears.

I'd rarely met men who were so soft-hearted and kind. In fact, virtually all of my past relationships with men had been horrific, and even after I'd returned from Turkey, things hadn't gone well. When I would be honest about my past, I could see it made most men feel uncomfortable, and the situation always became awkward. At best, they would avoid the subject and never want to talk about it. Since that kind of approach would never work for me, I'd assumed true love was something I would never know again, and I'd resigned myself to living alone.

Now, by meeting Robert in this small rural town, I had found a man who could accept my past non-judgmentally and also see the wonderful potential of new paths in my life. It was a blessing I hadn't expected, and one I only discovered when I stopped trying to control things and instead allowed God to weave the tapestry of my future.

Meeting Robert also helped restore other childhood dreams. Through his interests in outdoor activities like kayaking, I rediscovered my love of another of God's great blessings – nature.

Best of all, Rob's own three-acre homestead backed directly on 50,000 acres of forested land with riding trails, and he owned four beautiful horses! It had been nearly forty years since I'd been on a horse, but I felt the same excitement I'd experienced as a child. I couldn't wait to ride, and as we took weekend excursions into the serene forest near his house, I felt like I was truly living a dream.

Our kayaking excursions were amazing too. In them, I discovered peace and tranquility I'd never known before. On those trips we took on the crystal clear water, I felt I experienced a taste of heaven in the lush green stream banks, the rustling wind, the creaking tree boughs, the darting dragonflies, and the smells of the flowers and forest beyond. What an incredible contrast to the dark, course, discouraging world I had known before!

The fact that Rob and I were building something meaningful based on a friendship was a vastly new experience for me too. My mother had always encouraged this kind of approach to relationships with men, but I'd ignored her when I was young, and I'd paid a heavy price for my bad choices.

As I saw this more positive bond developing in my time with Rob, it confirmed what I knew about God's intentions for men and women – that refraining from sex before marriage was the better way to develop a real and lasting relationship. God's plan for humanity is often characterized as old fashioned or confining by the world, but it is actually the better path for us to take. Like a loving father, God is only trying to show us how to avoid the pain and hardships our more worldly choices tend to create.

While I was excited about how my relationship with Rob was evolving in the months that followed, I remained true to my commitment to God, and I continued to seek his daily guidance. If Rob was the man for me, I felt God's plan for us would unfold in His time and in His way. If God had something else in mind, I would be a peace with that too.

On June 9th, 2017, Rob popped the question. It was an especially memorable experience because we had spent that day with my family, celebrating my father's 75th birthday. To have all my family surrounding us when he knelt to propose is a moment I will never forget. It was as if God stood right there with us, celebrating the culmination of my childhood wishes – the treasured dreams I'd believed were lost to me forever during those darkest years of addiction and sin.

The following April, we were married at The Little Church of the West. My sister was able to fly in from Colorado, and with other extended family members present, it was a perfect day. We'd chosen the location so that Rob and I could honeymoon at the Grand Canyon and see some of the other beautiful natural landmarks in that area, including spending time on Lake Meade. I'd seen photos of these places, of course, but nothing had prepared me for the scale and majesty of it all. It was yet another reminder of the power and mercy of God, a love so large it could hardly be contained.

So, here I am today. More than a decade and a half have passed since my return from prison. I never feel regret for the years I lost because I know they were years God used to change my life and draw me closer to him.

Rob and I have a wonderful marriage, and I thank God for this blessing too. He has truly filled and restored every relationship as He promised. Recognizing His hand in these circumstances and expressing gratitude for every intervention remains an important way for me to cope with the challenges I still face in life, and I'd encourage any reader who finds themselves in moments of fear or doubt to use this approach too. When you are down or feel caught in a routine of sin, ask the Holy Spirit to remind you of the good times, and bring you to a place of gratitude for those blessings in your life. Then, lay your troubles before the Lord, seek his peace, and follow his promptings as you navigate through the challenges you're facing.

Above all, never give up. Never lose hope.

If you are still in a dark place or have a child who seems lost, I know those words can seem inadequate, but as you have seen, I do know how you feel. I have walked in the addict's shoes. I have been the wayward and destructive child. I know what it is to feel so trapped in sin that no option for recovery seems possible; no reason for hope exists.

But that is exactly the time and place for God.

Reach for the Bible. Saturate yourself with the word of God, and dwell in His promises. Speak to Him as you would a friend or loving father. Ask Him to guide you out of the dark places and break the chains that addictions or the world's damaging influences have placed on you. If you do this sincerely and remain grounded in Bible study and prayer, I believe you will be blessed too.

While in my darkest days, I felt certain my life and soul were unrecoverable, but I was wrong. I had underestimated the power of God to restore and transform. I now see my difficult journey as a kind of love letter from the Lord. He promised He would send His son Jesus to rescue the lost, and did exactly that in my life, reaching out to me with compassion, even at times when I pulled away or pursued my own selfish goals. He pursued me. He protected me. And, ultimately, He restored my lost soul.

Your life challenges or family circumstances may be much different than mine, but I believe His love and promises are meant for you too. Draw close to Him today, and be blessed by the peace and restoration only He can provide.

I'm thankful God's plan for humanity includes the incredible institution of the family. Family relationships have deep spiritual and emotional influences on us, and they shape us throughout our lives.

As I looked back on my own life and considered how my memoir might serve as both a cautionary tale and an encouragement to others, I realized I'd left out a critical element in the story. For this memoir to fully express how God recovers lost souls, it must include a chapter written from my parents' perspective.

God revealed this fact to me shortly after my return from Turkey. At that time, I gave my testimony at several gatherings, and afterward, parents with children struggling with addictions approached me. Most were just trying to make sense of the situation. Some had no idea where their kids were, and they were heartbroken to think they might be suffering as I had. Others were soul searching, wondering what they had done wrong. They wanted to know how they could bring their children back from the darkness. Was there really any hope for them?

Hearing these comments made me realize the addict is not the only victim of addiction; the sinner is not the only one to suffer from a sinful decision. Parents often have their lives turned upside down by such trials too.

In hopes of expanding my memoir to include my family's perspective on my life journey, I invited my mother to share her thoughts...

*   *   *

Philippians 4:13 has helped me many times through the years – I can do all things through Christ who strengthens me – and that passage served as a spiritual anchor for me each time our family faced a crisis.

No parent wants to hear a phone ring in the middle of the night. In fact, it's something we dread – like a night crier shouting, "bad news!" Unfortunately, my husband Jim and I have had a lot of those calls. Each was a horrible harbinger alerting us to an auto accident, a drug overdose, a terrible sickness, or something equally bad.

As terrible as all of those previous calls had been, nothing prepared me for the one I received on June 4, 2004. I was at my computer at the time and quickly picked up the phone. Someone on the other end – a voice I couldn't place – claimed she was calling from an American embassy. After asking me if I had a daughter named Shelly Lantz, the woman said, "Shelly has been picked up for a major crime and is being held by the Turkish government."

Ears burning and throat constricting, I couldn't immediately reply. It was as if my body and mind were frozen solid. Even without knowing any more, I could tell this call would forever change our lives, and I couldn't help but feel hurt, betrayed, frightened, confused, and angry. In the past, I might have immediately blamed myself for such a thing, but this time I felt no responsibility for Shelly or her actions – and I shed no tears. The days of mom and dad rushing in to fix things had run their course, and I distinctly remember that detached feeling. Shelly, your chances have run out. This is your burden to carry, came to mind.

The woman who called had mentioned Turkey. I thought I'd heard bad things about that country. Isn't it the one known for mistreating prisoners? In the back of my numbed mind, I wondered if I would ever see my daughter again. Even if I had felt compelled to protect her, what could I have accomplished? In Turkey, she was far beyond our reach.

After that first call, time seemed to slow to a crawl. It was strange, but we got no immediate word further clarifying Shelly's situation or condition. Then, one night around midnight, the phone rang. It was a terrible connection, and the person on the other end spoke undecipherable English. My husband and I tried to communicate with the person, but it was hopeless. After a few minutes, we hung up the phone in desperation, still uncertain what was going on.

A few weeks later, a third call came again in the middle of the night. As before, the connection was bad, and the caller incomprehensible. We hung up again, incredibly frustrated.

The next call finally shed some light on Shelly's situation, but it also made us suspicious. This time, the woman, on the other end, spoke English and claimed to be a lawyer. She said she wanted to represent Shelly. She asked for an absorbent amount of money and insisted we send it right away. We refused and hung up, guilt and despair welling up in our hearts. Only later did we learn we had probably made the right decision to refuse that call. By representing themselves, the girls actually achieved more than a lawyer might have accomplished.

Even though we didn't accept the offer from the professed lawyer, there was one positive outcome from the frightening call. The woman had mentioned the prison where Shelly was being held. With the name of that institution, we could locate a mailing address. Finally, we would be able to write to our daughter!

At about the same time, Jim's widowed mother, Lottie, came to live with us. She was a wonderful comfort to both Jim and me, and we spent many hours discussing if we were making the right decisions in handling Shelly's situation. It was a very difficult time, but Lottie stood by our side.

A couple of months later, we realized Shelly was not receiving our letters, and Lottie decided to write, hoping her messages might get through. They did, and she received a return letter from Shelly.

The exchange of letters between Shelly and Lottie developed into a wonderful relationship between granddaughter and grandmother, and we thanked the Lord for it. It was a blessing we had never expected, and in the months that followed, the two formed a powerful spiritual and emotional bond.

As Shelly has explained in her memoir, my letters went undelivered, and I now think that was what God intended. He had orchestrated a time of separation. Feeling that was the case, Jim and I stepped back and allowed God to work on Shelly without our intervention. We got our news through Lottie, and Shelly's letters gave us hope. We also learned about the many miracles that were transpiring during her stay in prison, and we saw that she had learned to seek comfort from God rather than from us. Those years of separation were a learning experience for us all, and I believe we were all molded and transformed by the hand of God through the process.

When Shelly's release from prison drew near, Lottie encouraged us to consider bringing her back into our home. She reminded us that Shelly was sober and had been able to live without drugs for several years. Our daughter had also developed a close and sincere relationship with God.

Were we not to act on her behalf, Shelly would have returned to the U.S. with no home address and no money to get back on her feet again. Lottie told us God was speaking to her heart and encouraging her to welcome Shelly back, and I understood what she was saying. I had the same sense of it too. That night, my husband and I made the decision to forgive Shelly's terrible actions in the past and bring her home.

To our delight, God continued to work in our daughter's life after her return. In her letters from the prison, she had mentioned a calling from God – a prophecy about helping one of our family friends with a serious kidney disorder. When she came back home, she brought this up again, telling us she still felt God wanted her to donate a kidney to David. At the time, I doubted she would be a viable candidate. I was aware of her drug use through the years, and like everyone else, I thought that would disqualify her. Still, I found it inspiring when she remained true to her belief. God had spoken to her, she would say.

As believers ourselves, we knew all things were possible with God. Perhaps the Lord really is in this, we thought.

To our amazement, the medical tests the doctors required prior to the transplant proved her right! I'll never forget the day I went to Miami with her. The doctor showed us Shelly's two beautiful, healthy kidneys on a diagnostic screen, and I was in awe. My mind and heart were filled with one phrase – "what a mighty God we serve!" Only He could make such a mistreated body whole again!

Perhaps that miracle alone sums up everything about Shelly and her journey. It is a testimony to God's sovereignty, His love, and transforming power. The God we worship seeks out lost causes and restores hope. The Lord was merciful to us and stood with Jim and me through our journey too.

No parent ever dreams her child will grow up to be a drug addict. Nothing prepares you for that. And none of us wants to believe the child we love and trust will seek to manipulate us with lies and deceitful behavior – but those things do happen.

The years Shelly wandered in the wilderness of addiction were incredibly difficult for her and for us. Without God in our lives – without knowing we could rely on His love and grace to uphold and comfort us – I think the experience might have broken each of us.

Looking back, I now know there were many things we might have done differently in Shelly's case. We should have practiced more "tough love" in our home, for example, and I would encourage other parents facing similar situations to learn from that mistake. Children do need boundaries. I mistakenly believed saying "no" to Shelly might drive her away – that I might lose her to the world – but the opposite was actually true. When I didn't stand by my convictions or enforce my own rules, I made it easier for her to explore the greatest temptations in the world.

I must also admit that while I love God, I didn't trust Him enough to release Shelly to Him. Rather than allow the Lord to use her hardships and suffering to teach and purify her at the very start, we provided safety cushions that softened the consequences of her actions.

The turning point was when Shelly came to our home, demanding her passport. That was the first time we truly "let go and let God." At that point, God separated us from her both emotionally and physically, and He was finally able to begin His good work in her.

Today, as I look back at the rut-filled road our family traveled to reach the place we stand now, I am happy we never cut ties with Shelly as some parents might have been tempted to do, and I praise God for the mercy He showed in drawing our daughter back to Him and to us.

If you are a mother, father, grandmother, or grandfather facing a similar situation in life, keep the faith and redouble your prayers for your child or grandchild. Understand that God may chasten, using the legal system or other painful repercussions to accomplish His ends. Only through prayer will you know when to act on behalf of your loved one and when to allow God to work in and through those trials.

My advice? Seek His peace at those times, and remember that withholding immediate assistance does not mean cutting all ties with your child – though he or she may, in anger, use that idea to threaten or manipulate you. Keep lines of communication open, and always let your child know your love remains strong and restoration is never beyond his or her reach. Like the father of the prodigal son described in Luke 15, you need not mount a rescue of your child in order to keep an open heart and welcome your son or daughter's eventual return.

I hope and pray Shelly's memoir will help both parents and children better understand how treacherous Satan is and how being drawn into "lesser" evils can quickly lead to greater sins – and eventually to overwhelming hardships. If your children are only beginning to dabble in drugs or other sins, perhaps you can share our daughter's eye-opening story with them to help them understand the risks they face by playing with fire. Even the most rebellious child can sometimes be reached by a peer who has walked his walk or known her pain.

Ultimately, Shelly's life was changed because God intervened, and because she chose to respond to His call. No matter how far gone you believe a son or daughter is, every breath that child takes still affords an opportunity for redemption. God healed our family and us. He can do the same for you and yours.

No one is unrecoverable.

ACKNOWLEDGMENTS

I wish I could say my life has been perfect since my conversion in the Turkish prison more than fifteen years ago. It has not. Although God is and always will be in control, living in this fallen world continues to present temptations and struggles, and I must face them like anyone else.

That's why I try to stay "plugged in" through prayer and the Church and why I surround myself with like-minded believers.

Living with my parents and grandmother when I returned from Turkey also bolstered my faith.

Even after my parents moved to another part of Florida, I remained with my grandmother, and it was a blessing to be her companion until she passed on to heaven at the age of ninety-three.

Though she was ready to join the Lord at that point, the separation was very difficult for me. We had become very close, and I relied on her as my accountability partner. She had always encouraged me during those years – but she also spoke the truth into my life. God used her to steer me back on the right path when I strayed off course. She had a wonderful way of gently but firmly steadying me when I wavered.

I hope and pray each of you is blessed with a similar spiritual mentor in your life.

As I close out this memoir, I feel compelled to recognize and thank some of the amazing people who have blessed my life. The first must be Grandmother Lottie Lantz. As you've learned in this memoir, she was a lifeline for me in prison, sending me compassionate letters every 10 days. I can't express how much her words strengthened me during my incarceration. As I've said, she never sugarcoated things but always spoke the truth in love. Thank you so much, Grandma – you are forever in my heart.

I also want to thank and honor my parents, Jim and Ruth Lantz. Sometimes I grieve over the family life I missed out on during my addiction, but I also consider myself blessed to have them both healthy and alive today. They live close by, and I see them on a regular basis.

My parents never gave up on me. They never lost hope that one day I would return to God and turn my life over to Him. As hard as it was for them, they eventually saw the importance of letting go and letting God take over – one of the most difficult choices a parent can make. No mother or father wants to see a son or daughter suffer, so most intervene. I'm very thankful they allowed God to work in my life.

Mom, I love you! Thank you for being the mother you were then and are today. I am so sorry you went through so much pain on my account, but I do believe the experience has also shaped you into the woman of God you are today.

Dad, I can't thank you enough! Thank you for marrying my mom and giving her the wonderful life you both have today. I have always been amazed by your selflessness. You adopted Kim and me and loved us as your very own children. In spite of all the horrible things I did, you never disowned me or distanced yourself to keep your own reputation unsullied. Instead, you supported me through my life and accepted the financial burdens I created with my treatments, hospital stays, and living arrangements. You never once condemned me for turning my back on you to seek out my biological father. You never once threw my foolish words back in my face or showed regret for the kindnesses you had offered. You loved me unconditionally, as God loves me, and I will always be deeply grateful for that.

The next person I want to honor is my sister, Kimberly. Kim, I know growing up with me was not easy. As the wayward child, I drew heavily on the attention of mom and dad, and that is never an easy thing for a sibling to accept. I know you had your share of difficulties too, and that's why I'm doubly proud of you today. Your thirteen years in the military are an amazing achievement! I'm deeply grateful for the ways God has healed and restored our relationship since my return from Turkey. When I got off that plane and saw you and your family there to greet me, I was lifted to the heavens. I love you so much, Kim, and I'm glad we talk almost every day. It is a blessing to have you there when I need encouragement, a listening ear, or a place to vent. Thank you for never giving up on me. I love you, my dear sister.

Many of you may wonder about the other members of my family – the half-brothers I mentioned and my biological father. My half-brother, Jeffrey, is gone now. He was forty-seven years old and ironically died in the same month, and at the same age, my biological father, Jeff Sr., passed away.

Jeffrey suffered from addiction for many years, just as I had. It broke my heart when I found out he was on life support. I didn't get a chance to say goodbye to him, but I will never forget the day he gave his life to Jesus. Jeffrey was sixteen years old at the time, and the excitement he expressed about the Lord at his conversion remains forever etched in my mind. Rest in peace, dear brother. Your suffering is finally over, and your new life has begun.

During my incarceration, Chad, the younger of my half-brothers, was deployed to Afghanistan by the military. His wife, Monica, who I'd not yet met, sent me many wonderful letters of support while I was in prison. Through her, I was updated on Chad's situation, and we got to share spiritual encouragement and build bonds as sisters in God. I'm grateful to Monica for loving me and writing to me during those years.

Chad retired four years ago, and I was blessed to be reunited with him after thirty-six long years apart. I'd dreamed about that reunion for so long, and it was an overwhelming experience when it finally happened. I have so much love and respect for Chad. It's hard to believe the child I once played with is now a retired military man – all grown up with six children of his own. For more than twenty years, he served the army by deactivating bombs in Iraq and Afghanistan. God bless you, my awesome brother. You are an incredible man of God.

In more recent years, I have met other people I'd also like to thank because they have played an important role in my personal ministry.

One is Robby Dilmore with Tru-Talk Radio. Robby is an awesome man of God, and he has a radio program called The Christian Car Guy. After hearing my testimony, he asked me to join him on the air, and I have shared my life story on his program many times since. Robbie, what a great encourager you have been to me! Thank you for hosting me on your program so your listeners could learn more about God's redemption and grace.

Others out there have also given me opportunities to speak and give my testimony, and I appreciate your support too.

For those who have taken the time to read my story, I hope and pray it has been a blessing. May God use it to speak to your heart and encourage you to never give up, never lose hope, and never forget how valuable your life is to God and your loved ones!

Last but not least, my thanks goes out to Brian Schutt, who helped me write this book. Brian is the co-founder of Cross International and Cross Catholic Outreach, two Christian charities that serve the poor in developing countries by supplying grants and resources to churches and ministries already operating overseas. It was my privilege to work at Cross from 2009 to 2016 as a school development officer, and I have a heart for their work.

I would have never been able to share my story without Brian's help. Thank you so much for believing in me, Brian, and for encouraging me when I thought I would not get it done. You did an amazing job helping me get this memoir on paper so it could be shared with others. You said you believed it would help both the addicted and the faithful parents who pray for them, and you have been like a big brother cheering me on. God bless you and your wife, Cindy, for taking the time out of your busy schedule to help me complete this project. My love to you both.

For more information on Shelly's story, please visit www.unrecoverable.info. There you can browse photographs and the diary from Shelly's time in prison. A portion of the proceeds from this book will be donated to the ministry of WellHouse, a program that provides safety and refuge for women escaping from human trafficking.

CPSIA information can be obtained
at www.ICGtesting.com
Printed in the USA
BVHW041104260523
664934BV00005B/103